TRIUMPHS AND DISASTERS

Other Frontline Books by Andrew Bamford

A Bold and Ambitious Enterprise:
The British Army in the Low Countries, 1813–1814

Gallantry and Discipline:
The 12th Light Dragoons at War with Wellington

With Wellington's Outposts:
The Peninsular and Waterloo Letters of John Vandeleur

TRIUMPHS AND DISASTERS

Eyewitness Accounts from the Netherlands Campaign, 1813–1814

Notes and commentary by

Andrew Bamford

Frontline Books

Triumphs and Disasters
This edition published in 2016 by
Frontline Books,
an imprint of Pen & Sword Books Ltd,
47 Church Street, Barnsley, S. Yorkshire, s70 2as

Edited text and commentary © Andrew Bamford, 2016

ISBN: 978-1-47383-525-2

CIP data records for this title are available from the British Library

For more information on our books, please visit
www.pen-and-sword.co.uk, email info@frontline-books.com
or write to us at the above address.

Printed and bound in Malta by Gutenberg Press Ltd

Typeset in 11.6/14.7 pt Arno Pro Small Text & 12/14.7 pt Arno Pro Display

Contents

Plates

General Graham, Lord Lynedoch. Print by Fry after Wright, 1815.
(*Anne S. K. Brown Military Collection*)

Sir James Carmichael Smyth. (*National Portrait Gallery, London*)

Thomas Slingsby Duncombe, by James Warren Childe, 1836.
(*National Portrait Gallery, London*)

Sappers & Miners, working dress, 1813. Watercolour by Charles Lyall.
(*Anne S. K. Brown Military Collection*)

A field officer of the Royal Engineers and a private sapper. Pen and
wash drawing by Charles Hamilton-Smith. (*Anne S. K. Brown
Military Collection*)

An officer and private of the 52nd Light Infantry. Pen and wash
drawing by Charles Hamilton-Smith. (*Anne S. K. Brown Military
Collection*)

Junior officer, Coldstream Guards, *c.* 1814. Living history re-creation
courtesy of The Coldstream Regiment of Foot Guards, 1815.
(*www.coldstreamguards1815.org.uk; photograph by Ellie Wout*)

Junior officer, 33rd Foot, *c.* 1814. Living history re-creation courtesy
of His Majesty's 33rd Regiment of Foot. (*www.33rdfoot.co.uk;
photograph by Ellie Wout*)

Junior NCO, 1st Foot Guards, *c.* 1814. Living history re-creation
courtesy of 1st Foot Guards (1815). (*www.firstfootguards.org;
photograph by Ellie Wout*)

Coldstream Guards 1814. Watercolour by Orlando Norrie, showing a
corporal and a pioneer. (*Anne S. K. Brown Military Collection*)

The attack on Bergen-op-Zoom. (*Engraving from the collection of Philip
J. Haythornthwaite*)

1st Foot Guards *c.* 1813–15, detail, from ink and watercolour by P. W.
Reynolds. (*Anne S. K. Brown Military Collection*)

Maps

Introduction

In 2013, I completed a history – the first book-length study of the subject in English for over a century – of the operations of the British forces sent to the Low Countries in 1813 and 1814 under the command of Sir Thomas Graham. This was published under the title *A Bold and Ambitious Enterprise*. In terms of scale these operations were eclipsed by contemporary fighting in Germany and France, not to mention the Peninsula, and overshadowed by the final struggle at Waterloo a year later. They are most often remembered – if they are remembered at all – for the disastrous defeat at Bergen-op-Zoom on the night of 8–9 March 1814, where a failed attempt to capture the French-held fortress led to over 1,500 casualties amongst the attackers. Yet prior to this repulse, Graham's operations had met with considerably greater success, helping to complete the liberation of much of what would become the Kingdom of the United Netherlands, and had introduced Britain's soldiers – and their military and political masters – to the complexities of working closely with allied forces. As such, they were rightly recognised by the great historian Sir John Fortescue as representing an essential precursor to the far more heavily documented actions of the Hundred Days.

As I began researching Graham's campaign for my earlier book, it quickly became apparent that there were surprisingly rich resources to be had when it came to eyewitness accounts of the fighting. With so many of Graham's troops being freshly recruited, and from battalions with little or no previous overseas service, this represented the first – sometimes the only – active service that these men would see. As a result, several accounts deal solely with this campaign, in the form of anything from short reminiscences in magazines and journals, to full-length books. For others, service with Graham formed a postscript to earlier adventures in the Peninsula, or else a precursor to the following year's experiences of the Waterloo campaign. A sizeable proportion of these accounts are, at the time of writing, available in print. Gareth Glover's publication of the letters and diaries of staff officer James Stanhope, and annotated re-issue of the letters of Royal Engineers subaltern John Sperling are two accounts that can be easily obtained; others, such as the anonymous and laboriously titled *Letters from Germany and Holland, During the Years 1813–14; With a Detailed Account of the Operations of the British Army in those Countries, and of the Attacks Upon Antwerp and Bergen-op-Zoom, by the Troops under the Command of Gen. Sir T. Graham*, are at least available in print-on-demand form. One of the classics, and also one of the longest memoirs dealing solely with this campaign, remains *Old Stick Leg*, Brigadier General H. H. Austin's edited version of his ancestor Lieutenant Thomas Austin's account of his service with the 2/35th under Graham, which is currently out of print although often cited in other works. However, using Austin's memoirs in the preparation of my own account of the campaign revealed a number of discrepancies that proved hard to resolve completely, a point I will return to in the appendices to this work. Another classic, although with service under Graham sandwiched between accounts of earlier adventures in the Baltic and later fighting at Quatre Bras and Waterloo, is Thomas Morris's memoir of service in the ranks of the 2/73rd, which is particularly valuable as being one of the few non-officer accounts of the campaign.

So, with a little effort, the interested reader could well assemble a decent library of full-length works dealing with the varying experiences of their writers during the operations in question. Less easy to come by, however, are some of the shorter but equally useful accounts of the campaign, many of which have either never been published or else are so long out of print as to be unobtainable. The primary purpose of this volume, therefore, is to bring together six of the most significant of these shorter accounts and present them, with introduction and annotation, as a single combined volume. I used three of these accounts during the preparation of my earlier book on the campaign; two of the others were unavailable at that stage – the one due to my inability to locate a printed copy, the other due to the temporary closure of the archive in which it was held – and the last was not known to me at the time that *A Bold and Ambitious Enterprise* was put together. Because there are elements of new information contained within these last three accounts, which add to our understanding of the course of the campaign, and because all six accounts touch upon aspects which, due to space considerations, could not be discussed as fully as I would have liked in the earlier work, this title also includes a series of appendices containing further analysis of these points. I am pleased to say, so far as the credibility of my previous book is concerned, that nothing in these new accounts has caused me to revise my understanding of the course of events; at the same time, however, greater detail is added on several points, so that these more focussed studies serve to complement, rather than supplant, the narrative of *A Bold and Ambitious Enterprise*.

The six eyewitness accounts cover almost the full range of ranks and roles within Graham's little army, from one of his senior subordinates to his infantry rank and file. Three accounts are absolutely contemporary, being composed of letters and diaries written at the time. A fourth also consists of letters, but letters that were tidied up for later publication. The final two are later memoirs, one being a full account in its own right – albeit a fairly short one – whilst the other is excerpted from a longer work. In all six accounts, the narrative deals as much, if not more so, with the experience of life on campaign and relations with fellow soldiers – British and allied – and with the Dutch population than it does with actual military operations. Thus, in choosing the title for this work, I was as much in mind of the personal triumphs and disasters of everyday life – a well-played practical joke, a romantic encounter, a good meal, or a successful day's shooting – as with success and failure on the battlefield. On the battlefield too, however, are to be found triumphs and disasters aplenty, from the pride taken in a well-conducted operation to the ignominy of being wounded and taken prisoner.

In the order that they appear, our six eyewitnesses are: Lieutenant Colonel James Carmichael Smyth, Royal Engineers; Ensign Thomas Slingsby Duncombe, 2/Coldstream Guards; Lieutenant Charles Shaw, 2/52nd Light Infantry; Ensign William Thain, 33rd Foot; Corporal Alexander Frederic Meuller, 2/1st Foot Guards; 2nd Lieutenant Dunbar Moodie, 2/21st Fusiliers. All six accounts are reproduced as closely to the original text as possible, be that source manuscript or printed copy. Occasional corrections and clarification have been added in square brackets. Spellings of place names have been left as per the original: in most cases it should be fairly obvious what the writer was trying for, but a footnoted confirmation has been added when a name first appears, and clarification is repeated for those places where the rendition is a particularly serious mangling of the actual spelling.

With those accounts that take the form of diary entries, or collected letters, I have where necessary added commentary at appropriate breaks in the text; for the accounts of Shaw and Moodie, designed to be read as single narratives, I have saved my commentary for the end or for the appendices. In all six accounts, I have used footnotes to identify persons mentioned in the text, and to elucidate any specific points on which confusion might otherwise arise were an explanation left for the commentary. Although not all of the six eyewitnesses were involved in every operation mounted by Graham's forces, their various accounts overlap to cover pretty much the entire course of the campaign. That being so, there is little point in providing a potted history of the actions as well, particularly since Carmichael Smyth's comprehensive account – presented first within this work – serves largely to fill that role. However, in order to give a basic overview, to enable the accounts to be read individually, and to place events in context, a chronology of the campaign and a series of maps showing the theatre of war and the course of the various engagements in which the British troops were engaged, all follow this introduction. Notes on the command structure and order of battle of the forces engaged form the first of the appendices.

*

The maps for the most part duplicate those to be found in *A Bold and Ambitious Enterprise*, and I must therefore begin the acknowledgements for this work by again thanking my wife Lucy for the original drawings, and David Beckford for the additional graphic work. Additional thanks for contribution to the research for this book, and for aid in locating the sources used, must go to the following: Carole Divall, Maggie Downie, Anthony Gray, Vic James, Clive Jones, Jan Kemperman, Kevin F. Kiley, Richard MacFarlane, C. W. A. Putter, Stephen Summerfield, John White and Ellie Wout. Some of these people are good friends and colleagues; others I have never met in person but are contributors to the excellent *Napoleon Series* online discussion forum. As well as helping me untangle the local geography, Ellie has also provided a number of photographs which feature in the plates section. For this I am extremely grateful, as I also am to the living history groups whose members posed for some of the shots. Details of these groups can be found in the list of image credits. Finally, I must once again thank my father, Mick Bamford, who has yet again served as my proof-reader; responsibility for any mistakes or omissions is of course mine.

Chronology of Events

1813

12 July	British troops under Gibbs sail for Baltic.
16–19 October	Battle of Leipzig; French begin final retreat from Germany.
Early November	First Cossack patrols enter the Netherlands.
1 November	Gibbs recalled from Baltic with four battalions.
9–19 November	Dutch rising against the French.
30 November	Prince of Orange lands at Scheveningen.
4 December	Sir Thomas Graham formally appointed to command British forces in the Netherlands.
6 December	Foot Guards under Cooke arrive at Scheveningen.
9 December	Breda falls to Russians under Benckendorff.
16 December	Graham's main forces begin to disembark.
19–22 December	Abortive French counter-offensive against Breda.

1814

1 January	Main allied armies begin their invasion of France.
8 January	Graham meets Bülow to plan operations against Antwerp.
10–12 January	British forces concentrate at Roosendaal and move on Antwerp in conjunction with Prussian offensive.
13 January	First Battle of Merxem; Prussian retreat compels withdrawal from before Antwerp.
19–20 January	Allied commanders agree plans for a renewed attack on Antwerp.
30 Jan.–1 Feb.	Second allied advance on Antwerp.
2 February	Second Battle of Merxem.
3–5 February	Bombardment of Antwerp.

6 February	Prussians under Bülow begin march for France; British under Graham fall back from Antwerp.
28 February	Gore arrives at Breda with last two battalions from Baltic.
7 March	Planning meeting agrees scheme for attack on Bergen-op-Zoom.
8 March	Bergen-op-Zoom attacked by troops under Cooke; assault fails with heavy losses.
9 March	Surviving British troops still inside Bergen-op-Zoom forced to surrender.
21 March	Minor action near Fort Lillo between British troops and French warship.
6 April	Preliminary operations against Fort Batz begin; news obtained of Napoleon's abdication.
3 May	Bergen-op-Zoom handed over to the Dutch.
5 May	British troops occupy Antwerp.

Maps

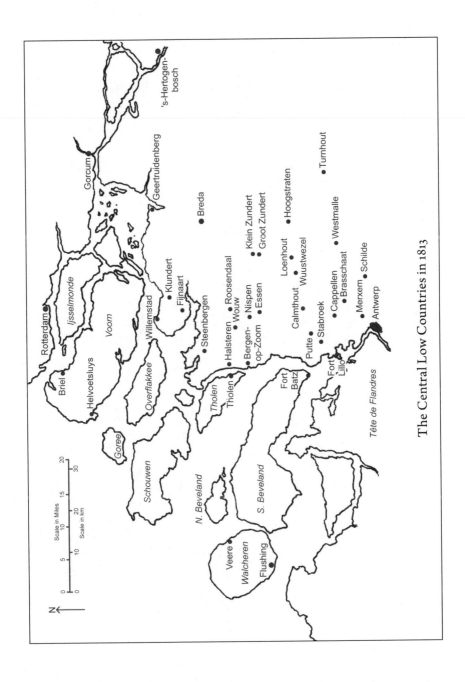

The Central Low Countries in 1813

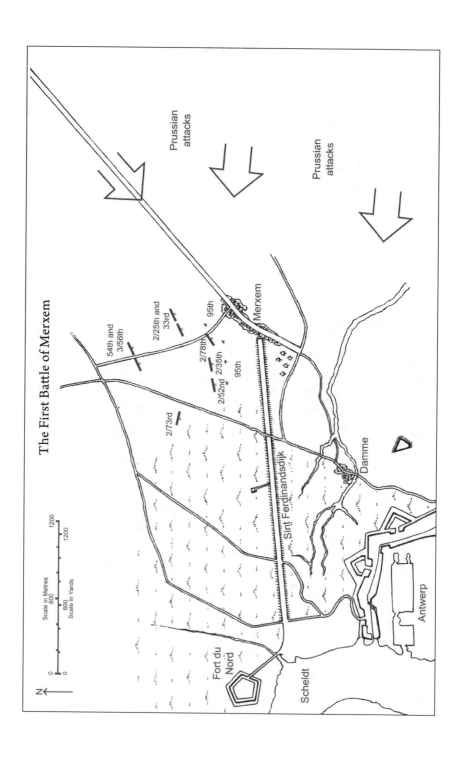

The First Battle of Merxem

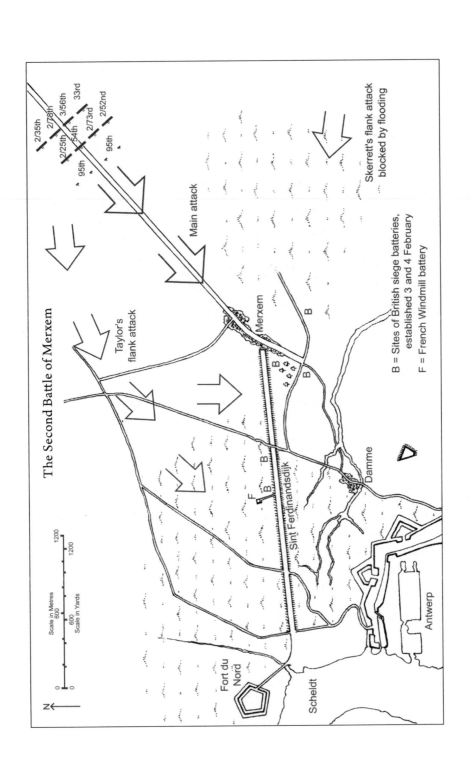

The Second Battle of Merxem

2/35th
2/7/8th
2/25th 3/56th
54th 33rd
95th 2/73rd
95th 2/52nd

Main attack

Taylor's flank attack

Skerrett's flank attack blocked by flooding

B = Sites of British siege batteries, established 3 and 4 February

F = French Windmill battery

Merxem

Sint Ferdinandsdijk

Damme

Fort du Nord

Scheldt

Antwerp

Scale in Metres
0   600   1200
Scale in Yards
0   600   1200

N

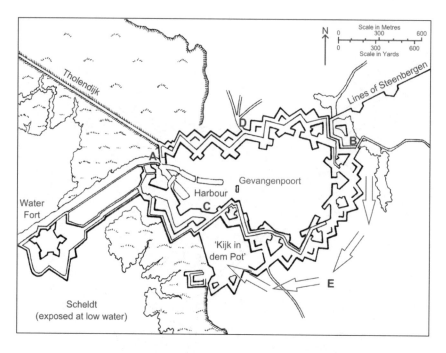

Bergen-op-Zoom – The Initial Attacks

A Right Attack (500 stormers and 600 supports, under Lt Col Carleton) to attack from Tholendijk across the harbour mouth.

B Centre Attack (600 stormers and 600 supports, under Lt Colonel Morrice) to attack across the frozen ditch between the 'De Zoom' Ravelin and the Breda Gate.

C Left Attack (600 stormers and 400 supports, under Colonel Lord Proby) to atack Bastion 'Oranje'.

D False Attack (650 men under Lt Colonel Ottley) to demonstrate against the Steenbergen Gate.

E Subsequent movement of Centre Attack survivors to join the Left Attack at Bastion 'Oranje'.

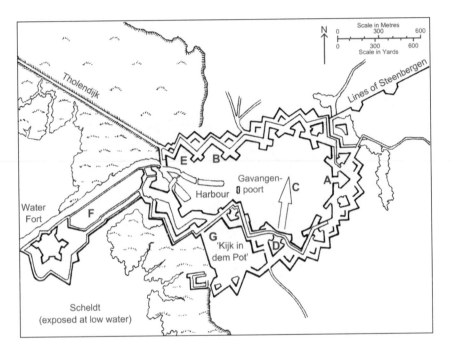

Bergen-op-Zoom – British Confusion and French Counter-Attacks

A Carleton's party dispersed around here, after making an anti-clockwise circuit from the harbour.

B Skerrett's advance clockwise from the harbour checked.

C Clifton secures the Antwerp Gate and advances into the town, but is killed and his party defeated.

D Survivors of Clifton's party try to hold the Antwerp Gate but are driven off.

E French counter-attack the survivors of Skerrett's party and regain control of the harbour.

F 4/1st are pinned under the guns of the Water Fort and are forced to surrender.

G Some survivors escape back down ladders from Bastion 'Oranje', where Cooke and remainder surrender.

Chapter I

Lieutenant Colonel
James Carmichael Smyth

Royal Engineers

Born on 22 February 1779, James Carmichael Smyth was educated at Charterhouse and then at the Royal Military Academy, Woolwich. Upon graduation from the latter he was commissioned into the Royal Artillery in November 1794, transferring to the Royal Engineers the following year. He spent most of the first decade of his service at the Cape of Good Hope, returning to England as a captain in 1803 when the colony was handed back to the Dutch. Three years later he was back in Africa, serving on Sir David Baird's staff when the Cape was captured for the second time. Carmichael Smyth returned to England in 1808, but was soon on active service again during Moore's Corunna campaign. Thereafter he served at home until his assignment to command the engineers attached to Graham's army in the Low Countries. His promotion to lieutenant colonel pre-dated this appointment only by a matter of weeks, being gazetted on 20 October 1813. He was then thirty-four years of age.[1]

The letters reproduced here are primarily those sent by Carmichael Smyth to his superior officer, the Inspector-General of Fortifications, Lieutenant General Gother Mann. These consist of a number of formal reports, sequentially numbered, as well as enclosures and memoranda sent with them. This correspondence with Mann, which runs through until after Waterloo, is taken from a bound manuscript letterbook, now held by The National Archives. Interspersed amongst these letters are memoranda by Carmichael Smyth with his opinion on the various siege

1. Biographical details primarily from R. H. Vetch, 'Smyth, James Carmichael (1779–1838)', *Dictionary of National Biography* (Oxford: 1885–1900), Vol. 53; now available online at http://en.wikisource.org/wiki/Smyth,_James_Carmichael_(1779-1838)_(DNB00).

operations mooted or undertaken, and also two letters from Colonel J. Rowley, Deputy Inspector-General of Fortifications, acknowledging the services of the Royal Engineers at Bergen-op-Zoom. With one exception taken from Sir Thomas Graham's correspondence, these all come from elsewhere in the Carmichael Smyth papers, and have been inserted into the sequence of letters at the appropriate points. Since these reports, even without the additional memoranda, form a continuous narrative of the course of operations, commentary is limited largely to personal details relating to Carmichael Smyth's activities during the campaign.

Carmichael Smyth to Mann   *Ramsgate, 2nd December, No. 1*[1]

Sir,

I have the honor to report to you my arrival at this Place and of my having (in obedience to the Master General's Orders as communicated to me in your Letter of the 23rd Ultimo) taken upon myself the duties of Commanding Engineer with the Army under the Command of Lt. General Sir Thomas Graham.

I beg leave to report to you that there are only nine Non Commissioned Officers present with the Company of Sappers instead of fifteen as mentioned in Lt. Col. Handfield's[2] Letter to me of the 27th Ultimo – there being a Deficiency of four Serjeants and twelve Corporals. As the Services of the Non Commissioned Officers are so essentially requisite I take the liberty of respectfully requesting that if it meet with your approbation, Non Commissioned Officers to complete the Company may be ordered to join it forthwith. Capt. Thomson (who has had Charge of the Company for some time)[3] particularly laments that Serjt. Hemmings and Corporal

---

1. TNA, PRO30/35/6, pp. 1–2.
2. Lt Col John Handfield, RE, who was assigned to coastal defence duty at the time; see Brown, Steve, 'British Artillery Battalions and the Men Who Led Them 1793–1815: Royal Engineers/Royals Sappers and Miners', *Napoleon Series* website, at http://www.napoleon-series.org/military/organization/Britain/Engineers/RoyalEngineers.pdf.
3. Capt. Robert Thomson, RE. First commissioned November 1804 and served throughout the campaign under Graham. The company in question was No. 4 Company, 2nd Battalion, Royal Sappers and Miners, day-to-day command of which was left to Sub-Lt Thomas Adamson whilst Thomson was

Burnet should have been transferred at the present moment as being very steady and intelligent. The Officers of Engineers have all joined with the exception of Captn. Sir George Hoste.[1]

Carmichael Smyth to Mann   *Klundert, 31st December, No. 2*[2]

Sir,

Nothing very particular has taken place in this Country since our Arrival, nor have any duties of a professional Nature been required from the Engineer Officers of sufficient importance to make it necessary to trouble you with any detail.

It was originally intended that the whole Armament should have Rendezvous'd at Helvoetsluys, or at any rate that those Regiments embarked on board the Men of War which were compelled to anchor in the Roompot for want of a sufficient Depth of Water off Helvoet, should have subsequently marched across the Islands of Schouwen and Over Flackee[3] to Helvoet & where the whole of the troops would have been equipped and arranged, the Artillery Brigades put in order, and from where such operations could have been undertaken as would be judged by the Commander of the Forces after his own arrival in the country most advisable.

Upon our anchoring on the Evening of the 15th, however, in the Roompot, Sir Thomas Graham received the very pleasing Intelligence that the enemy had evacuated the very important place of Williamstadt (which was already occupied by the Guards) & Tolen,[4] a town capable of some defence and close to Bergen-op-Zoom. He determined immediately to take possession of Tolen & to bring every thing forward from Helvoetsluys to

otherwise occupied as an engineer officer. See also De Santis, Lt Col Edward, 'Quartermaster Sergeant James McKay, Royal Sappers and Miners', at http://www.reubique.com/mckay.htm.

1. Capt. Sir George Charles Hoste, RE, born 1786 and first commissioned December 1802; younger brother of the noted frigate commander Capt. Sir William Hoste, RN. Served extensively in the Mediterranean including at Maida and at Alexandria in 1807. George Hoste's knighthood was in fact a Sicilian decoration, conferred after his gallant conduct as a supernumerary aboard the frigate HMS *Spartan* – part of his brother's squadron – during an action with a superior Neapolitan force on 3 May 1810.

2. TNA, PRO30/35/6, pp. 2–6.

3. Overflakkee.

4. Willemstad and Tholen.

Williamstadt (which we have now made our Depôt) & from Williamstadt to move and concentrate the troops as fast as they could be equipped in the Neighbourhood of Bergen-op-Zoom.

Until the 22nd Head Quarters were at Tolen, our Light Brigade at a village within a Couple of Miles of Bergen-op-Zoom & the remainder of the Infantry in Cantonments as near as accommodation could be procured & ready to act as Circumstances might require.

Our Guns both Field and Battering were however still at Helvoetsluys and we had no Cavalry – the latter want, was in a great measure supplied by the Russians who sent us two Squadrons of Hussars & a small body of about 150 Cossacks.[1]

The French garrison in Bergen op Zoom was unquestionably contemptible & I am in my own opinion convinced that had the unlucky easterly Winds not prevented our departure at an earlier period, not prevailed we should have got into the place without any trouble, & as easily as the Russians entered Breda. At Antwerp the Enemy had concentrated the whole of their disposable Force & our little Corps could not yet even attempt to invest Bergen-op-Zoom. The day after our arrival they threw in one new-raised Battalion & they have since sent in another. With, however, the addition of these Reinforcements I do not believe that the Garrison exceeds 2,500 men from every information I have been able to procure.

Upon the 22nd Intelligence was received that a French Corps of about 7,000 Infantry with Guns & 800 Cavalry had moved from Antwerp upon Breda occupied by a Russian Light Corps under General Beckendorff.[2] It is perhaps fortunate under our then circumstances without Guns that they did not move upon us.

This movement of the Enemy's had however the effect of compelling us to make a retrograde movement towards Williamstadt to hasten the disembarkation & Equipment of our Artillery & to enable us to move towards Breda to assist the Russians under the protection of the River Mark which we were to have kept upon our Right,[3] as it would not have been prudent to

---

1. See Appendix III for more details of these troops.
2. Maj. Gen. Alexander Benckendorff.
3. The Mark, also known as the Dintel, rises north of Turnhout and flows into the Scheldt delta by way of Hoogstraten, Breda, and Oudenbosch.

have marched across the open country by Rosendaal[1] from Tolen without Guns, and with a very small corps of cavalry with whom we were perfectly unacquainted

Head Quarters were in consequence removed to Williamstadt on the 25th. The French however fell back again from Breda and remain at Westwesel[2] & Hoogstraten evidently as a Corps of Observation to gain Intelligence of the Movements of the Allies towards Antwerp. Our march therefore to Breda became unnecessary. Our Field Brigades[3] have in the mean time been landed and prepared; some cavalry of our own have joined, and we will be able to move in conjunction with the Allies to take our own share of operations as may be determined on in a very few days.

I was sent a Day or two ago by the Commander of the Forces to examine the Fortress of Breda, & on a Communication to the Russian General Commanding in that Town. The appearance of the Russian Troops is uncommonly good, & I was also much gratified at seeing three new raised Dutch battalions. The Dutch are very willing & (as I hope) hearty in the cause. There is not, perhaps, that Display of Activity and Energy there would be in England, but the whole male Population of the Country is ordered to be enrolled & armed from 17 to 50, and they do talk of having 25,000 Men regular Troops ready in the Spring. We cannot expect to alter the National Character, but if they arm all their Population and give us a disposable force of 25,000 men I do not think we will have any cause to complain.

I regret much that the Engineer Stores detailed in the List of the 25th November as signed by you and ordered for the present Service have not as yet arrived. With a view to our subsequent operations it is highly desirable that both the Stores & the Ordnance should be expedited without delay. We have however in the mean time six Transports with a small Battering Train, originally meant for Spain and from which we will derive great assistance consisting of 5 24pdrs, 6 Howitzers, 4 Mortars, & 4 68pdr carronades, with the requisite Platforms and Stores.

1. Roosendaal.
2. Wuustwezel.
3. In this context, field batteries. The formation created by adding drivers to a Royal Artillery company to equip it for field service was known as a brigade, and was designated by the name of its commanding officer.

Although Carmichael Smyth began at an early stage in the campaign to make himself indispensable to Graham as someone who could be trusted to liaise with Britain's allies and to give an honest and informed account of their strengths, weaknesses and intentions, his primary function remained that to which he had been appointed, namely to be chief officer of engineers. Thus, once the threat to Breda had passed and serious thought could be given to striking against the fortifications of Antwerp, Carmichael Smyth was required to provide his professional opinion on how siege operations might best proceed:

Memorandum respecting the proposed Operations
against Antwerp.   *Oudenbosch, Jan 7 1814*[1]

In going over the Ground in Front of the Works of Antwerp, and within Mortar Range of the Basin with a view to ascertain the best Emplacement for our proposed Batteries; – if we begin upon our Right the remains of Fort Pimentel on the banks of the Scheldt seem to offer at once a very advantageous Situation for a Mortar Battery from whence the shipping in the Basin can be easily reached and the Fire of the Guns in the Fort du Nord and at the 7 Gun Battery at the end of Ferdinand's Dyke silenced; so that (at the first appearance) the occupying of the remains of Fort Pimentel would not only in itself afford a good situation for a Battery to forward the great object, but would materially assist us in becoming Masters of the Dyke St. Ferdinand, behind which Mortar Batteries to any extent might subsequently be established.

To counteract, however, these advantages there appear Reasons on the other side against the occupation of Fort Pimentel, & which, I confess, appear to me to throw the Balance against such a measure. In the first place since the Low Country between Merxem and the Scheldt is inundated, we could not communicate with or support any detached Corps in that Direction without going to the rear by Eckeren[2] and Wilmersdorf.[3]

In the next place, the advantages of silencing Fort du Nord is not very great as it is only mounted with six 12pdrs and two small Howitzers which if our right is at Merxem could not affect us. The Battery of the seven 24pdrs

1. TNA, PRO30/35/1, pp. 64–7.
2. Ekeren.
3. Unknown location.

which enfilades the inside of the Dyke St. Ferdinand it would entirely be desirable to dismount, but after all not more so than the Guns of any other Battery upon the Ramparts of the Place bearing upon Merxem. This Battery will be even more distant from us than the Body of the Place as also lower. The other advantage Fort Pimentel might be supposed to give, namely a favourable Emplacement for a Mortar Battery, may be found equally in front of Merxem without the disadvantages of detaching[,] by avoiding which our Corps can be well Kept together to repulse any Sorties or other operations the Enemy may undertake. Upon the Dyke however on which Fort Pimentel is situated a small Body might be posted as a Corps of Observation to give Information of any Movement the Enemy might attempt in that quarter.

The occupation of Merxem seems the Key to our operations, and in front of it, and on its left, there appear to be several situations where Mortar Batteries may be placed to great effect so as to take the Basin diagonally as also in its greatest length.

How far on the left it may be desirable to place one Battery to obtain the last advantage, namely of taking the Basin in its greatest length, the Commander of the Forces will be left to judge when upon the spot, and whether or not it may be advisable to place it on the other side [of] the Schine.[1] At any rate it will be requisite to have two Bridges established upon the River to communicate with the Prussians or with our own left should we cross it and occupy any ground on the other side.

At the Gap in St Ferdinand's Dyke it would appear that the Enemy have established a Battery with a Palisade in front of it. Once however in possession of Merxem it may be taken in the Rear should it not have been silenced during our Advance.

The five Bastions and three Ravelins counting from the Scheldt and by the Red Gate were only mounted with 20 Guns – 6pdrs, 8pdrs and 12pdrs when Capt. Gorcum left Antwerp.[2] There were no Mortars or Howitzers. As however there were plenty in the Town it is to be supposed that these Points are now completely armed. The Garrison consists of

1. The Klein Schijn brook, although Carmichael Smyth here upgrades it to the status of a river.
2. Van Gorkum, Jan Egburtus (ed. L. J. F. Janssen), *De Bestorming der Vesting Bergen op Zoom, op den 8sten Maart 1814* (Leiden: Hooiberg & Zoon, 1862).

18 Battns, 450 each	8,100
Two Companies of Sappers	180
Artillery	600

With Sailors and Veterans the whole were completed to amount to 10,000 Men. ⅞ of the Soldiers might be reckoned Conscripts.

The Citadel is represented as having been completely armed and provisioned ever since the allies first crossed the Rhine.

That Carmichael Smyth was able to provide such useful intelligence was in no small part down to Captain Jan van Gorkum, a Dutch officer of engineers in French service who deserted to the allies bringing with him detailed knowledge of the French defences at Antwerp as well as elsewhere. Van Gorkum, who left a useful account of the campaign, was commissioned into the new Dutch Army and served alongside Carmichael Smyth in the operations against Antwerp and Bergen-op-Zoom. With so many inexperienced subordinates, it is hardly surprising that Carmichael Smyth sought the opinion and cooperation of an experienced engineer officer with local knowledge. The two men evidently became good friends, continuing to correspond after the war, but it was perhaps unfortunate that van Gorkum shared Carmichael Smyth's sanguine opinion of the chances of achieving success against the French fortresses. Thus, as will be seen in particular when it came to the planning of the attack on Bergen-op-Zoom, the two men encouraged one another in their plans rather than allowing them to be tested against a more neutral professional analysis. For the time being, however, Antwerp remained the objective as Graham sought to act on the recommendations in his chief engineer's report. Because of the relative weakness of Graham's forces, it was necessary to enlist the co-operation of the Prussian III Korps, commanded by Generalleutnant Friedrich-Wilhelm von Bülow, in these operations.

Carmichael Smyth to Mann *14th January,*
Calmthout in Brabant, No. 3[1]

Sir,

The British Army in this Country advanced from the Cantonments they occupied upon the River Merke [Mark] on the 10th Instant in conjunction with a Prussian Force under the orders of Lt. General Bulow. The object of this forward movement was to dislodge the Enemy from the position he occupied at Westwesel, Hoogstraten, & Turnhout & if possible to cut him off from Antwerp. It was afterwards in contemplation to proceed upon Antwerp, and act as circumstances might require.

The British Column was directed (with a view to the above objects) on Calmthout, to the left and rear of the Enemy's Position. The Prussians in three Columns moved upon the three points I have mentioned above. The Enemy was Driven by the Prussians and lost about 2,000 in Killed and wounded. He however retired upon Antwerp by his right & avoided our Troops altogether notwithstanding every exertion was made to intercept him. These Attacks took place on the 11th.

On the 12th the Prussians were employed in closing up their Columns (which were a good deal lengthened out by their long and harassing Marches) and on the 13th we again moved forward in conjunction with them to attack the Enemy who occupied the Villages (in force) in front of Antwerp. The Village of Merxem which came to the share of the British and one end of which is within 400 yards of the Works of Antwerp was carried by the Bayonet, the French General who commanded with about 150 of his Men being Killed, and as many taken.[2] The Vicinity of Antwerp offered every facility for the escape of the Enemy, or a very considerable number of Prisoners would have been taken.

The Garrison of Antwerp consists (including the Corps now driven in) of about 12,000 men. They are however of a bad description most of them young Conscripts & 2,000 of them Sailors

The force we had of British and Prussians was adequate to have kept the Enemy within the works, but General Bulow was afraid of his Left, as

1. TNA, PRO30/35/6, pp. 7–11.
2. The French in Merxem were under Général de Division Jean-Jacques Ambert, who survived the battle; the officer killed was his second-in-command, Général de Brigade Antoine-Sylvain Avy.

Marshal McDonald is still on this side [of] the Rhine and might move suddenly upon him. Under these circumstances we retired, & the Prussians are to occupy Breda, & the British Cantonments in the Country about Rosendaal for the present.

Our Advance upon Antwerp has afforded me an opportunity of seeing the Works of the Place, and I have no hesitation in giving it as my decided opinion that whenever circumstances will allow us to advance in front of Antwerp for 48 hours we can burn the Naval Arsenal and the fifteen sail of the line now moor'd within the Docks or great Basins lately excavated. The Ships lay with their broadsides touching each other, or nearly so. There are several most advantageous Positions for Mortars & Howitzers within so short a range as 1,500 and even 1,300 yards. Great works have been projected by the French, and in particular one or two detached Forts with a view of occupying some commanding Ground & of Keeping an Enemy at a distance from the shipping, but none of them have been executed. They have merely added Redoubts to the former Fortifications of Antwerp on the Face looking down the Scheldt & these are not in a finished state. A Lieut. Colonel and a Captain of Engineers the latter of who has been stationed at Antwerp for two Years (Dutchmen by birth) came over to us during the Affair of Yesterday & they have promised to add to a plan of Antwerp (which I already have) all the French Improvements. I will take the liberty of sending you a Copy by the first opportunity.

In my opinion of the Practicability of burning the fleet and Arsenal both these gentlemen agree. I am happy also to add that Lieut. Col. Sir George Wood Comm'g the artillery is decidedly of the same opinion.[1] I mention the above circumstances least you might imagine that I was too sanguine in my Expectations. But I trust that whenever the operations of the Allies compel McDonald to retire across the Rhine, or that we shall be strong enough to advance & remain for a short time before Antwerp that I shall have the honour of reporting to you the Destruction of the Fleet, and Naval Arsenal.

I take the liberty of mentioning to you that in the Engineer Stores belonging to a small Battering Train originally meant for Spain but sent to this Country there are Platforms for four 68pdr Carronades, fourteen

---

1. Lt Col Sir George Wood, RA. Commanded the artillery under Graham
    throughout this campaign, and served Wellington in the same capacity in 1815.

24pdr Guns, six 8-Inch Howitzers & four Mortars, complete and with a proportion of Spikes, but neither Hammers or Augers. I conceive it my duty to report this circumstance as (however trifling these Articles) yet most serious delay might have arisen from the want of them.

The Carronades, Mortars & Howitzers were ordered up, & if we had remained another Day at Antwerp would have been required. There must have been an oversight or Neglect on the part of the Person appointed to ship the Stores which might have exposed the Service to considerable Inconvenience.

In a former letter I reported that instead of five Serjeants I have only one, & instead of five first Corporals only three, there being consequently a Deficiency of four Serjeants & two Corporals in the Company of Sappers in this Country. As I am obliged so frequently and constantly to detach small Parties, the complete number of N.C. Officers is particularly required, and as you were good enough to say that the Company should be completed I take the liberty of again mentioning the subject.

I am happy to add that in the Duties we have hitherto had to perform I have experienced very great Zeal & Willingness on the part of the young officers.

I enclose a Sketch of the Country where the Affair of Merxem took place.[1]

Because of the concerns Bülow entertained about his flank, the initial advance on Antwerp failed to achieve its objective. Nothing daunted, Graham began planning for a renewed offensive, and dispatched Carmichael Smyth to the Prussian headquarters at Breda in order to obtain Bülow's renewed cooperation now that it was known that the French forces under MacDonald had in fact moved away from the theatre of operations. As well as Bulow's cooperation, it was also important to secure that of his chief of staff, Oberst Leopold Hermann Ludwig von Boyen, a distinguished officer who later rose to the rank of *Generalfeldmarschall*; both Prussians were also keen to coordinate their operations with the arrival of the leading elements of the Saxon corps commanded by General der Kavallerie Karl-August, Herzog von Saxe-Weimar-Eisenach, which was moving into the Low Countries to

1. This sketch not copied in the letterbook.

reinforce the allied troops there. This was all covered in Carmichael Smyth's report to Graham upon his return from the conference.

Memorandum by Lt. Col. Smyth on returning from Breda
27th Jany. 1814[1]

Lieut. General Bulow said (after reading Genl. Sir Thomas Graham's letter) that he still considered Antwerp as the immediate object of the proposed forward movement; & that in advancing upon Louvain or Malines (should it be necessary) his plan was to throw back the Enemy in order that his left Flank might be secure and that we might not be interrupted in our operations before the place.

He said that the time when he would be able to advance would depend upon the movement of those Battalions lately employed at Bois le Duc who were ordered to march upon Tylbourgh that the moment they arrived at Tylbourgh the whole would advance together,[2] that he did not intend to wait for the Saxons as their arrival was very uncertain in consequence of the difficulty in passing the Waal, but that they would follow his movements & support him where necessary

He added that in every respect the spirit of the arrangement as provisionally drawn up the day before yesterday would be adhered to, that his Head Quarters would be the first day's march at Westwissel & that if Sir Thomas Graham would place his at Calmthout on the same day; he would communicate with him that evening & either proceed towards Antwerp as agreed upon or move towards Lier & Malines according to the information he expected to receive from General Borstell[3] who had sent a strong reconnaissance of cavalry towards Lier which he was ordered if possible to occupy.

With respect to the Mortars & heavy stores at Breda he still wishes them to move one day's march in his rear upon the great causeway – as they will consequently not have left Breda on the Evening of the first day's march when he will communicate with Sir Thomas Graham, orders can be sent to delay them should he leave the Antwerp road and move towards Malines;

---

1. TNA, WO1/199, pp. 533–40.
2. Tilburg; Bois le Duc, mentioned earlier, is now known by the Dutch name 's-Hertogenbosch.
3. Generalmajor Karl von Borstell, commanding 5. Brigade, III Korps.

JAMES CARMICHAEL SMYTH   13

or they can be suffered to advance to West Wessel if it should be prudent to allow this.

In answer to the observation I made respecting our situation at Calmthout should the Prussians march towards their left; Genl. Bulow said that he could leave two or three battalions to reinforce us; & that as the Saxons were not to move with him he would direct them to join us. He also said that if he moved towards Malines he should at any rate go through Braeschaat & that he would there leave a post of observation.

In going over both to General Bulow & to General Boyen the probable details of the operations before Antwerp, I pointed out in consequence of recent information, Sir Thomas Graham might perhaps judge it right to make some alterations in the first plan & that it might be advisable to occupy the remains of the Fort Pimentel on the banks of the Scheldt; which would thus be the *point d'appui* upon our right.[1] Genl. Bulow stated that it would make no difference – and both he and Genl. Boyen afterwards stated (in another room) that we ought not to embrace a greater front than our means would allow and that wherever we placed the left they would place their right & General Boyen assured me that if requisite they would cordially cooperate in the attack upon Merxem; the possession of which appears so indispensable to our success.

The result of this conference was an agreement for a renewed advance on Antwerp, leading to the Second Battle of Merxem. The course of this attack, and the subsequent bombardment, is related in Carmichael Smyth's next report to General Mann.

Carmichael Smyth to Mann   *Braeschat, near Antwerp,*
                                          5th Feb, No. 4[2]

Sir,

General Sir Thomas Graham having determined to make an attempt to destroy the Fleet and Arsenal at Antwerp, & having concerted with the Prussian General Bulow the Details of the Different Movements & the co-operation we were to receive from his Army, the British Troops were

1. 'Point d'appui'; literally meaning fulcrum, here signifying a point of assembly or concentration.
2. TNA, PRO30/35/6, pp. 12–17.

put in motion on the 29th Ult. and concentrated in the Neighbourhood of Braeschaat on the Evening of the 1st Instant. On the morning of the 2nd the Village of Merxem of which we had possession upon the former occasion was attacked and carried with the utmost gallantry notwithstanding the Enemy had constructed several Field Works, Abbatis [sic], and Entrenchments for its defence and by inundating the Country to a considerable extent confined our approach to a smaller front. A Convoy of Wagons with intrenching [sic] Tools followed the attacking Column and as soon as the Enemy were driven into Antwerp I selected the Situation for our Batteries, with a view to destroy the Fleet, which were immediately traced and commenced upon. The next forenoon (on the 3rd) we opened a fire upon the enemy from 17 Mortars, two Howitzers and six 24pdrs – four of the latter of which fired with hot Shot.

It was impossible to sustain the most sanguine hopes of a favourable Result, notwithstanding however the utmost Exertions of every Officer and Man in the Army and the very excellent Practice made by the artillery who threw more than 2,000 shells & a continued fire of three Days we have not obtained the objective in view. The ships were repeatedly on Fire, several Fires Kindled in Buildings round them, and a large Store Room containing the Biscuit and Provisions for the Fleet being destroyed by being put on Fire. The Vessels themselves, however, have not been burnt and I am afraid it is not possible to destroy them without much larger means than we at present possess. The Enemy kept a number of People on board of these provided with Buckets and Fire Engines, and as fast as a fire was kindled it was extinguished. It appears therefore absolutely necessary to ensure success that we should not only have Mortars enough to set fire to the shipping but to enable us to throw such an overwhelming quantity of Shells as to render it totally impossible for any men to work whilst exposed to it. Congreave Rockets have been requested as peculiarly adapted for this sort of Service but as I have never seen them used I cannot give an opinion. We have none with this Army, or they would unquestionably have been made use of, and had a fair trial.

The Prussian Army having received orders from the Head Quarters of the Grand Allied Army to advance immediately, we have been obliged to break up from before Antwerp this morning, & to return to Cantonments (for the present) on the Frontiers of Holland, as we are not strong enough to keep the Garrison of Antwerp in check and carry on the Bombardment by ourselves.

I enclose,

 1st. A Copy of the Orders regulating the disposition of the Attack on the morning of the 2nd.

 2nd. A copy of the General Orders issued by General Sir Thomas Graham as far as concerns this Department.

 3rd. A tracing of the Plan of Antwerp with the Situation of our Batteries.[1]

No. 1. Copy of the Disposition for the Attack on Merxem by General Sir Thomas Graham 2nd Feb'y, Braeschaat.

The Attack on Merxem will be made this morning by the 2nd Division, having a Brigade of Guards of the first Division in Reserve on the great Chaussée. Major General Skerret's [sic] Brigade with the three Flank Companies from Denthoust[2] will move from that place by the most direct paths leading on Antwerp to the left of Merxem, but as nearly parallel to the great Road as possible.

As far as circumstances of ground will admit light troops will be detached on each side of the Chaussée from the head of the second Division so as to endeavour to get in by the Flanks of the Village. Care will be taken however that the troops so employed shall always have support in Reserve, and frequent reports will be sent in from the officers to the head of the Column.

Sir George Wood will take care that the heavy artillery shall be ready to be brought up in case it shall be found necessary to employ it against the village of Merxem.

As soon as the Enemy is driven out of the Village, the avenues leading into it from Antwerp will be strongly occupied and Lieut. Colonel Carmichael Smyth Commanding the Engineers will lose no time in forming Barricades and such other Works as he may think necessary to defend it against any attempt by the Enemy.

As it may be expected that the Enemy will throw shells from the Ramparts of Antwerp, the Village will at first be occupied with all attention to find shelter for the troops from the effect of such Bombardment, no more

1. This plan not copied in the letterbook.

2. Den Hout; these were the flank companies of the 2/21st and 2/37th, the remainder of these battalions being in garrison.

being allowed to remain in the Village and within range of the Artillery of the place than what are necessary for its defence and for carrying on the works already mentioned.

Lieut. Colonel Smyth will likewise mark out such Mortar Batteries as he may think necessary and will send in to the Adjutant General a detail of such working parties as he may require.

No.2 Extract from the General Orders issued by General Sir Thomas Graham   dated Braeschaat, 6th Feby. 1814

Circumstances having occurred since the Commencement of the late operations which render it indispensably necessary to desist from the Enterprise against Antwerp, the Commander of the Forces cannot omit this opportunity of expressing his entire Approbation of the Conduct of the Troops and returning his thanks to the General Officers and Men on this occasion. It must have been evident to the whole Army that the Commanding Officer of Artillery Sir George Wood and Commanding Engineer Lieut. Col. Carmichael Smyth with all the Officers and Men of their respective Corps deserve the highest Praise – there never was any occasion where better Arrangements for the ready Execution of the Service or greater Exertions in the course of it were made by those distinguished Corps. The want of success can only be attributed to the want of time and of greater means.

Carmichael Smyth to Mann   Braeschaat near Antwerp, 7th Feb, No. 5[1]

With reference to the late transactions before Antwerp, I beg to report to you that Serjt. Stevens of the Company of Sappers and Miners is the only Serjeant present with the Company. He is a remarkably good Man, and having superintended the laying of Platforms and made a Splinter Proof Magazine under a heavy fire with Coolness and Courage I am fully justified in recommending him to your Notice to be made Colour Sergeant to the Company & which appointment (I believe) is extended to the Companies of Sappers and Miners by His Royal Highness the Prince Regent's last Regulations on the subject.[2]

---

1. TNA, PRO30/35/6, p. 18.

2. Stevens received the promotion, and, after further distinguished service in 1815,

I also beg to recommend Acting Serjeant Melbourne (a Corporal in the Company) to be made a Serjeant in consequence of his activity and good conduct.

In due course, these reports would meet with the following message of approval from Carmichael Smyth's superiors in London.

Colonel Rowley to Carmichael Smyth   *Pall Mall,*
                                              15th February 1814[1]

Sir,

By Lieut. General Mann's desire I have to acquaint you that your report (No. 4) dated 6th Instant has been laid before the Master General who has been pleased to express his full Approbation of the Zealous Exertions of yourself and the other Officers of Engineers, as well as the Officers, Non Commissioned Officers & Privates of the Royal Sappers and Miners under your Command in the late endeavours to destroy the Enemy's fleet &c at Antwerp, of which approbation you will be pleased to make the necessary Communications to the Brigade under your Command.

The Prussian troops having been called away to join the main allied armies in France, Graham was obliged for the time being to give up thoughts of mounting a direct attack against Antwerp. This did not, however, prevent the British commander from giving up all hope of offensive operations, and it was decided to explore the possibility of making an attack against some of the outlying fortifications that acted as satellites to the main enemy concentration around Antwerp itself. Carmichael Smyth was naturally called upon to furnish his professional opinion of the best means of attacking either Fort Batz or the town of Lier. Fort Batz stood at the south-eastern tip of South Beveland from where, along with Bergen-op-Zoom, it covered the northernmost passage of the Scheldt estuary. Lier lies ten miles southeast of Antwerp, and control of it was felt to be important for covering the flanks of any operation against Antwerp, and, in the event that more troops became

obtained a commission on Carmichael Smyth's recommendation. See also Connolly, T. W. J., *The History of the Corps of Royal Sappers and Miners* (London: Longman, Brown, Green & Longman, 1855), Vol. I, p. 207.

1. TNA, PRO30/35/1, p. 90.

available, facilitating effective cooperation between two wings of a force besieging Antwerp on both banks of the Scheldt.

Memorandums [sic] Respecting Batz

Groot Zundert
17th Feby. 1814[1]

The Fortifications of Batz consist (according to the best information we have been able to get) of a large square Work with Redans on three sides to afford a cross fire. The fourth side, which is the one opposite the Water, is perfectly straight and mounted with a considerable number of heavy Guns for the defence of the River and to impede the Progress of Vessels towards Antwerp. The Fortifications are entirely of Earth without any Revetment surrounded by a broad and deep Ditch. They are moreover well palisaded. The extent of the Fort is not accurately Known nor is there any information respecting its Profile, but from the Depth and Breadth of the Ditch it may reasonably be conjectured that there would not be much probability of breaching an Earthwork of such magnitude. The interior of the Work contains Barracks for 1,000 or 1,500 Men with several public Buildings; lately the Enemy have constructed Bomb proofs or a sort of Blindage to afford cover for the Garrison.[2]

The only mode to attack a Work of this nature appears to be to silence its Defences by constructing Enfilading Batteries and to destroy or weary out the Garrison by Shells. The Depth and breadth of the Ditch precludes the idea of any attempt to carry it by assault even if it should be found possible to destroy the Palisades by previous Fire.

A Battery of six 24pdrs appears to be necessary in the first Instance to enfilade and silence the western Front. This done effectually, would give us the command of the Western Dyke which affords cover to approach and establish a Battery to enfilade the Northern or land Front. For the above objects, including the first proposed Battery, twelve 24pdrs appear to be necessary. Two Mortar Batteries each consisting of 4 Mortars might also be established at any convenient situation and continue animated from the first; some 8inch Howitzers with Spherical Case might also be usefully employed, so as to distract the Enemy and contribute to the Surrender of the Place.

1. TNA, PRO30/35/1, pp. 67–70.
2. 'Blindage': a protective screen or cover.

For the above purposes and reasoning upon the Information which we at present possess it is supposed that the following would be pretty nearly the amount of the Military Means requisite for the Reduction of Batz.

1st – 12 24pdrs

2nd – 8 Mortars

3rd – 4 8inch Howitzers, Field Guns with Spherical Case

4th – Entrenching Tools and Engineer Stores in proper
Proportion for the Construction of the Batteries.

To afford a relief and to work the Ordnance with Promptitude it does not appear that with less than 200 Gunners the Service could be undertaken; but as the Navy would be able to afford great assistance of Seamen for the Guns, perhaps one company of Artillery might answer the purpose.

With respect to the number of Troops as not only a sufficient number to construct the Batteries &c and to contain the Garrison would be required, but also to be able to repel any attempt either from Flushing or Antwerp to relieve the Place or reinforce the Garrison; it is impossible to make any Calculation as that must depend entirely upon Circumstances and Contingencies of which the Commander of the Forces is the sole and the best Judge. Without any view, however, to any attempt from Flushing or Antwerp and solely to furnish the Working Parties and Guards to contain the Garrison 1,200 Men appear the least number with which the Reduction of Batz could be attempted.

Memorandum Respecting Lier   *Headquarters Groot Zundert,*
22nd February 1814[1]

Lier is a considerable town with a great deal of open space, and in consequence occupies a much larger extent of ground than from the number of its Inhabitants (which are stated to amount only to 10,000 Souls) might be otherwise supposed. It is surrounded by an old rampart (built as far back as the Duke of Alva); a wet Ditch is in front of about half the Extent of the Works the other half is secured by the Nette,[2] one Branch of which flows around that part of the Town whilst another (the principal one) runs through it and admits Vessels or rather Craft of considerable Burthen from the Scheldt.

1. TNA, PRO30/35/1, pp. 88–9.
2. The River Nethe.

The great difficulty in making a Post of Lier would be the extent of its Ençiente [sic].[1] I am confident I am within Bounds when I calculate it at one Mile and a half. It occurred to me at first that perhaps it might be only necessary to arm and repair as also to guard that Front facing Antwerp; as Lier may be said to be à cheval upon the Nette and might be supposed (in consequence) to have its rear and its Flanks secured by that River. There are Bridges, however, upon the Nette at the Villages both above and below, and of course excepting they were destroyed and the Villages occupied, any Troops left in Lier would have to attend equally to the whole Circumference of the Town.

The Country between Westmalle and Santhoven[2] is flat, wooded and intersected with Roads. From Santhoven to Lier, though more open, as you approach Lier, yet there are so many Roads leading from Antwerp upon this Line, and upon the whole so many Plantations that it would be a very difficult Task to patrole [sic] it properly; nor would it be possible to prevent the Enemy from Antwerp (if disposed) acting upon that Line of Communication when and where he pleases and constantly harassing our Convoys. The Enemy now patrole to within a few Miles of Lier.

In the event, the operations against Lier and Fort Batz were not carried out, and attention instead turned to the possibility of making a move against Bergen-op-Zoom. The planning of this operation, and its outcome, were detailed by Carmichael Smyth in his next formal report to Mann.

Carmichael Smyth to Mann   *Calmthout, 10th March, No. 6*[3]

Sir,

Some reinforcements having joined this Army from England, as also the Brigade from Germany under B Genl. Gore the Commander of the Forces determined to advance from the Cantonments we had occupied upon the frontiers of Holland ever since our return from the attack upon the fleet at Antwerp; and a few days ago, in consequence, our Right was placed at Fort Frederick close to Lillo upon the Scheldt and our left at the village of

1. The *enceinte*; that is to say, the main defensible perimeter of the place.
2. Zandhoven.
3. TNA, PRO30/35/6, pp. 19–24.

Braschaet. At Fort Frederick a battery secured by strong palisades, trous de loup[1] &c has been constructed to cut off all communication by water from Antwerp to Bergen-op-Zoom and Batz; and the village of Braschaet upon our left has been strengthened by field works. It is also in contemplation to secure Eckeren and Donk by strong works so as to enable us by a chain of posts to prevent the Garrison of Antwerp deriving any succours from the Country on this side of the Scheldt. By means also of these posts a larger proportion of our force is rendered disposable and a greater assemblage of course may be made upon any one front.

The greatest deficiency however in making any arrangements for forward movements was the fortress of Bergen op Zoom which could not be left in the rear without a considerable corps to mask it. Its capture also, with a view to the security of Holland should any reverse of affairs take place is so very evident that Sir Thomas Graham was induced to make a considerable effort to gain possession of this important fortress.

We have not as yet the means for a siege of so much importance. The season indeed which prevents our landing and receiving our stores would not enable us to use them if we had them. A scheme was therefore proposed and digested for an assault at night, which may be said to have completely succeeded and a considerable Corps of troops were introduced into the body of the place.

It is not for me to offer any remarks on its subsequent evacuation. I enclose a sketch of the town showing the different points of attack and which will render the following details more intelligible.[2]

The Column attacking at A had to ford the small River called the Zoom, and which forms the harbour of Bergen-op-Zoom.[3] The River at the point where it enters the town is not more at low tide than 1 foot or 18 inches deep. As it was low tide on the night of the 8th instant, about 10 o'clock, this was the general hour fixed for the whole of the attack.

The obstacles to be got the better of were; an armed vessel with a guard on board at the harbour mouth. The Ford of the river was moreover covered with Harrows. A row of strong palisades also runs from the flanked angle to its gorge of that bastion to the right of the storming party as they came in.

1. That is to say 'wolf pits', holes dug to impede access to a defensive position.
2. Map not copied in letterbook; however, see maps 4 and 5 in this work.
3. See the account of 2nd Lt Moodie in this volume.

These Harrows were removed, and the palisades cut down by a detachment of sappers under Lt. Sperling Royal Engineers,[1] who was the Engineer attached to this Column and who conducted himself in a most manly and gallant manner.

The Guards who made the attack at B were conducted to the point of attack by Captain Sir George Hoste of the Engineers assisted by Lieutenant Abbey,[2] having a detachment of sappers with axes to cut down the palisades of the Covertway [covered way] and also charged with the carrying and placing of the ladders required to descend the counterscarp as also to ascend the Escarpe [scarp]. These duties were executed with great coolness and decision, and the Guards mounted the ramparts with very little loss. This attack, as being the central one, I accompanied myself.

The Column destined to attack at C did not succeed. They descended the counterscarp and placed the ladders to ascend; but the principle [sic] officers having been killed or wounded it was judged proper to withdraw the regiments.[3] They were however ordered to the point A[4] to follow the Guards and ascended by the same ladders without any opposition.

As I had no Engineer officer present with this Division of the Army to attach to this Column Capt. Mitchell of the Artillery volunteered and requested of me to be employed as such.[5] I cannot say how much I am obliged to him, and how gallantly he performed the duty he had undertaken. He received three severe wounds at the foot of the Escarpe. As he was acting with us I hope there will be no impropriety in my requesting of you to Mention his name to the Master General along with the Engineer Officers employed upon this occasion.

You will perceive by the foregoing narrative that with the exception of the Officers and Men disabled by casualties we had every soldier within

1. Lt John Sperling, RE. First commissioned December 1811, served throughout Graham's campaign and also during the Waterloo campaign. His own account of his experiences, based on his letters home to his father, was later published; see Sperling, John, *Letters of an Officer of the Corps of Royal Engineers from the British Army in Holland, Flanders, and France to his Father, from the Latter end of 1813 to 1816* (London: James Nisbet & Co., 1872).
2. Lt Charles Abbey, RE.
3. See the account of Ensign Thain, reproduced in this volume.
4. In fact he means point B.
5. Capt. Edward Mitchell, RA.

the works intended to have been brought there, or whom it had been proposed to employ upon any of the assaults.

We had tranquil possession of the Rampart as far as we extended. The firing was apparently completely at an end. About 4 o'clock in the morning I went out of the town to report to Sir Thomas Graham the state of things and at the same time [was] authorized by M General Cooke to say that his intentions were to keep his people well together and as little exposed as possible until day light when he would be enabled to see what the enemy were about and he would then act accordingly.

I saw Sir Thomas Graham and was returning back again a little after Day light with a message to M. General Cooke to recommend that he should send in to the Governor some person to point out the folly of any further resistance which would only irritate our Soldiers to give no quarter. I was also to have conducted in 500 more of the Guards & the 35th Regiment. Impressed as I was in point of fact that the Town was already ours and that as soon as it was broad day the Garrison must lay down their arms, you will judge my mortification at seeing some of our regiments retreating by the Water Port Gate and at hearing that the Royals had Surrendered. The Guards soon afterwards re-descended their ladders.

As all the Casualties that had happened had already taken place previous to my leaving the town, and as by keeping possession of those Bastions the fire of which could bear upon the scaling ladders we had a sure road to secure reinforcements (if it was thought we were too few to attack the Garrison after having scaled the ramparts) I am at a loss to conceive the reasons for evacuating what we had gained with so much credit and with so much loss.

I trust the conduct of the officers of the Engineers will meet with your approbation. The officers employed were Captain Sir George Hoste, Lieutenants Abbey and Sperling.

Lieut. Abbey is severely wounded & I am afraid will not live.[1] Sub Lieutenant Adamson of the Sappers and Miners is killed as also I believe about twenty of the men.[2] I have not yet got a correct return but will forward one the first opportunity.

1. See Bamford, *Bold and Ambitious Enterprise*, pp. 201–2.
2. Sub-Lt Thomas Adamson.

Carmichael Smyth to Mann   *Calmthout, 10th March, No. 7*[1]

Sir,

In reporting to you the death of Sub Lieutenant Adamson of the Sappers and Miners who was killed at the foot of the Escarpe at Bergen op Zoom on the evening of the 8th March I should wish to solicit you in favour of Acting Serjeant Major Adam of the Royal Artillery who is with the Artillery in this Country and who is most strongly and highly spoken of by Sir George Wood. I am aware that you must have many applications for these appointments and that I have no claim upon your notice; but from the character I have heard and what I have myself seen of the Serjeant Major I think he will be a useful officer to the Sappers and Miners.[2]

Carmichael Smyth to Mann   *Calmthout, 25th March, No. 8*[3]

Sir,

I have the honor [*sic*] to lay before you a Return of the Killed, Wounded and Prisoners amongst the Company of Sappers in this Country in the late assault at Bergen op Zoom. I could not have the return made out sooner as some of the wounded and all of the prisoners were in the Enemy's power.[4]

The prisoners are to be sent home by the earliest convenience under an engagement not to serve in Europe until exchanged – but their Services are applicable to all other parts of the world. As the Company is so much reduced (having also lost two Men severely wounded at Antwerp) I beg you will have the goodness to order it to be completed again as soon as convenient as their Services are understood to be likely to be again soon required.

I beg leave very respectfully to return my thanks for your attention to my recommendations respecting promotions, & more particularly for that of the vacant Sub-Lieutenancy.

1. TNA, PRO30/35/6, p. 25.
2. This was James Adam, who was subsequently commissioned as a sub-lieutenant on 21 March 1814. He served through the Hundred Days campaign, but was placed on half pay from 1817.
3. TNA, PRO30/35/6, p. 26.
4. Return not copied in letterbook, but casualties amounted to two dead and ten taken prisoner. Around fifteen men, including some of those taken prisoner, were wounded. See Connolly, *Royal Sappers and Miners*, Vol. I, p. 208.

In the aftermath of the Bergen-op-Zoom disaster, Graham again turned his attention to Antwerp. With his own forces severely diminished, it was evident that a substantial allied contribution would be needed: attempts were made to secure the cooperation of Dutch, Saxon and Prussian forces, but little actual assistance was forthcoming. Nevertheless, Carmichael Smyth was busily employed working out the engineering requirements of such a siege, and, as an alternative, those that would be needed for an attempt to reduce the rather more manageable objective of Fort Batz.

Memorandum respecting the number of Engineer Officers &
Sappers & Miners required for the Siege of Antwerp, supposing
that it should be deemed advisable to approach from both sides of
the Scheldt at once   Calmthout, 25 March 1814[1]

	Captns. RE	Subns. RE	Sappers.
In constructing the Batteries & carrying on the approaches of the principal Attack there ought to be constantly employed 2 Captns., 4 Subns., and 60 Sappers, which to give the necessary reliefs requires:	6	12	180
Do. Do. the second Attack which it is supposed will not be so extreme, will require nevertheless 1 Captn., 3 Subns., 30 Sappers, constantly which to have the relief:	3	9	90

	Captns. RE	Subns. RE	Sappers.
We have in the country	2	4	60
and under orders	2	–	–
	4	4	60
	9	21	270
	4	4	60
	5	17	210

1. TNA, PRO30/35/6, p. 27.

We consequently require an addition of 5 Captains 17 Subalterns & 210 Sappers. As however several Officers from the Line may be expected to be procured to act as Assistant Engineers, the number of Subaltern Engineers may perhaps be diminished; but I do not think the number of Captains or sappers can be reduced.

Memorandum respecting the Estimate of the time that may probably be required for the reduction of Batz   Calmthout, 31 March 1814[1]

The two Mortar Batteries may be constructed and the Platforms laid in

	24 Hours
The first Gun Battery required to enfilade the Western Front	24 –"–
It may be proper to allow this Battery to produce the effect desired	48 –"–
The construction of the 2nd Gun Battery	24 –"–
Time for the Battery to play	48 –"–
It may be proper to allow for accidental unavoidable delays, damage by the Enemy's fire	48 –"–

Hours 216
or Nine Days

Eventually, when it became clear that there was no likelihood of being able to mount operations against Antwerp, Graham authorised an attack on Fort Batz, albeit with rather smaller resources than outlined by Carmichael Smyth. In the event, however, this operation was incomplete by the time that news was received of the abdication of Napoleon and the consequent cessation of hostilities.[2] Carmichael Smyth's remaining correspondence therefore deals for the most part with administrative measures relating to the occupation of Antwerp, and his report on the state of the fortifications at that place. He must, however, have been both gratified and relieved to find that the following communication from London provided official endorsement and commendation of the role of the engineers under his command at Bergen-op-Zoom.

1. TNA, PRO30/35/1, p. 82.
2. For a brief account of this undertaking, see the memoir by Lt Shaw in this volume.

Colonel Rowley to Carmichael Smyth   *Pall Mall, 2nd April 1814*[1]

Sir,

Lieut. General Mann desires me to inform you that His Lordship the Master General, before whom your report of the late gallant though unsuccessful attempt upon the Fortress of Bergen-op-Zoom has been laid, has expressed himself highly satisfied with the zealous conduct of yourself and the Officers of Engineers, as well as the Officers, Non Commissioned Officers & Soldiers of the Royal Sappers and Miners on the above occasion.

I am also desired to convey a particular approbation of the gallantry and ability shewn by Lieutenant Sperling while attached to the advanced party which first entered the Fortress under the immediate command of the late Colonel Carleton.[2]

You will be pleased to make known this Communication to the Officers and Men under your orders.

Carmichael Smyth to Mann   *Head Quarters Graven Wesel,*
30th April 1814, No. 9[3]

Sir,

I have the honor to report to you that the Commander of the Forces has been pleased to grant two Months Leave of Absence to Captain Thomson to enable him to return to England on account of his private affairs from this day's date.

Carmichael Smyth to Mann   *Antwerp, 5th May, No. 10*[4]

Sir,

I have great pleasure in reporting to you that His Majesty's Troops this morning took possession of Antwerp, the Citadel, as also the Redoubts and Forts upon the Scheldt in its vicinity.

1. TNA, PRO30/35/1, p. 91.
2. Lt Col Hon. George Carleton, 44th Foot, was the nominated commander of the Right Attack at Bergen-op-Zoom but since that column was accompanied by Generals Skerrett and Gore, Carleton had instead led its Forlorn Hope. In this capacity he was killed after leading a small party around the ramparts. See Bamford, *Bold and Ambitious Enterprise*, pp. 190–200.
3. TNA, PRO30/35/6, p. 28.
4. TNA, PRO30/35/6, pp. 29–30.

In consequence of the agreements or convention entered into with the French Government respecting the Low Countries, General Count Kunigl (an Austrian Officer) arrived here a few days ago with full powers on the part of the allies to receive the different Fortresses, and to make the necessary arrangements (conjointly with a French Commissioner) for the withdrawing the French Troops within the prescribed limits. The Commander of the Forces sent me into Antwerp on the 2nd, to receive the Plans, Models, and every thing relative to the Engineer Department, as also to examine the state in which the Defences were about to be left by the French Garrison.

I hope in a short time to be able to transmit a full and detailed statement of every thing relative to the fortifications of this Important Station, which information cannot but be desirable to have in our possession into whatever hands the navigation of the Scheldt may ultimately fall. I propose also to avail myself of the present opportunity of ordering copies to be made, without delay, of the best of the plans and Sections in the Office here, and also causing such others to be carefully taken as may be found requisite to give complete information relative to the place.

Carmichael Smyth to Mann   Antwerp, 15 May 1814, No. 11[1]

Sir,

I beg leave to inform you that the Commander of the Forces has been pleased to grant one month's leave of absence from this day's date to Major Sir George Hoste to enable him to return to England on account of his private affairs.

Carmichael Smyth to Mann   Antwerp, 7 June 1814, No. 12[2]

Sir,

I have the honor to forward to you a detailed Report of the Fortifications of this place and of its dependencies, as also plans and sections according to the accompanying List, of every part of the works which appeared to me at all necessary to be Known should we ever have again to undertake any hostile operations upon the Scheldt.[3]

1. TNA, PRO30/35/6, p. 30.
2. TNA, PRO30/35/6, pp. 31–3.
3. This report is not copied in the letterbook.

Having submitted the report to the Commander of the Forces, as also the plans he has thought it advisable that I should forward them to you by an officer of Engineers. I have selected Lieut. Sperling for this duty as I believe him fully competent to afford any additional explanation that may be required. I trust you will have the goodness to permit him to return to this Country as soon as convenient, with any orders or instructions you may think proper to favour me with.

General Lord Lynedoch returns to England tomorrow for a short time.[1] His Lordship mentioned to me, in private, that the Fortifications of this place as also the Basin and Dock Yards would be in all probability to be destroyed, and ordered me to take the requisite steps that there might be no delay on our part, as soon as the orders should finally be received. Under these circumstances I take the liberty of reporting to you that we will require eighteen chests of Miner's Tools complete, which may be forwarded to Ostend with a Clerk or Conductor of Stores, from which place to here there is a canal. I do not think any Entrenching tools will be wanted from England as we have found a considerable number in this place left by the French and which at any rate will serve us for some time.

I propose to begin by drawing off all the water from the Ditches and then to cause the escarpe [sic] and counterscarpe [sic] to be blown up into them. It appears to me that if the water is then let in again, the ramparts will be so shook and undermined, that they will be perfectly useless, and we may then Trust to Contractors to level them and to fill up the Ditches under proper superintendence.

The Basin in the same manner I propose destroying, namely by first drawing off the water and then blowing the Masonry of the sides into the bottom. By the[n] again letting in the water and again draining it off, the sides divested of their masonry will become so rotten and hollow that I should think it would be easier to excavate a new basin than to repair the one so destroyed. The Pillars of the Flood Gates will of course be afterwards blown up.

The above are the methods which appear to me upon the first blush of the business to be the readiest modes to be adopted. But I trust (as the object is so very important, and one upon which the Eyes of all the Military part of

---

1. Graham had been ennobled as Baron Lynedoch as a reward for his Peninsular service.

Europe will be directed) you will favor me with your sentiments upon the mode I have proposed, and oblige me by at least some general Instructions for my guidance.

I also take the liberty of adding that if another Company of Sappers & Miners can be spared as also some additional Officers to superintend the different operations, the object in view will be much sooner accomplished. Independent of the very extensive works, Antwerp and the Fortifications of the other side of the Scheldt, I presume Lillo, Liefkenshoek, & Batz, will also be to be destroyed.

In fact, no such measures were required to destroy the docks and fortifications, as the eventual peace settlement would leave Antwerp as part of the new Kingdom of the Netherlands. During the coming months of peace, Carmichael Smyth remained on the continent carrying out a series of inspections that served to enhance British understanding of the fortresses in the region. Having been so engaged, he was still in the Low Countries when the return of Napoleon brought about renewed hostilities, and was ideally placed to serve as commanding officer of the Royal Engineer forces under Wellington. Having seen action at Waterloo, he accompanied the allied army in its advance on Paris. After hostilities were over, Carmichael Smyth remained in command of the Royal Engineers on the continent until December 1815, when he went on half pay. In August 1821, on Wellington's recommendation, he was created a baronet, and two years later was employed to conduct an inspection of the fortresses of the Low Countries. He subsequently carried out similar inspection tours in the West Indies and Canada, winning plaudits for his report on the defences of the Canadian border. In 1825 he became a major general. From 1829 he served as a colonial governor, first of the Bahamas and then of British Guiana. Whilst still occupying the last post, he died suddenly on 4 March 1838, after having contracted a fever. He had married in 1816, and was survived by his wife and son.

Chapter II

Ensign Thomas Slingsby Duncombe

2nd Battalion, Coldstream Guards

Tom Duncombe was the son of a Yorkshire squire, born in 1796 at the family's estate near Knaresborough. His uncle, Charles Duncombe, was the effective head of the family and an established Tory politician, and with this wealthy and well-connected background it is unsurprising that the young Thomas made his way from Harrow to the fashionable and expensive Foot Guards.[1] His first commission, as an ensign in the Coldstream, was gazetted on 17 October 1811, before he left school, and he was still only seventeen years old when he embarked upon the brief spell of active service that is covered by the diary extract reproduced here: the extract is itself taken from a biography of Duncombe by his son, published in 1868.

That he merited a biography had little to do with his military career, during which the six months covered by this diary were his only active service, but would be justified by his extensive political career, of which more later.[2] For the time being, however, it is to give away little of what follows to emphasise that Duncombe had already, in his youth, acquired the rakish character for which he would be known throughout his life, nor that the diary that follows represents a fairly harsh indictment of the level of professionalism displayed by some young Guards officers,

1. Officers in the Household regiments, above the rank of ensign, held their commissions under a dual-rank system which, as well as a lower rank representing their regimental role, gave them a higher rank, and the seniority that went with it, in the Army as a whole.
2. Duncombe, Thomas H., *The Life and Correspondence of Thomas Slingsby Duncombe, Late MP for Finsbury* (London: Hurst & Blackett, 1868), Vol. I, pp. 5–21. For further biographical information, see Fisher, David R., 'Duncombe, Thomas Slingsby (1796–1861), of 20 Queen Street, Mayfair, Mdx.', *History of Parliament Online*, at http://www.historyofparliamentonline.org/volume/1820-1832/member/duncombe-thomas-1796-1861.

and of the disdain with which they affected to treat the rest of the Army. Whilst some of these aspects make for unpleasant reading, they give the diary a frankness and honesty that makes it stand out from many later, sanitised, memoirs.

1813
21 November:

Marched at nine o'clock from the Birdcage-walk to Greenwich, where we embarked on board smacks for Harwich. I was on the rear-guard from London to Greenwich, and never were men more drunk than the major part of the Coldstreams.

25 November:

On board the smack.

26 November:

On board the smack; sick.

27 November:

Arrived in Ouzely Bay, twenty miles below Harwich, and went on board the *Dictator*, Captain Croften, with whom we dined.[1]

28 November:

On board the *Dictator*; dined with the lieutenants – a bad set, but a good dinner.

29 November:

On board the *Dictator*

30 November:

Set sail for Holland.

1. Completed in 1783 as a 64-gun ship of the line, HMS *Dictator* was re-rated as a troop ship in June 1813. The ship's commanding officer was Capt. Hon. George Alfred Crofton, RN; see O'Byrne, William Richard, *A Dictionary of Naval Biography* (London: J. Murray, 1849), pp. 257–8.

1 December:

On board the *Dictator*; bad wind.

2 December:

On board the *Dictator*; do.

3 December:

On board the *Dictator.*

4 December:

On board the *Dictator*; a calm.

5 December:

On board the *Dictator*, and anchored within six miles of Schevelinge.[1]

6 December:

Landed at Schevelinge at eleven o'clock, and then marched to the Hague, where we were most handsomely received by all; was billeted upon a Mr. Mirandole; a good house, and I had their state bed-room, without a fire – what a bore! Dined at Lady Athlone's with Bentinck;[2] ate an enormous dinner, and was much pleased with the Hollandois cooking; plenty of hock, champagne, and claret got all my baggage safe; went to my billet; supped with my patron, and went to bed in state. John, my servant, says he 'never seed' such people, that they would give him anything they had, but could not make them understand, as he could not speak Dutch.

1. Scheveningen. It seems a common error by British writers to add an unnecessary l to their attempts to render this place name, apparently in attempt to reproduce the Dutch pronunciation in print.
2. Capt. and Lt Col Charles A. F. Bentinck, Coldstream Guards, then serving as adjutant of the 2nd Battalion. He had previously served with the same battalion at Cadiz and Barossa. His father was Maj. Gen. John Charles Bentinck, and his mother was Lady Jemima de Ginkel, daughter of the 5th Earl of Athlone and his wife, Anna-Elizabeth-Christienne, Baroness de Tuill de Seeroskerin. It is the latter, Dowager Countess since her husband's death in 1808, who was the hostess of this party. See Courthope, William (ed.), *Debrett's Complete Peerage of the United Kingdom of Great Britain and Ireland* (London: J. G. & F. Rivington, 1838), pp. 533–4. The Bentincks had been created counts of the Holy Roman Empire, and Duncombe also uses this title for the son.

7 December:

Slept well, got up and went down to breakfast, and found my patroness and daughters, who gave me some thimble tea-cups of bad tea, and sweet plum biscuits; then went to parade at eleven, determining not to breakfast with my patroness again; after parade went with Gooch[1] to the 'Marechal de Turenne' hotel, and had some chocolate and mutton-chops to make up for my bad dejeuner; passed the morning in looking about the place, and was much pleased by it; dined with my patron, who gave me a pretty fair dinner; played three rubbers of whist with that party, and won two of them; then supped and went to bed.

8 December:

Breakfast in my own bed-room, and then went to the parade; went and ordered some dinner at the Marechal de Turenne; bought a horse; took a walk with Cuyler, and then dined with Walton, Shawe, Wigston, and Drummond[2] at the Marechal's; tea; went home to supper, and then to bed.

9 December:

Breakfasted in my own room; went to the parade; we took a march to Schevelinge and back; took a ride with Cuyler and Poingdestre;[3] dined with my patron; went to see the bivouac of the Cossacks, a very curious sight; went to the comedie; saw given *Le Retour du Prince d'Orange, ou les Pecheurs de Schevelinge;*[4] supped with my patron, and went to bed.

1. Ensign Henry Gooch, Coldstream Guards.
2. Ensign Augustus Cuyler, Lt and Capt. William Lovelace Walton and Lt and Capt. Charles Augustus Shawe, all Coldstream Guards; Lt and Capt. R. H. Wigston, 3rd Foot Guards. The last officer mentioned is either Lt and Capt. William Drummond, or Ensign Barclay Drummond, both 3rd Foot Guards. Walton and Shawe were both Peninsular veterans who had served in 1/Coldstream Guards under Wellington; Wigston and William Drummond had likewise served with the 1st Battalion of their regiment.
3. Ensign J. H. Poingdestre, 3rd Foot Guards.
4. 'The Return of the Prince of Orange, or, the Fishermen of Schevenigen'.

10 December:

Breakfast in my own room; went to the parade played a game at chess with my patron's son; saw sugar made from mangel-worsel;[1] took a ride; pretty well pleased with my bargain; dined with my patron; a bad dinner; nothing but fish, so that I suppose they were Roman Catholics, and this was a fast-day, which did not suit me, so I went with Gooch and Cuyler, and got some good dinner at the Marechal de Turenne's; returned home to supper, and went to bed early, as we were to march the next morning to Delft.

11 December:

Marched at nine o'clock to Delft; sorry to leave the Hague; Gooch and I got a bad billet at a gin-shop, so we had it changed for one of the best houses in the town, and had a good dinner and supper with our patron, and a good bed.

12 December:

Marched to Maynsluys;[2] a very fine frosty day; but a bad town and bad billet; dined; then went and supped and smoked a pipe with Smith.[3]

13 December:

Marched to the Brill;[4] had an uncommon wet march, and unpleasant crossing the Maze;[5] had a tolerable billet; but unfortunately the patroness had her husband in the French service, as well as her son, so that of course she was not very agreeable; but we had a good dinner and a good bed; Brill is a very strong fortified place.

14 December:

Marched to Helvoetsluys; a fine frosty day; and a very strong place; went out to see if there was any skating, but found none; the French had been here seven days before us; dined at the inn with Gooch; had a good dinner,

1. Not mangel-wurzel but sugar beet, the commercial use of which had been extensively promoted under the Napoleonic regime as a means of counteracting the effects of the British blockade but which was unknown in Britain.
2. Uncertain location; most likely Maasslyus.
3. Assistant Surgeon George Smith, Coldstream Guards.
4. Briel.
5. The River Maas.

and found some port wine; went home to my billet at a tallow-chandler's shop.

15 December:

Stayed at Helvoetsluys; a stupid place; wrote to England; dined at the inn with Gooch, Powys, and Eyre, and Smith;[1] went to bed at eight, intending to be called at three in the morning.

16 December:

Got up at three o'clock, and got some tea, and went on board a smack to go to Williamstadt,[2] where we arrived about two o'clock, after a very cold passage; marched the company to the barracks; got my billet; had a room with a fire and bed; went and bought some beef and fish; boiled them both, and made a good dinner; wrote this; went to bed.

17 December:

Marched to Steenbergen; a very long march, very dirty, and much rain. Crossed two ferries; got to Steenbergen about three, on the rear-guard, and most of the old men were knocked up;[3] got my billet at a tobacco shop; very civil people; gave me a good dinner of beef-steaks; had some coffee; went to bed on the ground, not having my bed with me (as all the heavy baggage was ordered to be left at Williamstadt).

18 December:

Got up; had my breakfast, went to parade; we halted here for one day; went out shooting with Walton and Gooch; got one shot at partridges, but was driven home by the rain; read; got my dinner (fried beef); Gooch came and drank a bottle of wine with me; had some tea and went to bed.

---

1. Ensigns Thomas Powys and Francis Eyre, both Coldstream Guards.
2. Willemstad.
3. A drawback inherent in the fact that the 2nd battalions of all three Foot Guards regiments, being configured primarily for the home depot role, had a higher than normal proportion of older men: see Bamford, Andrew, *Sickness, Suffering, and the Sword: The British Regiment on Campaign 1808–1815* (Norman: University of Oklahoma Press, 2013), pp. 137–9.

19 December:

We marched from Steenbergen, to make room for the Thirty-third, to some farmhouses about two miles off; our company had two good barns; Talbot[1] and I got a good dinner off two fowls, which we had just killed at an adjoining farmhouse, and eggs and bacon; smoked a pipe; Shaw and Gooch came and sat with us; gave them some tea, and went to bed with straw and sheets and greatcoats.

20 December:

Remained here and got a good farmer's breakfast; went with Talbot to Steenbergen to get provisions in a cart; brought home plenty of wine and meat; had a good dinner Shaw came to sit with us and smoke a pipe till bedtime.

21 December:

Got up; and at breakfast Bligh[2] arrived with all our heavy baggage, to our great delight; went with him and Talbot in a cart to Steenbergen for more provisions; had a good dinner; and found our own beds a great comfort.

22 December:

Had a famous breakfast upon veal kidneys; went shooting with Smith; we never saw a head of game; his dog was worth nothing; went home to dinner. Bligh dined with us; got a letter from England; had a good dinner, then tea, and bedtime.

23 December:

Breakfast; Mills[3] called upon us; went out with him with my gun, hearing there was a covey of birds near us; a very bad day; remained in the farmhouse; and at ten o'clock all our baggage was taken away, as the French were advancing; and we were ordered to be ready to march at a moment's warning.[4]

1. Lt and Capt. John Talbot, Coldstream Guards, a Peninsular veteran who had served at Cadiz and Barossa with the 2nd Battalion and then transferred to the 1st under Wellington for the 1812 campaign. The same officer is frequently identified as 'Jack Talbot' in subsequent entries.
2. Lt and Capt. Thomas Bligh, Coldstream Guards, a Peninsular veteran of two years' active service with the 1st Battalion.
3. Ensign John Mills, Coldstream Guards.
4. The French advance referred to here was part of their operations against Breda.

24 December:

Got some boiled milk, and went to the village to hear the news, but heard none, excepting that we were about two miles from the French, and that the Coldstreams was the advance, as all the other troops had moved off to Steenbergen and Williamstadt; returned to my company, and found Loftus[1] with orders for our marching to another farmhouse nearer Steenbergen; got the company out. Graham[2] came by, and asked me where I was going, and a few questions about where the villages were, &c.; marched to another farmhouse about a mile from Steenbergen, and then got upon my horse to go there for provisions, and a few dressing things for myself and Talbot; got home about five. We dressed our own dinner – hashed rabbit and fowl, and boiled leg of mutton and turnips; Loftus and Mills dined with us; Talbot got a bed, I got a mattress, and took the window curtains for sheets, and went to bed.

25 December:

Slept well; had a good breakfast upon the hashed mutton and boiled milk; took a walk to Mills's; I had some luncheon there; we marched then to Steenbergen, where I got my billet. It was refused at first; but I sent to the Burgomaster to know whether it was good. He said it was, so I broke into the house with my servants, licked the patrons for their impudence, and made them give me a fire; treating them *a la Cossacque*, as they were very much against the English, and said they wished the French back. I asked for a piece of bread, and the man showed me a baker's-shop, upon which I reconnoitred his kitchen – found some bread, cheese and butter, and Geneva, which I made free with; dined with Hawkins at half-past six; there was Mills and Lake there;[3] came home and went to bed. One way of passing a Christmas day! Got all our baggage back.

26 December:

Had some breakfast, and foraged the patron's kitchen for it; I am on the main guard; lunched with Talbot and Mills; walked on the ramparts with

1. Capt. and Lt Col Henry Loftus, Coldstream Guards.
2. The commanding general, Sir Thomas Graham.
3. Lt and Capt. Henry Hawkins and Ensign Charles Lake, both 3rd Foot Guards. Hawkins was another Peninsular veteran, having served for two and half years with his regiment's 1st Battalion before returning home in early 1812.

Cuyler turned out the picquet to Graham, and hashed a hare for dinner, with Cuyler and Bentinck; had a good dinner – soup, fowls, and the hare; went to my old patron, and ordered my baggage to be packed up, and rowed him for his principles; went home to Cuyler's house, and sat there all night, as I could not go to bed, being on the guard.

27 December:

At five o'clock turned out the guard to the picquets coming in; we marched to Old Castel[1] at ten o'clock; I was on the rear guard; we left Steenbergen to its fate, and the people very sulky; we had a good march; arrived at Old Castel about four; found a room without flue, but soon had the carpenter to make a chimney; dined with Loftus; came home, and had my own bed down.

28 December:

We remained at Old Castel; had the parade at eleven; tried a pointer, and bought it; went riding, and dined with Mills, Talbot, and Loftus.

29 December:

Remained at Castel; breakfasted with Cuyler; went to the parade, and mounted the main guard; dined with Talbot and Mills; and returned to the guard.

30 December:

Was relieved by Powys; went out shooting with Mills; found very few birds; came home and dressed for dinner; passed a pleasant evening, and went to bed.

31 December:

Went out shooting after breakfast with Mills; killed a few birds, but too foggy to shoot; so came home and had a good dinner with Perceval,[2] and Mills, and Talbot; we drank 'the old year out and the new one in.'

1. Oud Gastel, a village three miles west of Oudenbosch.
2. Lt and Capt. George Harvey Perceval, Coldstream Guards. Had served extensively with the 1st Battalion in the Peninsula, October 1810 to March 1813.

1814

1 January:

Remained at Old Castel; Loftus and Mills went out shooting with me; much pleased with my pointer; exchanged my single-barrel gun for Mills' double; we all got into the ditches, and had famous fun; Mills and Talbot dined with me.

2 January:

Had a parade; went out shooting with Perceval and Gooch; I killed four ducks, one dog and one cat, one partridge – a good day; dined with Cuyler and Bentinck; we went and roused up the doctors about twelve, and they turned out of bed; we nearly got fired upon by the inhabitants, as they were convinced we were the French.

3 January:

Mounted the main guard; had my breakfast; turned out to Cooke and Mackenzie;[1] sat with Jack Talbot went to dress for dinner; we dined by ourselves; went to the main guard, where I laid down.

4 January:

At five o'clock went to breakfast with Bentinck and Cuyler, who were going to the Hague (commenced acting as adjutant); went to Adams;[2] was relieved by Powys on the main guard; had my breakfast; went to Finart for pay, but did not find Jones;[3] heard the shocking news from Spain, and got a letter

---

1. Maj. Gens George Cooke and Kenneth Mackenzie, respectively commanding the First and Second Divisions.
2. Capt. and Lt Col Lucius Frederick Adams, commanding officer of 2/Coldstream Guards. Adams had previously served in the Peninsula, March 1809 to February 1812, generally as a company officer but also with a brief spell as brigade major in the latter part of 1809.
3. Capt. and Lt Col Leslie Grove Jones, 1st Foot Guards. Had previously served with the 3rd Battalion of his regiment in the Corunna campaign, and with its 2nd Battalion at Cadiz and Barossa. Challis gives his middle name as George. The village in which Duncombe sought Jones is in fact Fijnaart, and his failure to locate him meant a wasted round trip of some eleven miles.

from England;[1] went to the orderly-room, and gave out the orders; dined at home with Jack Talbot; and went to bed.

5 January:

Got up; a rainy morning; wrote to England, and began a letter to White;[2] breakfasted; gave out the orders; nothing but snow; sat at home; I dined with Perceval and Bligh, and went home to bed.

6 January:

Had a parade; went to Adams for orders; went to breakfast; gave out the orders; went to Finart for pay with Perceval; got it; coming home we found the ferry overflooded; obliged to go across in a small boat; left the cart and horse behind; drove down the stream a long way; at last arrived; waded through mud up to our knees; found a couple of cart horses saddled on the other side; got upon them; and arrived at Old Castel to dinner at seven o'clock with Adams; and went to bed, and slept sound after the fatigues of the day.

7 January:

Had the parade; went to breakfast; went out shooting; killed a leash of birds; dined with Adams; went to bed; just going in Adams sent for me; the French had licked the Prussians near Breda; went and doubled all the picquets; sent patrols; and visited the outposts and picquets at twelve and three; did not go to bed; the battalion turned out at five; I stayed till eight, but nothing happened.[3]

8 January:

Had the parade at ten; got my breakfast; we had two courts-martial; dined with Talbot; and went early to bed.

1. It is not clear what this 'shocking news' was; certainly, the allied forces suffered no setback at this time.
2. Unidentified.
3. In fact, although there was action around Breda, this alert was a false alarm.

9 January:

Bentinck returned; gave up my adjutancy; we marched to Steenbergen; had quarters with Mills and Talbot; and Hawkins, Jones, and Barnet[1] dined with us; and went to bed.

10 January:

We marched to Wouw – a horrid bad place; Talbot went to Tholen with the old men;[2] got quarters with Cuyler and Gooch, and dined with Bentinck; then returned home.

11 January:

Remained at Wouw; was on the main guard; went to skate; rode with Cuyler, and bought fowls; dined with Cuyler and Gooch.

12 January:

Remained at Wouw; had our breakfast; went and skated; called upon Mills; dined with Gooch; and went to bed early.

13 January:

Called up at three with orders for marching; we got up and marched to Achterbrook,[3] near Antwerp – a miserable hole; got quarters with Cuyler by turning out the Deputy-Deputy's Postmaster-General, who was in a great rage; but we soon convinced him, by *vi et armis*, that His Majesty's Guards had a preference to quarters before him; had some dinner; and went to bed at eight.[4]

---

1. Lt and Capt. Charles John Barnett, 3rd Foot Guards, who had previously served in the Peninsula, November 1809 to May 1812.
2. This transfer of unfit men to garrison duty was implemented across Graham's army, although for most of the line battalions those so detached were young and unseasoned rather than older and worn out. In fact, so ineffective were these men that they could not even do garrison duty, and the 2/44th had to be pulled out of the line to help man the defences at Tholen. See Bamford, *Bold and Ambitious Enterprise*, p. 104.
3. Achterbroek.
4. The post of 'Deputy-Deputy's Postmaster-General' did not exist; Duncombe is evidently being facetious but no doubt his victim was one of the many unsung

14 January:

Called up at three o'clock for a picquet on the Antwerp road; was relieved at nine by the Fifty-fourth; followed the battalion to Wouw; got my old billet; and Taylor[1] gave me the orders for marching the following day to Steenbergen; Cuyler and Bentinck dined with me.

15 January:

Marched at nine to Steenbergen; got my old quarters; had my dinner; and went to bed early, not sorry to have left that barbarian country.

16 January:

Remained at Steenbergen; took Cuyler into my quarters, as he was turned out of his; Lambert dined with us.[2]

17 January:

Remained at Steenbergen; went upon picquet at Coveing.[3]

18 January:

Was relieved at four o'clock, and got home about six; dined with Lambert; and not sorry to get to bed.

19 January:

Went to parade; skated and wrote letters; Lambert, Bentinck, and Talbot dined with us; did not sit late.

20 January:

Remained at Steenbergen; was on the barrack duty.

individuals filling the junior staff posts without which the army in the field would not have functioned.

1. Maj. Gen. Herbert Taylor, commanding the Second Brigade.
2. Lt and Capt. Sir Henry John Lambert, Bt, 1st Foot Guards. Had previously served with the 2nd Battalion of his regiment at Cadiz and Barossa, and with its 1st Battalion from May 1812 to June 1813, being part of the time detached as an ADC to Col William Wheatley commanding a brigade in the First Division.
3. Unknown location.

21 January:

Duke of Clarence arrived, and inspected us; was sent on picquet towards Bergen-op-Zoom – a miserable hovel; was relieved pretty early the next morning.

22 January:

Was relieved by the First Guards, and went out shooting; Hawkins lent me his gun, but found no game; dined at home, and had a regular blow-up with the mistress, who wanted to turn us out, but we barricaded the house, and showed fight. The Burgomaster came; he went out quicker than he came in, and said he should speak to the General.

23 January:

Slept without being disturbed by the patroness; had a parade; went to church at one; went and skated, and wrote letters; dined at home.

24 January:

We remained at Steenbergen, and carried on the war with our patroness.

25 January:

Remained at Steenbergen; went out shooting not much sport; dined with Hesketh.[1]

26 January:

Went on picquet, and relieved the Third Regiment;[2] nothing extraordinary there.

27 January:

Was relieved by the First Guards; went and skated; dined with Dashwood.[3]

---

1. Lt and Capt. Robert Bamford Hesketh, 3rd Foot Guards. Had previously served with his regiment's 1st Battalion under Wellington, April 1809 to December 1811.
2. That is to say, 2/3rd Foot Guards.
3. Ensign Augustus Dashwood, 1st Foot Guards.

28 January:

Still at Steenbergen; we went out with Mills' troop, and charged some woodcutters to great advantage; dined with Talbot.

29 January:

A monstrous bad day; no parade; nothing but snow; Loftus, Hesketh, Drummond, Perceval, and Cuyler dined with me at my new quarters, which I have changed by turning men out and putting them in my deserted house; and we have much the best of the bargain.

30 January:

Ordered to march; went in a carriage with Perceval to Esschen,[1] and arrived about four o'clock; had pretty good quarters with Mills and Perceval.

31 January:

Marched by daybreak to West Wesel; I was on the baggage guard; arrived there about three; a most wretched and deserted village; having been just romped by the French; got miserable quarters.

1 February:

Marched to Westread,[2] about four miles from Antwerp; a bad and wet march; arrived there about three; we got bad quarters.

2 February:

Marched at daybreak to attack the French at Merxham, about a mile from Antwerp; the light division attacked about eight o'clock,[3] and we supported; and about twelve we drove them from their village into the town, taking a good many prisoners, and killing as many. I was on a covering party immediately after we arrived, and the rest began to erect batteries against Antwerp. They shelled us a good deal; I was then detached with fifty men to a post on the right of the village, to defend

1. Essen, a village to the east of Bergen-op-Zoom and a march of 15 miles from Steenbergen.
2. Unknown location.
3. The attack was actually made by the Second Division under Maj. Gen. Gibbs, which comprised the Second and Light Brigades.

our right, and there I found a snug house; but the balls rattled about it a good deal.

3 February:

Jones visited me in the morning, and we went to attack an enemy's picquet in a wood, but we found there was treble our number, so we returned without firing a shot at them, though they kept up a brisk fire against us. I was relieved about two o'clock by the Twenty-fifth,[1] and then marched to the cantonment, as we were fairly shelled out of the village; had some dinner; went to the top of a windmill to see the battering, which was very hot on both sides; and then laid down in my cloak pretty tired.

4 February:

Went on picquet again under a very heavy fire; lost a few men; laid down under the bank; the firing ceased towards night; procured a cold chicken and some brandy about nine, and got through the night pretty well, but was excessively cold.

5 February:

Was relieved about seven in the morning; part of our village on fire, and some of our guns dismounted; things going on very badly; marched the men up to their cantonment; the batteries were opened again, but they said to no use, as they never hurt the fleet. I was rather unwell; sent for the surgeon; he seemed to think it was a touch of the ague; advised me to go to bed. As there was none to be found, Adams sent me to Breschat,[2] to the baggage; I relieved Cuyler from that duty, and he went up to the battalion; got some tea, and went to bed.

6 February:

Much better by my night's rest; had a row with some officers of Engineers and the Trotters,[3] who wanted my quarters, but I told them they must burn the fleet first before they should turn me out; they went off in the pouts,

1. 2/25th Foot.
2. Brasschaat.
3. 'Trotters' is a mystery; whilst evidently disparaging slang, it is unclear exactly who Duncombe is using it to refer to. Possibly officers of the commissariat, since so much of the Army's equipment was supplied by the ubiquitous John Trotter.

saying, 'that the Guards always got the best quarters, and that nobody cared where they were.' I told them I was sure *I* did not; Worrell[1] arrived, and said, 'that the battalion was coming, and the siege was to be raised;' about two o'clock Perceval, and Mills, and I got our old quarters; and went to bed very early after the fatigues.

7 February:

Remained at Breschat; Mills set off for England;[2] horrid stupid work.

8 February:

Marched at five to Jundau;[3] a monstrous wet day; got bad quarters with Perceval and Bentinck, and the young one came.

9 February:

No parade; rode over to Breda with Perceval, Bentinck, and Lambert, in about an hour; got some luncheon, and made a few purchases; saw the Saxon army; a dirty town.

10 February:

Marched at seven to Rosendaal; a nasty foggy day, and bad roads; got pretty good quarters to myself; and dined with Perceval.

11 February:

Parade; took a ride towards Bergen-op-Zoom; and dined with Bentinck, Adams, and Park,[4] &c.

1. Assistant Surgeon Septimus Worrell, Coldstream Guards.
2. Mills had obtained permission to return home on leave; see MacKinnon, Colonel, *Origins and Services of the Coldstream Guards* (London: Richard Bentley, 1833), Vol. II, p. 207.
3. Uncertain location; Duncombe's son corrected it to Jerensdam in the 1868 printing, but although this name appears in other Victorian publications it is not in modern use and it is unclear what name has superseded it.
4. Park is a mystery; no officer of that name appears in the returns for the regiments under Graham's command, or on his staff.

12 February:

Remained at Rosendaal; rode over to Steenbergen; water almost all the way; saw Jack Talbot and Loftus; dined with Cuyler.

13 February:

Remained at Rosendaal; wrote some letters; church; dined with Shaw.

14 February:

Rode over to Nipsen;[1] Adams, Bentinck, Perceval, and Bligh dined with me.

15 February:

On a general court-martial at Rosendaal, on two men of the Third Guards; dined with Perceval.

16 February:

The court-martial continued at Rosendaal; I was not quite well, having a sore throat; dined with Walton, our Acting Major.[2]

17 February:

Still at Rosendaal; the court-martial concluded.

18 February:

Went over to Steenbergen; dined with Talbot; and stayed there all night.

19 February:

Returned to Rosendaal, and Jack Talbot came back with me to stay a day; we dined by ourselves; got rather beery, as usual.

---

1. Nispen, a round trip of ten miles from Roosendaal.
2. That is to say, acting second-in-command of the battalion. The men holding the small number of substantive field officer posts in the Foot Guards regiments tended to have already risen to higher things by virtue of their rank in the army; thus the posts were filled by more junior men acting up. The substantive first and second majors of the Coldstream Guards at this time were John Calcraft, who was unemployed as a lieutenant general, and Kenneth Howard, who was a major general commanding the First Division in the Peninsula.

20 February:

Went to parade; then to church; we dined with Perceval.

21 February:

Went back with Jack Talbot to Steenbergen, and dined with him and Loftus, and then went to the ball; capital fun; the young lady shopkeepers affected fine; waltzed with some; and went to bed about one.

22 February:

Stayed at Steenbergen; went shooting with Loftus; he killed three couple of ducks and I two; very fair sport; I was well pleased with my new purchased gun; we dined with Loftus, and Perceval and Hesketh came.

23 February:

Returned with Perceval to Rosendaal; dined with him; and found my cook dead drunk.

24 February:

Went out duck shooting; killed a couple of mallards; the frost very severe.

25 February:

Went out shooting with Cuyler, but could get no shots; the ducks were too wild; dined at home by myself – something extraordinary – but I had refused two invitations.

26 February:

Cooke inspected the Brigade; I went out shooting; only killed a teal; and dined with Bentinck.

27 February:

Parade; wrote a letter home; went to church; and dined at home.

28 February:

We moved from Rosendaal to Nipsen; pretty good quarters.

1 March:

Marched about one to Kalmont;[1] a very rainy day.

2 March:

Marched about two to Stabrock;[2] was on the baggage guard; the French had been here this morning; dined at home; got a capital house with Perceval.

3 March:

Remained at Stabrock; took a ride; dined at home.

4 March:

Still at Stabrock; went shooting; up to our necks in water, and killed nothing; the ducks too wild.

5 March:

At Stabrock; rode out; Adams, Hesketh, Count Bentinck, and Barnet dined with us.

6 March:

Got up early to see the working party go off to work at Fort Hendrick;[3] was Acting Adjutant for Bentinck, as he had gone to the Barrosa dinner.[4]

7 March:

At Stabrock; rode up to Berendeith;[5] dined with Hawkins.

1. Apparently Calmthout.
2. Stabroek; a march of six miles.
3. This fort stood on the east bank of the Scheldt, downstream from Fort Lillo; it therefore served as an ideal location from which to keep watch on the French garrison of the latter, and over river traffic more generally.
4. Evidently a celebration of Graham's victory at Barossa, 5 March 1811. Alone of his current command, the three Guards battalions had also served under Graham on that occasion so no doubt the Peninsular veterans amongst their officers – of whom Bentinck was one –were heavily represented at the festivities.
5. Berendrecht; now a suburb of Antwerp.

8 March:

Went on picquet at half-past three in the morning at Fort Hendrick; very bad fun; stayed there all day and night.

9 March:

Not relieved; heard that Bergen-op-Zoom had been stormed with great loss.

10 March:

Not relieved; very tired.

11 March:

Not relieved; took the Burgomaster of Lille's papers; was sick of the picquet, as we had not been to bed or changed our clothes.

12 March:

Was relieved, to our great delight; we marched to Putte, and remained there all night; very happy to have got into bed again.

13 March:

We joined the battalion at West Wesel, and fired a feu de joie for the news of the allies.

14 March:

At Wesel; was Acting Adjutant, as Bentinck was Acting Brigade Major, in the place of Stothert,[1] wounded; very bad quarters here.

15 March:

At Wesel; Macdonell,[2] our new Commanding Officer, joined us; and he dined with Perceval and me.

1. Lt and Capt. William Stothert, 3rd Foot Guards, wounded at Bergen-op-Zoom. Had previously served in the Peninsula, May 1809 to January 1812.
2. Capt. and Lt Col James Macdonell, Coldstream Guards. Macdonell had already served extensively in the Peninsula both as a regimental officer and on attachment to the Portuguese Army; prior to that he had served with the 78th Highlanders, with which regiment he had seen action at Maida. Later won fame as the defender of Hougoumont, and ended his career a general and a knight.

16 March:

West Wesel; took a ride; dined at home with Perceval.

17 March:

The Steenbergen detachment arrived; Jack Talbot dined with us.

18 March:

Rode to Loenhout; a much better place than this.

19 March:

At West Wesel; went out shooting with Barnet, but found nothing.

20 March:

Perceval went to Brussels; wrote letters; and dined with Macdonell.

21 March:

Rode with Bentinck to Breschat to see the work there; never was there so poor a fortification;[1] came home, and set off with Talbot to Calmhout[2] to dine with Sir T. Graham; we got there about seven. I was glad to find we were in time, as six was the dinner hour; the roads were terribly bad; the dinner rather dull, and Graham seemed low. We came home about one in a spring waggon and four horses, as we were afraid of going in the cart, being dark, and bad roads; we were nearly overturned in the waggon. We knocked up a bos at the first house, and made him wade through the mud with a lantern;[3] luckily we found ourselves safe again at West Wesel.

22 March:

Went to parade, and then went out shooting with three beagles; had a good run or two; I shot only one rabbit, a plover, and a pigeon; dined at home alone, and went to bed pretty early.

1. This comment relates to the field works being constructed to enable Brasschaat to function as the main British outpost facing Antwerp. Duncombe was not alone in not rating the quality of the position; for a more professional view, see Sperling, *Letters*, pp. 50–1.
2. Calmthout.
3. Evidently implying a local farmer/peasant, the precise etymology of 'bos' is unclear but may perhaps suggest a forester (Dutch *bosopzichter*) or woodsman.

23 March:

At West Wesel.

24 March:

At West Wesel; sent for my portmanteau to Williamstadt; went out with the beagles; had a short run, but did not kill.

25 March:

At West Wesel; went out shooting with Berkeley Drummond,[1] but killed nothing; dined at home.

26 March:

Stayed at home nearly all the day; turned out the battalion just before dinner-time, and marched up to the chaussee, but found that it was a false alarm. N.B. The greater part of the battalion was drunk. Dined at home.

27 March:

At West Wesel; a bad day; dined with Hesketh; and wrote letters to England.

28 March:

Still at West Wesel, though it had been reported that we were to have marched every day; wrote official letters to the Paymaster for Macdonell.

29 March:

At West Wesel; nothing extraordinary.

30 March:

In *statu*[s] *quo*; went out with the beagles; had not much sport, being a hot day.

31 March:

Went out with the beagles; had a large field; Macdonell was out with us; there was one or two bad falls; Perceval and party came home from Brussels; I dined with Jack Talbot and suite.

1. Ensign Barclay Drummond, 3rd Foot Guards; the fact that Duncombe here specifies the full name of the junior Drummond suggests that when the surname alone is used, as above, the senior man is meant.

1 April:

At West Wesel; a very bad day; had not much sport with the beagles.

2 April:

More rain; we fired a feu de joie for the news of the allies; dined with Hawkins and Barnet.

4 April:

At West Wesel; rode over to the fort at Breschat, to see Perceval.

12 April:

We gave a dinner party to Adams, &c.

16 April:

Marched at six o'clock, to our great delight, to West Maarle – a nice village;[1] dined with Adams.

17 April:

Marched on to Lier – a good town, and was billeted at a priest's house, who bothered me with his too great civility.

18 April:

At Lier; rode out towards Antwerp.

19 April:

Saw the lace manufactory; was introduced to General Ferguson,[2] and dined with him.

20 April:

At Lier; rode out and dined with the General.

21 April:

At Lier – a very bad, rainy day; played at billiards and dined with General Ferguson.

1. Westmalle.
2. Lt Gen. Ronald Craufurd Ferguson, Graham's new second-in-command.

22 April:

Rode down to see the Chateau de Buckhout,[1] and dined *avec le* General.

23 April:

Joined General Ferguson at the Chateau, and like it very much.

24 April:

Took a ride out with Boldero;[2] a large dinner party.

27 April:

Sir T. Graham dined with us at the Chateau.

30 April:

Went to see the Guards fire the *feu de joie* for the opening of Antwerp.

1 May:

Rode over to Brussels with Boldero – a very good town; dined at the Belle Vue with Trench,[3] and went to the play, which was miserably bad.

2 May:

Returned from Brussels to the Chateau, and lunched at Malines with some of the Guards.

3 May:

Drove to Leir with Webster,[4] and from thence into Antwerp, without a passport, but got through without much difficulty; had some luncheon; saw the garrisons of Bergen-op-Zoom, Batts, Lille, &c.,[5] march in, and returned home to dinner.

1. Château de Bouchout, near Meise in present-day Belgium. Begun in the twelfth century; extensively rebuilt in the seventeenth.
2. Most likely Lt Henry Boldero, 3/56th Foot, ADC to Ferguson, although Lt and Capt. Lonsdale Boldero, 1st Foot Guards, was also serving in the Netherlands.
3. Lt Col Frederick Trench, Deputy Quartermaster General to the forces in the Netherlands.
4. Lt Henry Vassal Webster, 9th Light Dragoons, extra ADC to Ferguson. Later served as extra ADC to the Prince of Orange at Waterloo.
5. That is to say, Fort Batz and Fort Lillo.

4 May:

Rode to head-quarters, and dined with Ferguson there – a very bad dinner.

5 May:

Went into Antwerp in state with Sir T. Graham, &c.; rode round the ramparts, citadel, &c., and came home to dinner.

6 May:

Rode out with Ferguson, and a large party at dinner at home. Generals Halkett, Gibbs, &c.[1]

7 May:

Went with General Ferguson to dine at General Cooke's, to meet the Austrian commissioner – a grand dinner; all the Bigwigs present.

8 May:

Drove Ferguson's German waggon with my two Dutch horses, with Boldero, into Antwerp, and took Jones home with us.

9 May:

Rode with Ferguson to Antwerp; saw a most beautiful collection of pictures, and bought a few books rather cheap.

10 May:

Dined at home, and went to the play at Antwerp.

11 May:

Stayed at Antwerp, and dined with General Cooke.

12 May:

Rode home to Buchout, and dined there.

16 May:

Went to a ball at Antwerp, which was rather gay.

1. Brig. Gen. Colin Halkett and Maj. Gen. Samuel Gibbs, commanding the Third and Second Brigades.

20 May:

Left Buchout, and went to Antwerp, and dined with General Cooke.

21 May:

Set out at six o'clock by a Dutch schuyt to Flushing, where we arrived about five o'clock – a fair wind and we saw Leivinsuch, an amazing strong fortress;[1] got good beds and dinner; the party consisted of the General, Jones, Colonel Smith and his aide-de-camp,[2] and me.

22 May:

Went round the ramparts and town – well worth seeing, but a wet day; went to Middelburg, where we dined and slept; rather a good inn and town.

23 May:

Looked about the town; went to Tarvere,[3] but in consequence of the weather and a gale of wind, we could not put to sea, so returned to Middelburg, and looked into all the curiosity shops.[4]

24 May:

Still windbound at Middelburg, as it was blowing a most boisterous gale.

1. Fort Liefkenshoek, on the west bank of the Scheldt below Antwerp.
2. That is to say, Carmichael Smyth. The officer identified by Duncombe as Carmichael Smyth's ADC was in fact Lt Sperling, RE; however, Sperling in his own account of the trip refers to Duncombe as 'Duncan', so neither officer got it quite right. Sperling also confirms that 'Jones' was Capt. and Lt Col Leslie Grove Jones, 1st Foot Guards, now released from the captivity into which he had fallen at Bergen-op-Zoom, for whom see above. See Sperling, *Letters*, pp. 69–73.
3. Veere.
4. It is worth noting that Sperling comments on this, remarking that 'As some of our party are much interested in old books and prints, we have been ransacking the treasures which this out-of-the-way place affords. It has furnished us with very pleasant occupation during the rain. Considerable purchases have been made from tempting portfolios.' Sperling, *Letters*, pp. 71–2. Evidently, Duncombe did display some interests beyond the chase and the bottle.

25 May:

The weather had improved; we went to Tarvere, where we embarked for Bergen-op-Zoom, and arrived there about five o'clock; got our dinner, and went to bed early.

26 May:

Walked round the town and ramparts; saw the different places of attack, &c., well worth seeing; went to Antwerp in a coach and four, and dined with General Cooke.

27 May:

Set off to Brussels, and got in in time for dinner; then went to the play.

28 May:

Got a pretty good billet, and went through the regular routine of fashion here; dinner at three; *Allee Verte* at five; play at eight.

With this return to peacetime routine, Duncombe's diary comes to an end. He would, however, remain on the continent for a little while yet, continuing to serve as part of Ferguson's military household. What Duncombe was not, however – at least, not in any formal sense – was the general's ADC. For a start, Ferguson already had three of these, which was one more than he was entitled to and which caused the junior man, Webster, to be carried as an unpaid extra, but more pertinently Duncombe was too junior to hold such a post officially. That said, there was nothing to stop an officer serving unofficially as an additional unpaid aide if his own commanding officer was happy to release him from regimental duty: this loophole allowed Duncombe to join Ferguson's staff but did not allow him any of the financial benefits that would accrue to the general's official aides. Thus, the monthly returns for Graham's troops continue to list Duncombe as serving with his battalion until he received leave with effect from 14 July to return to England on private affairs: this leave was to run until 13 September. Duncombe's departure coincided with Ferguson leaving the theatre, so it can be inferred that the young officer followed the general home. Before his leave had expired, Duncombe received orders to join the regiment's 1st Battalion, which had returned from the Peninsula and was now back in London. As a result of this posting, he missed the Waterloo campaign and saw no further active service.[1]

Duncombe remained in the Army until 1819, having risen to the rank of lieutenant and captain in November 1815. However, peacetime soldiering evidently had little appeal, and he left the service and entered a new life as a man-about-town and, ultimately, a politician. He quickly became known in late Regency society for his heavy gambling, for his skill as a gentleman jockey, and for his enthusiastic pursuit of women of dubious morals and negotiable affections. Considering this reputation, which is reinforced by the tone and content of his diary, it might reasonably be expected that the rest of his life consisted of mindless dissipation, but in fact this is actually some way from the mark. True, he retained throughout his life a reputation as a rake and a dandy, but, as time went on, he also became increasingly radical in his politics and something of a champion of the working man. When one considers that this change set him up in direct political opposition to his own family, it becomes even more surprising.

One possible source of the radical influence is Lieutenant General Ferguson, who combined his military career with Whig politics, but it has also been suggested that a fellow patron of the turf, John Lambton, MP for County Durham, may have encouraged him into more radical political views. It was as a Whig that Duncombe was elected MP for Hertford in 1826, and, having lost that seat in 1832, again as a Whig that he successfully stood as MP for Finsbury in 1834. This time he retained the seat until his death on 13 November 1861, which came after a long and debilitating struggle with a severe bronchial condition. He was survived by his only son, but details of his marriage – beyond the fact that his wife was a great beauty but considerably his social inferior and shunned as a result – are not forthcoming. Even his son, writing his father's biography, fails to provide any details.

Over time, Duncombe's politics became increasingly radical. He was a strong supporter of the reform movement that led to the Great Reform Act of 1832, but he continued to fight for the rights of the

---

1. See Monthly Returns for Graham's forces in TNA, WO17/1773; MacKinnon, *Coldstream Guards*, Vol. II, p. 207.

common man even in the revised parliamentary system that followed the act's implementation. A dandy to the last, he nevertheless enjoyed great popularity amongst his largely working-class constituents, using his eloquence and debating skill to argue in favour of religious toleration and of the new movement towards unionisation of labour. Quite evidently, he gained in later life the maturity that was an essential counterpart to the lively and boisterous character that his diary indicates as the key feature of his youth. It would be fair to say that Tom Duncombe added little to the military profession during his brief service, and, taken alone, his diary is one of the least palatable contemporary accounts left by an officer of this period. Judging by his later life, however, Duncombe's military service did at least form part of a growing-up process that ultimately produced a far more likeable and well-rounded character than the callow and irresponsible youth who served through the Netherlands Campaign.[1]

1. Later life summarised from Fisher, David R., 'Duncombe, Thomas Slingsby (1796–1861)'.

Chapter III

Lieutenant Charles Shaw

2nd Battalion, 52nd (Oxfordshire) Light Infantry

Unlike most of the other eyewitnesses whose accounts feature in this work, Charles Shaw needs little by way of introduction since the opening passages of his autobiography, the first five chapters of which are excerpted here, provide much of his background as well as his motivations for seeking to follow a military career. This eventually took him to the crack 52nd Light Infantry, into which he was commissioned as an ensign on 23 January 1813; he subsequently rose to lieutenant on 9 December of the same year, by which time he was already on active service in the Low Countries. It need only really be added by way of further introduction that Shaw was born in Ayr in 1795, the second of three sons of Charles Shaw, who was clerk of the county, and his wife Barbara, née Wright.[1] With that basic information in place, we can let Shaw take up his own tale.

I

It has often been remarked how, at an early age, the smallest circumstances give a tinge and colour to the unformed character. The boy who is educated near a trout stream acquires a taste for angling, which only dies with himself. The happy hours which it was my lot to spend, fishing in the rivers Ayr and Doon, made me look forward with delight to the day when I should be a man; when no schoolmaster could interfere with me; and in my choice of a profession I was guided in my views, by considering in what line of life I could best indulge myself in my favourite sport. I had heard that the lawyers have a vacation of six months in the year, in the best fishing and shooting season; and the thought of this so delighted me that, after *mature*

---

1. Vetch, Robert Hamilton, 'Charles Shaw', in *Dictionary of National Biography*, Vol. 51; available online at http://en.wikisource.org/wiki/Shaw,_Charles_ (DNB00).

deliberation, I resolved to become an advocate of the Scotch bar.[1]

To Edinburgh College I was sent, to be well grounded in Greek and Latin; but the river Tweed so interfered with these necessary branches of learning, that, as I was found to have forgotten even what I had been taught at school, it was wisely determined that I should go to St. Andrew's College, where it was supposed there were no temptations to idleness. Placed under the celebrated Professor Jackson in that University, before the session was finished, I became a proficient in the athletic game of golf. I now began to doubt the wisdom of the learned, on finding that all the rules for instruction in Latin and Greek, were given to boys in these two languages, instead of in English; the reason for which absurdity, I have not to this day been able to comprehend.

The great object was now to calculate the particular day on which the Professor would examine; and, having once ascertained this, the previous night was spent in hard study; and thus, by dint of a little manoeuvring, it was easy to keep up a respectable character for learning among the students. Thus my studies ended – the most valuable of my acquirements at the two Universities, being some sincere friendships, which, I am proud to say, endure to the present day.

At the period of which I speak, there was a depôt of French prisoners at Pennicuik, about ten miles from Edinburgh.[2] Six of these unfortunate fellows had escaped, and were retaken near St. Andrew's. These men excited much interest in my mind; an interest increased to pity by their re-capture, and I attribute half the romance and love of adventure which have developed themselves within me, to the operation of this trivial circumstance on a mind naturally ardent and sanguine. I well remember wishing myself to have been a French prisoner, in order to have escaped and to have proved the impossibility of retaking me.

I now began to hate the idea of law; but, fearing to offend my friends, I determined to leave the arbitrament of my fate to chance.

At St. Andrews, there is a large pool, called the Witches' Lake. The local traditions state, that reputed witches were for ages thrown into this pond.

1. There may well have been rather more to it than that: the family had a legal background, and one of Shaw's brothers did qualify as a lawyer.
2. The town is in fact Penicuik; the main depot was housed in the old Valleyfield paper mill, which was bought by the government for this purpose in 1811, but prisoners were also housed at Greenlaw House and – briefly – at Esk Mills.

If the poor wretches who were thus treated sank, they were drowned; if on the contrary they swam, they were to be burned. The stories told by the fishermen of the dances of old women on this pool, lighted by blue flames ascending from the surrounding rocks, interested me much; and often did I gaze into its depths to endeavour to see some of these drowned hags.

'Well,' said I to myself, shortly after the affair of the French prisoners, 'suppose I test my profession in the same way as that in which the witches were tested of old. I will throw myself into the pool – if I sink, they may make a lawyer of me if they please, but if I swim, I will make myself a soldier.'

Fatigued with the weary duty of hunting out words in the Greek Lexicon, I made up my mind to get rid of it somehow. One morning rising very early, I went down to the pool. Never can I forget the superstitious dread I had about plunging into this lake; but, shutting my eyes, I made a desperate leap. Instead of sinking as a lawyer (thanks to my happy stars) I swam out a soldier. From that day forth, I threw back my shoulders, buttoned my jacket to my throat à la militaire, and nearly suffocated myself with tight neckcloths. My sleeping dreams were of old Ascanius: my waking ones of Charles XII.[1] This military turn did not please my friends. They thought it would wear away; and did not prevent me from reading Cæsar's Commentaries, because of the elegant Latinity, but my own taste led me to the despatches of Sir John Moore and the Duke of Wellington.

About this period, the late Lord Moira left England to assume the government of India.[2] By the exercise of a little interest on the part of my friends, I might have accompanied his lordship; but European battles were more to my taste than Eastern; and my chief ambition was, like that of every other English school-boy at the time, to fight the French, who were then called our 'natural enemies.' What a sad perversion of terms! But, thank God, I have lived to see this feeling die nearly wholly away.

My early ambition was soon after gratified. On the 23rd of January 1813, I was gazetted Ensign, by purchase, in the 52nd Light Infantry. What

1. Ascanius was a heroic figure of Roman legend; Charles XII the eighteenth-century warrior-king of Sweden. Both achieved great deeds at a young age, which may explain their particular appeal to Shaw.
2. Francis Edward Rawdon-Hastings, Earl of Moira at the time of his appointment to India, but later created Marquess of Hastings. Served with distinction in the American Revolutionary War, and eventually rose to the rank of general; Governor General and Commander-in-Chief in India, 1813–23.

pleasing recollections arise in my mind when I think of that splendid regiment! The high-minded, honourable, soldier-like feeling, which actuated all the subalterns, the strict discipline, the gentleman-like bearing of the Commanding Officers to their juniors, all conspired to make the 52nd the beau ideal of what soldiers ought to be. I joined the 2nd battalion at Shorncliffe barracks, in March 1813. It was at that time commanded by Captain Diggle, now one of the officers at Sandhurst College.[1] I was provided with a very strong letter of recommendation by my friend Colonel George Napier,[2] to which I attribute my warm and cordial reception; and, on my arrival, was attached to Captain Love's company, an officer who now commands the 73rd.[3]

All the light regiments at this period in England, were quartered at Hythe and Shorncliffe, under the command of General Mackenzie.[4] The barracks were consequently full; and it fell to my lot to take up my quarters at an hotel, in company with Mr. Gleig, the clever author of the 'Subaltern.'[5] How strange and mysterious after all is the destiny of man! Thinking on this subject, I am often tempted to reverse the remark of Ophelia, and say, 'We neither know what we are, nor what we may come to.' Who could have then imagined that within a dozen years – least of all Gleig or myself – that he would become a

1. Charles Diggle, joined 52nd as a lieutenant February 1805, promoted to captain May 1810. Served extensively in the Peninsula 1808–12 and with the 2/52nd under Graham, then reverted to company command in the 1/52nd in which capacity he was severely wounded at Waterloo.

2. George Thomas Napier, joined 52nd as a captain in January 1804, serving extensively with the regiment thereafter until his appointment to command the 1/71st Highland Light Infantry in March 1814. The nature of his connection with the Shaw family is unclear.

3. James Frederick Love, joined 52nd as a lieutenant June 1805, promoted captain July 1811. Served in the Peninsula 1809–12, with the 2/52nd under Graham, and with the 1/52nd at Waterloo, where he was wounded four times. Commanding the 73rd Foot at the time Shaw wrote his memoirs, Love later became a full general, a knight, and Inspector-General of Infantry.

4. Maj. Gen. Kenneth Mackenzie, who would later command a division under Graham.

5. George Robert Gleig, then a lieutenant in the 85th Light Infantry. Gleig, who rose to become Chaplain-General of the Forces after taking holy orders, later wrote his own memoirs which were published, as Shaw notes, under the title *The Subaltern.*

minister of the Gospel, and I, a civilian of the city of Edinburgh. Be this as it may, I remember as though it were yesterday the many long conversations we had at the inn at Hythe. Whole nights were passed in determining how nobly we should act on first encountering the enemy.

No officer was allowed to do duty in the 52nd, until he was completely drilled in every branch of his duty. The regimental regulation was six months at six hours a day; and, at the end of this period, every subaltern was perfected as a private and non-commissioned officer. It resulted that none of the juniors of the regiment ever displayed that ignorance which is the cause of the want of much moral respect on the part of the soldier. I remember to have seen the effects of this ignorance once exhibited on parade, at Shorncliffe, by Sir _____ _____, of the _____, who commanded. This 'officer but no soldier' got the regiment into square, but how to get them out again was the chief puzzle. He applied to the adjutant of the 52nd, who whispered to him what to do, but it was all Greek to the military tyro. In this emergency the would-be *militaire* ordered the bugler to sound the 'disperse,' and a few minutes after the 'assembly,' when they were again in column. This ignorance produced a great effect on my mind, and I resolved, by an assiduous study of my profession, never to place myself in such a predicament.

From Shorncliffe, we removed to Hythe barracks, where my delight was to witness the officers of the reformed 85th, many of whom had been years in the Peninsula, practising the goose step.[1] At Hythe, we spent our time in drill and athletic exercises, and I will venture to say, that a more active body of young men were never seen than the officers of the 43rd, 52nd, and rifles. The 2nd battalion of the 52nd was at this time so weak, (being composed chiefly of boys and convalescents,) that the idea of the battalion being sent on foreign service never entered the mind of any one. However, about the end of November 1813, as we were quietly sitting at mess, an express arrived, much to the surprise and joy of all, ordering the regiment to hold itself in readiness for foreign service. The news was received by officers and men with a shout of delight, and in less than half an hour an order arrived, to march at twelve that night.

1. The 85th had had its entire officer complement replaced *en masse* in 1813 due to disciplinary and other problems; no doubt it was amusing to Shaw to see the picked veterans who made up much of the regiment's new commissioned leadership being put through the same drills as any new officer.

II

No sooner did we receive the order to march, than the regiment was in instant commotion. A pack of hounds in full cry was but a feeble type of the noise and hubbub which split the ears of all those who were within a quarter of a mile of us. Then the running to and fro, returning this and reclaiming that; this man seeking for his clothes brush – that for Muller's Fortifications – here an outcry for an odd volume of the last novel – there for the Dictionary of the Bible.[1] Neither was this confusion rendered less confounding by the sudden influx of visitors and tradesmen; the former to bid many of us a last adieu, the latter to be paid for a recent order, never again to be repeated. There was something so pleasant, yet withal so mournful, in this double kind of excitement, that I remember it made a deep impression on me. Yet, is not the scene of human life, in every situation, made up of a crowd of incidents such as these? Is it not, after all, a queer game of packing and unpacking, of coming and departing, until we fairly journey to that last sad home 'from whose bourne no traveller returns?' Are we not, whether civilians or soldiers, here to-day and gone to-morrow? But a truce to sermonizing, which I had not inflicted on the reader, but that I had all my 'traps' packed up in ten minutes, and was thus afforded an opportunity of observing the ups and downs, the chances and changes, the packings and unpackings; in a word, the domestic felicities to which soldiers are exposed. I had often heard at public dinners and elsewhere the song 'How merrily we live that soldiers be,' but I never knew what it meant till this moment.

At twelve o'clock, on the memorable night of which I speak, we marched for Deal. We arrived there at daybreak, while the inhabitants were as yet wrapt in 'Nature's soft restorer, balmy sleep.' It was a cold and raw morning, and there was something in the cheerless and uninhabited air of the town which gave me a prejudice against it. I have often since remarked that I never could very much like a city which I entered on a rainy day; and I am as little disposed to relish any town or village which I have traversed after the inhabitants have retired to rest, or before they have risen in the morning.

1. The first work mentioned is *A Treatise Containing the Practical Part of Fortification*, by John Muller, first published 1755; the latter most likely *A Complete Concordance to the Holy Scripture*, by Alexander Cruden, first published 1737. Both works ran to multiple editions.

This is doubtless owing to the cheerless, dull, and uninhabited look which such places wear. To mend the discomfort attendant on so early an arrival at Deal, we found the transports not ready to receive us. We were, therefore, forwarded by express – the officers in post chaises, and the men in wagons, to Ramsgate. The cleanliness of this town, its bracing air, and healthy site, pleased me much. There was then neither discontent nor distress among the substantial farmers or worthy yeomen of the Isle of Thanet; and as I saw the ruddy peasantry and noble teams, laden with corn, entering the streets of Ramsgate, I could not help remarking that England was indeed 'a land all flowing with milk and honey.' To be sure there were then war prices; but I heard it remarked at the time, and I fully believe the fact, that the farmers of the Isle of Thanet did not launch out into those extravagances which distinguished the same race in the other parts of England. Their daughters, to use a vulgar phrase then much in vogue, were neither 'Frenched nor musicked' and not one of them had a dozen of foreign wine in his house. Though we spent ten days in Ramsgate, and much money into the bargain, and were credibly informed that many of the bourgeoisie of the island had fortunes of £20,000 and £30,000, yet we did not mix at all in their society: for Colonel Gibbs,[1] who had assumed the command of the battalion, introduced us to the highest circles in the town, which was then, as well as now, a highly fashionable watering-place. It is impossible to forget the kind manner in which this excellent man behaved to the young officers, or the anxiety he evinced for their personal and social comfort. I could not, however, help regretting the useless despatch with which we had been hurried away from Hythe and Deal, more especially when I reflected on the great inconvenience which it caused to very many officers.

The 52nd gained golden opinions at Ramsgate, and departed amidst the regrets of the inhabitants. On the 9th December, the detachment to which I was attached embarked on board the *Dictator* troop ship, Captain the Hon. Charles Crofton. There were also on board detachments of the Guards,[2] of

1. Edward Gibbs, joined 52nd as a major in February 1808, breveted to lieutenant colonel February 1812 and obtained regimental lieutenant colonelcy April 1813. Served extensively in the Peninsula 1809–13, commanding a brigade in the Light Division at the storming of Badajoz, where he lost an eye. Commanded 2/52nd in the Netherlands, but did not serve at Waterloo. Brother of Maj. Gen. Samuel Gibbs.
2. One of the Guards officers being Ensign Duncombe; see above.

the 44th, and 56th, under General Skerrett, (afterwards killed at Bergen-op-Zoom,) together with the commissariat and medical departments. Our destination was the coast of Holland. The misery endured on board this ship, especially by the subalterns, was dreadful in the extreme. There was not even sitting room for the officers in the gun-room, and this was the more lamentable, as from the roughness of the weather sea-sickness was deplorably prevalent, and our only provisions pease-pudding and red-herrings.

On the 19th of December we landed at Tholen-land. The 52nd was the first regiment to disembark, and as I was a tolerably good French and Latin scholar, I was sent with the first boat. Arrived on Dutch ground, I saw standing on the shore a fine soldierly looking officer. I inquired who he was, and was struck with mingled awe and admiration when I learned it was Sir Thomas Graham, (now Lord Lynedoch,) of whom I had heard so much in my childhood.

The beach was crowded with native women, with blowsy cheeks, manifold petticoats of ample dimensions, and wooden shoes of impenetrable thickness. They wore for the most part a profusion of gold or brass ornaments, which in no degree contributed to their adornment. Although Sir Thomas still remained on the beach witnessing our disembarkation, yet such was the irresistible drollery of these figures, that neither officers nor men (both of whom were, however, very young) could refrain from repeated bursts of laughter. The girls could not at first understand it; but as laughter is infectious, especially between young men and women, the shore became one uniform scene of merriment. I was sent forward with the quarter-master; the latter had left the Highlands while yet a boy, but he could scarcely speak a word of English. On the strength of his Erse and Gaelic, mixed with a little Portuguese (for he had served a short time in Portugal) he fancied himself a great linguist. I found him haranguing a burgomaster of one of the villages in very villainous Portuguese, of which the said burgomaster understood not one word. My friend, however, was evidently impressed with the idea, that if he spoke Portuguese to any foreigner he must of course be understood.[1]

1. This was John Campbell, who had been Quartermaster of the 2/52nd since 1805. In that capacity he had served with the battalion on both its deployments to the Peninsula, August 1808–January 1809 and March 1811–March 1812. Campbell survived the war, and from 1824 until his death at Canterbury on 10 October 1830

Having taken up quarters for the regiment, we marched next morning for Halteren,[1] meeting on the way with a regiment of Guards returning from a reconnoissance [sic] of Bergen-op-Zoom. About three miles from the latter place, we again quartered in the village church of Halteren, huddling both officers and men together. At day-light, I was surprised by shouts of laughter. It was a young scamp who had dressed himself in the gear of one of the female images, and was holding forth to his comrades. Though none of us had before visited a Roman Catholic country, we took the precaution of shutting the church doors, in order to prevent the inhabitants from entering, and thus seeing their religious prejudices shocked. Before mid-day, we moved out on a 'reconnoissance' party. The sub-division to which I was attached was supported in front by some Cossacks and Russian hussars, and it was now for the first time that I heard a ball whiz by me. My attention was, however, more called to the zeal with which several respectable men were digging in their gardens. I soon divined the cause, on hearing an old Peninsula soldier call his comrade to mark well where the boxes were buried; of course, they contained treasure. On our return to Halteren, we found many more Russians had arrived, and a very superior class of Cossacks, who spoke Latin among themselves. There were many young men from Eton, Harrow, and Westminster in the 52nd; but their Latin was Hebrew to the Cossacks. My Scotch pronunciation caused my barbarous Latin to be understood. The Cossacks got on uncommonly well with our regiment: we alternately assisted each other very cordially, and I understood the greater part of what our friends talked about, but I never could comprehend the meaning they attached to the words 'meum' and 'tuum.'[2] In fact, to speak without circumlocution or disguise, they showed a very ill example to our soldiers. I recollect particularly well the manner in which they hunted some very agile turkeys, who had no particular wish to die prematurely. These fellows used to lower their lances the instant they spied the bird; sometimes, they speared them with the point, but it oftener happened that the turkeys escaped. Our fellows, of course, followed their example, not only in killing turkeys, but, in fact, making free with what they

was a military knight of Windsor, a ceremonial position that allowed him a small pension.

1. Halsteren, on the opposite side of the channel separating Tholen from the mainland.

2. That is to say, 'mine' and 'yours'.

could lay their hands on. A great proportion of our soldiers were young; the only veterans being those, who either from wounds or ill health had been sent home from the Peninsula, and who were knowing enough to put the young ones forward, while they alone contrived to reap the produce of this marauding. The officers were likewise youths, and we did not view this conduct as so serious a breach of discipline as we should have done. The commanding officer and the seniors, however, soon pointed out to us the absolute necessity of preventing the smallest approach to predatory doings.[1] There were two or three gentlemen of this army put under arrest, and some tried for permitting depredations, and even punished, whereby their characters were in some measure hurt, while really their sole cause of error was ignorance, and the bad example of the Russian and Cossack officers, who were allowed to do what they chose with impunity.

The style of living of these half-savage soldiers was not only clean but luxurious. Both English and Cossacks were equally bad at the Dutch language, but the latter fellows often after showed great quickness of conception. I was one day explaining to my landlady (a Dutch woman) that I wished a frying-pan to cook a beef-steak. She either could not or would not comprehend me; when one of the Cossacks, who was at my elbow, spying a *papier maché* tray, laid hold of it and put it on the fire directly. His astonishment was great indeed when the heat caused a crackling tatt-tatt, accompanied with a saltatory motion of no mean altitude.[2]

About this time, reports became rife that the French were to attack us. We accordingly made a night march. It was the custom for the company mess to carry a bottle of old rum, to be used in case of illness among the officers. It was my fate to be seized with sudden illness, and the surgeon ordered me to have a drink out of the bottle, which was carried by my brother Sub, now lieutenant-colonel _____, commanding the _____. I saw him look rather queer; he gave me the bottle without saying a word, and I was too ill to speak. On putting it to my lips, there was not a drop in it; for on a cold night it is difficult to resist the temptation of Brandy. Unable to move on, I remained behind the column, expecting to be taken prisoner; but an officer of the Rifles, who was well mounted, perceiving my situation, rode up to me,

---

1. It was, of course, essential to maintain the goodwill of the populace; Wellington was pursuing a similar 'hearts and minds' policy in southern France at this time.
2. Saltatory: dancing, or proceeding by leaps.

and although he could himself walk with difficulty, dismounted, and, tying his horse to a tree, bade me mount him when I found himself a little better. I had never seen this officer before; I had no kind of acquaintance with him, nor he with me; and it may be imagined by those who have been in similar situations how I appreciated such conduct. I should do but half my duty did I not record the name of this good and generous man. It was Colonel James Fullarton, of the Rifles, who died about two years ago, in command of the 96th regiment. A better man or a braver soldier never served king or country. Something may be gained by adulation of the living, but what avails it to flatter the 'dull cold ear of Death.'[1] Colonel Fullarton is beyond the reach of my praise, and the expression of my gratitude is now valueless to him; but, in holding up such a character for example, I only perform my duty to the living.

III

I had not long remained seated on the ground before I recovered, and mounting Colonel Fullarton's horse, rode on and overtook our men. In the morning, we arrived at Oudenbock;[2] and, on the 9th of January, 1814, marched to Rosendaal.[3] Having heard that there was a corps of about 10,000 French moving towards Antwerp, it was determined that we should make a combined movement with the Prussians to intercept them. Accordingly, we made a forced night march, and arrived at Capelhutte on the borders of a vast moor.[4] In a short time, a cannonade commenced to our left. We instantly formed, though the ground was covered with snow, and the cold intense. Hearing the rattling of artillery on the hard road, we threw out videttes, (German and Hussars). Those of the supposed enemy soon appeared, and, to the astonishment of both, the videttes met in a friendly

1. James Fullarton; ensign 51st Foot December 1802, served with that regiment at Corunna then obtained a captaincy in the 95th Rifles, May 1809. Served with 3/95th at Cadiz, Barossa and in Portugal before returning to England due to ill health. Served throughout Graham's campaign and then saw action in the Hundred Days, obtaining his majority as a result, before being promoted to lieutenant colonel in the 96th, September 1827. Died at Halifax, Nova Scotia, 8 March 1834. The quotation is from Gray's 'Elegy in a Country Churchyard'.
2. Oudenbosch.
3. Roosendaal; a march of five miles.
4. Apparently Cappellen; a march of sixteen miles.

manner. The truth was the Prussians had come down upon us, never supposing we were British. The mistake arose thus. Our men, owing to the cold, had worn their great coats; so that no portion of the scarlet uniform was to be seen; and the Prussians inseparably connected a scarlet uniform with British troops.

We marched onwards towards Antwerp. I was this night put on picquet on the road which lies between Antwerp and Bergen-op-Zoom. The cold was intense; and the snow deep on the ground; but hearing the Irish brigade were in Bergen-op-Zoom, and fearing some trick or blunder, I was all night on the move.[1] The sentries were relieved every hour; and the patroles every half hour. I recollect being much amused with one fellow whose post was on a very cold spot at the comer of a wood. He challenged me: – I answered patrole. His patience could not stand it. He halloed out 'D--n the patrole, I thought it was the relief.' The sentries were at this period ordered to put searching questions to prevent deceit; and, as there had been some complaints about always having biscuit, he put the question, 'When was last tommy day?' (soft bread).

The bread we did get was of the blackest rye. When we first landed, I met an officer of the 2nd German Hussars, who told me that during the Duke of York's campaign in Holland, the frost was so severe that it froze the bread, so that it became impossible to eat it. This was thought a regular bouncing traveller's story, but this night, to our very great discomfort, proved its truth. The next morning, we marched for Antwerp, and made an attack on the village of Merxem, which was carried in a very splendid manner, by the Rifles under Fullarton, and the 78th regiment under Colonel M'Cleod.[2] The ground was, as I before remarked, covered with deep snow, and I recollect the astonishment of all of us on seeing the wounded Highlanders lying

1. There had been no 'Irish Brigade' in the French Army since the Revolution, but the 3/3e Régiment Étranger, previously the Légion Irlandais, was serving in the Low Countries at this time. They were, however, in garrison at Antwerp, not Bergen-op-Zoom.

2. Col John Macleod, 2/78th Highlanders. Strictly speaking, Macleod was in command of the whole 2nd Brigade, and the battalion was led by Lt Col Martin Lindsay. Macleod had entered the Army in 1793, and served almost exclusively with the 78th. Wounded at Merxem, he returned to command the battalion on garrison duties during the Hundred Days. He died in 1851, having risen to the rank of lieutenant general.

at full length on the encrimsoned snow, none of the light brigade having heard of their having landed in Holland.[1] The Prussians looked on them as English Cossacks; because all strange and savage-looking fellows amongst us were called Cossacks.

Many strange mistakes were often on the point of occurring from the ignorance of the different variety of uniforms. It was in these cases that the advantage of being a good linguist was so strikingly apparent. This ought to be a lesson to all military. It was Charles the Fifth, I believe, who said, 'So many languages as a man knows, so many times is he a man,' and the truth of this remark has been strikingly exemplified to my various scenes of blood and strife.

The 52nd were now ordered into the village to relieve the Rifles and 78th, and, as they were entering with their great coats on, a Prussian regiment met them. Each took the other for an enemy; but Colonel Gibbs, who was an excellent German scholar, prevented a collision which might under other circumstances have taken place. I think it was on this occasion that I had a conversation with his present Majesty.[2] The regiment had removed to the left, and I was with the rear company, when a gentleman dressed in a blue coat with white lining came up. From his dress I thought he was one of the Commissariat, but remarking two musket shots through his coat, I thought him a rather rash commissary. I felt inclined to be offended when, addressing me in a loud commanding tone, he asked, 'What regiment is that? Who commands it?'

'That gentleman,' said I, pointing to Captain Diggle.

'Is he the Commanding Officer?'

'No! Colonel Gibbs commands.'

It was odd that the men should have had the same idea of the mysterious stranger as I had myself. They, too, supposed he must be a Commissary, and began muttering something about 'Bread Bags better in the rear,' when my

1. The 2/78th had only landed on 10 January and had joined the army in the field by forced marches, only catching up on the eve of battle. See Davidson, Major H. (ed.), *History and Services of the 78th Highlanders (Ross-shire Buffs) 1793–1881* (Edinburgh & London: W. & A. K. Johnston, 1901), Vol. I, pp. 95–122.

2. William IV, who in 1814 was still the Duke of Clarence. In fact, if true, this anecdote must relate to the Second Battle of Merxem; see Appendix IV for commentary on this issue.

friend Captain Anderson of the Artillery suddenly rode up.[1] What was my astonishment on seeing him salute the supposed Mr. Commissary Bread Bags in the most respectful fashion, uttering at the same time the following words: – 'If your Royal Highness moves a little more to the left you can have a little better view of the enemy. Sir Thomas Graham is in the steeple of the Church.' I, in a whisper, asked Anderson, 'What Royal Highness is this?' when he informed me it was the Duke of Clarence who had landed from England the day before. The Duke's courage continued to be the talk of the army for some days; but I said little, thinking I had gotten into a scrape for having mistaken his Royal Highness for a Commissary.

This evening, we were again on the march. All the troops were over-powered with fatigue. The night was intensely cold, and before morning each man was marching as suited his own convenience. There was but a brigade of our men in the road, but this sample of service gave me some idea of what Napoleon's army must have suffered in its retreat from Russia.

We remained quietly at Rosendaal for some time, after our return to that place. On the 30th January, during a most tremendous hail and sleet storm, we commenced our march for Westwesel.[2] The weather was so dreadful that I am convinced the troops could not have withstood it, if they had not been convinced they were marching for France. As we approached Bracht, the road was one long pool of water; but, nevertheless, all went on with spirit till the steeple of Antwerp appeared in the distance. We reached Donk that night. It is a pretty village about three miles from Antwerp. At Donk we, for the first time, heard that we were to attempt to burn the fleet at Antwerp; but our hopes of success abated much on learning that Carnot, the celebrated republican, and still more famous engineer, was in the citadel of the town, and had come expressly to render it impregnable.[3] The order next morning was that the Rifles, supported by the bayonets of the 52nd, should carry the village of Merxem. At the moment of attack, and when the ugly order of 'medical men to the Front' had been given, Sir Herbert Taylor

1. Capt. William Cochrane Anderson, RA. First commissioned November 1807, served on the Walcheren expedition and would later also serve at Waterloo.
2. Wuustwezel.
3. Lazare Carnot, once Minister of War under the Revolutionary government, had been hastily re-commissioned as a *général de division* and given the command of the Antwerp garrison.

carried us to the right to make a diversion.[1] In this manner, we escaped the musketry; but were exposed to the more nervous and harmless round shot. At the same time, we had an opportunity of observing and quietly admiring the good conduct of all the troops engaged. Driving the enemy before us, we formed under cover of a dyke, but, no sooner were we there, than he commenced with round shot, knowing the exact range to a nicety, and causing us many ugly casualties. This night while the mortar batteries were erecting, the 52nd and Rifles were employed in the covering party. The weather being frosty, and the ground of a damp and spongy nature, the only way to get shelter from the shot was by digging holes in the dyke. Tools being put into our hands this was speedily done; but, as the wet continued dropping from the upper part of the holes, and froze as it fell upon us, our position was anything but pleasant. I was in the same hole with my brother subaltern, now Major M'Dowall of the 44th,[2] and I well remember we lay on each other in turn in order to keep our bodies warm; meanwhile, the enemy kept up a very sharp fire of shot and shell. Many ammunition waggons were near the batteries, and never shall I forget the gallantry of a Major Mitchell of the Artillery[3] in extinguishing the fire of a shell which had struck into the centre of a waggon of ammunition. In the attack on Bergen-op-Zoom, Lord Lynedoch (then Sir Thomas Graham) speaking of this same officer says – 'He fell covered with honour and with wounds, but still there is a slight hope that the services of this gallant soldier may be spared to his Country.' Our attempts to burn the fleet at Antwerp were unsuccessful; and we retired, passing through the same country by which we had advanced.

IV

Though the country through which we had advanced had suffered little from the march of our troops, yet I cannot say that the steps of our enemies had fallen as lightly as though they had trodden on flowers. On the contrary, the Dutch suffered severely from the ravages of a brigade of Saxon Cuirassiers. Amongst others, a family with which I had been quartered, and had left in

1. Maj. Gen. Taylor was commanding the 2nd Brigade; although he directed this flanking movement, which drew on troops from the Light Brigade as well as his own command, it was Graham who instigated the manoeuvre; see Bamford, *Bold and Ambitious Enterprise*, pp. 135–9.
2. Ensign Dahort McDowall, 2/52nd Light Infantry.
3. Capt. Edward Mitchell, RA. Shaw made a mistake regarding his rank.

perfect happiness, suffered in the most shocking manner. Our regiment was now attached to the brigade of that excellent man and lamented officer, General Gibbs, who afterwards fell at the disastrous affair of New Orleans.[1] We took up our quarters at Groot Sandert,[2] and here the Prince of Orange joined the army. Though his Royal Highness appeared to be heart and soul in the cause, and full of the eager and believing enthusiasm of early manhood, yet his subjects gave no indication of being actuated by feelings so generous and laudable.

At Groot Sandert we had a good deal of drill; and here I may remark, that, among the many officers I encountered in the army, I never met with one who had so much the knack of turning the minds of young men to useful military details as General Gibbs. It was a frequent custom of his, to ask young military men to his table; and, here in the easy confidence of a generous hospitality, he pointed out to them, with the air of one who was really interested in their welfare, the advantages which would result to them, as officers, from the study of languages and mathematics. On parade, his favourite amusement was to employ two young subalterns, in skirmishing companies, against each other; and in this manner infused a military spirit into those under him. The 56th was then in his brigade. It was commanded by a character well known in the British army. I mean Lieutenant-Colonel Brown of the 28th, who, it is said, purposely allowed his regiment to be surrounded at Barrossa [sic].[3] Most officers would have felt nervous in such a situation; but it is reported Brown addressed his men thus: – 'Twenty-eighth! what d----d lucky fellows you are! This day you must be either extinguished or distinguished. Do as you like.' The 28th took their Colonel at his word. The rear rank turned to the right-about, and repulsed the enemy; and now the 28th wear the number of the regiment

1. For details of the new organisation of the forces, see Appendix I.
2. Groot Zundert.
3. One of the Army's greatest characters, Lt Col John Frederick Brown had served extensively in the Peninsula with the 28th Foot, but his command at Barossa was a flank battalion made up of light and grenadier companies from several regiments. He obtained a brevet lieutenant colonelcy in July 1810, and was promoted to substantive rank in the 56th in March 1812. In 1813 he was given command of the newly raised 3/56th and led this battalion throughout Graham's campaign: he was therefore no longer 'of the 28th' when Shaw knew him.

both in the front and the back of their schakos [sic].[1] Colonel Brown, at the period of which I speak, was rather given to the vice of swearing. The parson of the brigade, a Mr. James,[2] was a most excellent and conscientious man, and, despite the severity of the weather, regularly celebrated Divine Service in the open fields. On one of these occasions, James delivered one of the most impressive sermons I ever heard against the vice of swearing. The only fault the sermon had (if fault it had at all) was, that the preacher descended too much to minute particulars. The discourse over, General Gibbs gave orders for the brigade to return to quarters, directing Colonel Brown to move off first. Brown ordered his regiment to move off from the right. The grenadiers made some mistake, when the Colonel thundered out a volley of oaths; but, instantly recollecting himself, and turning to the clergyman, he exclaimed, 'Beg pardon, Parson; but look there! – D----n me! could you yourself help it?' This appeal was irresistible; the whole brigade burst into fits of laughter, and thus the effects of the sermon were entirely destroyed.

About the end of February, a small party of the Rifles and 52nd were sent to Westermalle, to attempt a surprise on a party of French.[3] The roads were heavy and fatiguing; and, although there was a bed where we halted with three mattresses, the senior officer kept all to himself, not allowing the junior officers to lie down. 'My ancient' had a fine new pair of strong shoes, so I thought 'tit for tat' all fair. As soon as he was asleep, I took his shoes, and having ordered a cauldron of boiling water, cleaned them carefully while it was getting ready. When the pot was at a boil, I flung in the shoes, simmered them well for half an hour, and before morning they were clean, and at his bed side, outwardly as large as ever, but so swollen in the inside, that his feet could not enter. My senior officer had to make the next day's march in a pair of clogs, lent him by an artillery officer, I having distinctly proved to him that the snow water always produced a contracting effect on English leather. This may appear a scurvy-enough trick to have played, but the intense selfishness of the man merited so sharp a reprisal. We soldiers

1. Shaw is here confusing two stories; the 28th gained their 'Back Badge' through gallantry at Alexandria in 1801, under circumstances much akin to those Shaw attributes to Brown's men at Barossa.
2. This was Rev. Maurice James, Chaplain to the Forces, who was in fact the only clergyman to serve with Graham's army for much of the campaign.
3. Westmalle; this was not a major operation, but rather part of the ongoing war of outposts between the British Second Division and the Antwerp garrison.

would go to perdition for a gallant, generous, self-denying fellow; but we loathe and detest those selfish men who think only of their own comforts.

On the evening of the attack on Bergen-op-Zoom, we got an order to march to relieve the Guards, who had taken that city. About four o'clock in the morning, we heard the melancholy truth. On this subject, I do not care to dwell. I shall only state what were the general reports in the army; namely, that Lord Lynedoch, with the greatest talent, had put the troops in the town, and, by some sad mistakes, they lost it.

We now marched to Starbrock,[1] where we were along with the 25th or King's Own Borderers. At this time, that regiment was not in great repute, but they were most careful in giving all their designations and additions on the walls of the picquet houses, which had always the 'rd' of Borderers changed into 'th' by the relieving regiment. Thus, there were many squabbles, and much rivalry, among our men.[2]

Starbrock lies at little distance from Fort Lillo. It is only approachable by a dyke which runs alongside the river. On this dyke we had erected a battery, to prevent communication between Antwerp and the fort. About the 21st March, a French ship of the line dropped down the river to destroy the battery.[3] The Rocket Brigade, which had been employed at the battle of Leipsic, now joined Lord Lynedoch's army.[4] They were brought to destroy this ship. The rocket that was fired, hung for a few seconds above the ship, but returned with the same velocity, falling among some ice a few yards in the rear of the spot from whence it was discharged. Worst of all, too, the shell attached burst, and dispersed the numerous amateurs who congregated around.

Several years after this event, when in the 90th regiment, I dined one day at the table of Admiral Gore,[5] at Chatham. A naval officer present told the story of this very affair of the rocket. His account was received with a loud laugh of incredulity; but, when I asked him some corroborative questions,

1. Stabroek.
2. The 2/25th not being in good repute may refer to their having inadvertently burnt down their billets at Groot Zundert, leading to a substantial claim being lodged for compensation. See Graham to Bathurst, 6 March 1814, in TNA, WO1/200, pp. 77–9.
3. L'Anversois, 74 guns; see Bamford, Bold and Ambitious Enterprise, pp. 343–4.
4. This was the 2nd Rocket Troop, Royal Horse Artillery.
5. Vice-Admiral Sir John Gore, Commander-in-Chief, The Nore from 1818 to 1821.

I never saw a man more relieved. Every one knows the uncertainty of rockets, but I must confess this was a singular case.

About this time, an order came for 100 volunteers of the rifles, and 100 of the 52nd, to go to South Beveland, in order to storm Fort Batz. By the kindness of Lord Harris, who then commanded the 73rd,[1] I was allowed to go as Adjutant to the detachment. By some mistake, we were delayed two days in Tholen. The town is surrounded with ditches filled with green putrid matter. The owner of the boiled shoes, which had contracted from the contact with snow water, was of the party. I leaped a rather broad ditch, but in 'mine ancient's' attempt to follow me, he dropped heavily somewhere about the centre, stirring up the 'rankest compound of villanous smells' that ever offended the nose of Christian.[2] He had no luggage with him; but we had a rare delight in prevailing on him to take off his uniform in order to have the unsavoury smell boiled out of it. While his clothes were yet boiling hot in the cauldron, the order for a sudden march arrived. The affected sympathy of his juniors, whose dissatisfaction at this lucky *contretemps* was but ill-disguised, was irresistibly ludicrous to those who knew the real relish with which they regarded the disagreeable man's misfortune.

It was at South Beveland we first saw the Russian sailors, who had been taken in the Tagus, drilling as soldiers. It was shocking to see the brutal and unfeeling manner in which they were treated by their officers. It was at South Beveland, too, that we saw Commodore Owen,[3] with his sailors and marines. The Russians and Marines were formed under fire of Fort Batz, losing men, when luckily General Gibbs arrived to inform them of an armistice. It was arranged that we were to make the attack next day.

War being thus over, at least as far as regarded this expedition, we amused ourselves exactly as we pleased, the inhabitants being so happy and contented, that they would make no complaints. Although it was breeding time, they allowed us to shoot the game, and to gallop their waggons along their dykes; in short, they treated us in every respect with the greatest possible kindness. I happened, at this time, to be quartered in a wealthy

1. Lt Col William Harris, commanding the 2/73rd. Harris was the son of Gen. George, 1st Baron Harris, Commander-in-Chief, Madras, during the Fourth Mysore War, and succeeded to his father's title in 1829.
2. Shaw is here quoting from Shakespeare's *Merry Wives of Windsor* – right down to the mis-spelt villainous.
3. Capt. Edward Owen, RN, commanding HMS *Cornwall*.

farmer's house. Looking out of bed one fine morning, on which I awoke rather earlier than usual, I perceived a high narrow barrel, at the top of which, alternately there appeared, the head and tail of a dog. This was a churn. Near to the top of the barrel, was a moveable lid on a sort of hinge. The dog being put there, feels himself falling down tail foremost; he exerts himself with an effort, and up he comes; however, it is but to go down again as he did before, and thus the poor animal continues up and down, stirring the milk, until butter is made.

Leaving South Beveland, we rejoined the regiment at Donk by a very pleasant march.

Williamstadt was, at this time, the *dépôt* for the convalescents and wounded of the army. Each regiment furnished an officer for this duty. Many regiments made it a point to allow skulkers to take it, or to send officers who did not agree well with the mess, but in the 52nd, there were none such, and it accordingly became a regular routine duty, each man in his turn. I was despatched to relieve a Lieutenant Mitchell in his duty.[1] The commandant was Major [Evatt], who had placed no less than thirteen officers under arrest, on the morning of my arrival.[2] I was introduced to him, when, in a harsh voice, he said 'Who are you?' I said 'Lieutenant Shaw, 52nd, sent by Colonel Gibbs, to relieve the other officer.' On this, he flew into a violent passion saying, 'Go instantly about your business, and tell Colonel Gibbs I shall not trouble myself to teach his officers their duty. Go about your business.' This man, in officer's uniform, never said more grateful words to me. I instantly obeyed, and starting out of the gates, never halted until I arrived at my regiment. I thus got rid of a month's disagreeable command.

V

I had hardly arrived at our quarters, before this disagreeable Commandant reported me for having quitted the garrison without orders. Owing to his impertinent message to his superior officer, and his ungentlemanlike conduct to myself, the affair went off quietly. It were, perhaps, well to put officers of this stamp in the rear, in order to make it disagreeable to skulkers.

1. Lt Edward Mitchell, 2/52nd Light Infantry.
2. His name disguised by an ellipsis in the original, the identity of the Commandant at Willemstad is revealed in the Monthly Returns (TNA, WO17/1773) to have been Capt. (Brevet Maj.) George Evatt, 55th Foot. See also Appendix II for further comment on this officer.

While [we were] quartered at Donk, the garrison of Bergen-op-Zoom marched through, on their way to France. We had a very pleasant day with the officers, to whom we gave a dinner; from this we marched to Malines. There was quartered in that town, a brigade of the division of French, which had been with Davoust to Hamburgh. Each brigade furnished a subaltern and thirty men for the town guard. I happened to be the officer of the Guard, and, although it was almost unnatural to see such recent and inveterate enemies doing the same duty, we, nevertheless, got on remarkably well.

Whilst we were at Malines, the regiment of the King of Rome marched into the town. It was composed of very young boys, but we were all astonished at the superior manner in which they exercised.[1] Our brigade was now ordered to Brussels. The whole town turned out in the *Allée Verte* to receive us. The admiration of the inhabitants for the army in general, was great, but it was turned into astonishment, the moment the 78th Highlanders made their appearance in their kilts. The first emotions of the Bruxellois were those of wonder and affright, which soon changed into uproarious laughter.

The 78th had not been long in the town, before they became the greatest favourites. They fully deserved their popularity, for it was impossible to find anywhere a better behaved regiment; the inhabitants of Brussels over-powered both our officers and men with every species of kindness. The conscription had been so severe, both in France and Belgium, that every one was obliged to enter the army without either regard to family or rank, and the gentry and *bourgeoisie* of Brussels supposed our army was similarly composed. It was the custom for the officers to visit the different billets, to see that the men were conducting themselves properly; and I have often, on such occasions, seen common uneducated soldiers sitting at table with most respectable families; of course, this did not last long; for, though these people could not exchange a word with our men, they must have seen, from their demeanour and manners, that they were not fitting companions for them.

1. This is a reference to the remaining elements of the Pupiles de la Garde – specifically, the 2e, 3e, and 4e Bataillons – which had been serving under Général de Division Maison in that officer's defence of the Low Countries against the allies. These battalions were composed of the sons of soldiers; the bulk of them had been used to help rebuild the Young Guard in 1813, leaving only the youngest boys in the three remaining battalions.

At this period, I obtained leave of absence and proceeded straight to Paris, where I had an opportunity of seeing the capital in a state of complete confusion, caused by the entry of the allied troops. I returned by way of Lille, at which city I had intended to have passed a day; but some boys, who discovered I was English, gathered a crowd round the hotel, when they commenced singing a song, the chorus of which was 'The Destruction of the English, at Bergen-op-Zoom.' This was anything but pleasant to my ears and feelings, and, hastily quitting the town, I proceeded to Antwerp, and thence to Bergen-op-Zoom, with a view of examining the works of that celebrated fortress. My military pride was here much offended by the guide, a Scotchman named Stewart, pointing out the marks still on the ramparts, by which the British had escaped. This is a disagreeable subject, but I convinced myself that Lord Lynedoch was fully justified in the attempt, and that, in fact, he did succeed in the object, though the troops lost it. I do not say that blame is to be attached to any quarter. It was a misfortune, perhaps arising from our having no reserve.

From Brussels, our regiment marched to do garrison duty in Antwerp; and, such was the innate dislike that Subs had to the guards in the citadel there, that I dare say many, like myself, experienced no great sorrow at hearing that the French destroyed it in 1833.[1] We left the place without regret, and marching through Ghent arrived at Tournay. We were everywhere well received by the people. In Tournay, we remained in very pleasant quarters during the whole autumn, with excellent shooting to boot. From that city we marched to Yprés, which town we were informed, boasted of the best society in Brabant. We had not been long there, before it was determined to give a ball to the inhabitants. It was thought necessary in the regiment to make the lieges of Yprés know, what a fine set of fellows we were; so, before going to the ball, it was agreed among ourselves, that our conversation to the ladies should be of the amiable qualities of our brother officers. We spoke with such effect that a ball was given in return for ours, and the houses of all the inhabitants were thus opened to us amiable young men. While we remained at Yprés it was carnival season, and many queer circumstances occurred, which I dare not here enumerate.

1. This relates to the French siege of Antwerp during their intervention in the Belgian Revolution. The siege, which included an intensive mortar bombardment, in fact ended in December 1832.

There is a curious custom at this place, which afforded us much amusement, but of its origin I have not the remotest conception. A cat is taken to
the top of the high steeple in the square; about twenty blown bladders are
then attached to its body, when it is flung into the street below. The poor
creature sails quietly and slowly through the air, mewing piteously all the
while. As it approaches the earth, all hands are extended ready to seize it,
for the lucky person is free from municipal taxes during the ensuing year.
The cat's claws and feet are left at liberty, and it sometimes happens that the
happy man who is to pay no taxes, gets well scratched for his pains.

With the relation of this bizarre custom, Shaw's account of his service
under Graham comes to an end. Indeed, Graham had already handed
over his command and returned home, and, as Shaw goes on to relate,
he and his comrades had every expectation of doing likewise. Instead,
however, news was soon received that Napoleon had escaped from Elba
and that hostilities had resumed. Shortly afterwards, in April 1815, the
1st Battalion of the 52nd arrived in Flanders, whereupon Shaw and most
of his comrades were drafted into the senior unit and the rump of the
2nd Battalion sent home. Shaw would make the Waterloo campaign
under the command of Colonel John Colborne, but missed the battle
itself due to being detached on baggage-guard duties in Brussels, a task
that he did his best to evade, but to which he was specifically ordered
to return by an ADC to Sir Henry Clinton, the divisional commander.

After the end of hostilities, and the reduction of the 2nd Battalion of
the 52nd, Shaw went onto half pay before receiving, in 1817, an appointment to the 90th (Perthshire Volunteers) Light Infantry, of which Lord
Lynedoch was colonel. A further reduction soon had him again on half
pay, and Shaw entered the wine trade at Leith, where he also served
in the local Volunteer unit. In 1831, he took service on the Pedro-ite
side during the Portuguese Civil War, serving initially as an officer of
marines and then on land; by 1834, he was commanding a whole brigade
of British mercenaries, and would be knighted by the victorious Dom
Pedro the following year. He subsequently served in Spain with the
British Legion during the First Carlist War, finally returning home
in 1836. Two years later, he received a British knighthood to go with
his Portuguese honours. In 1839, with Chartism spreading amongst
the working classes in England, Shaw received an appointment as

Commissioner of Police in Manchester and Bolton, where he combined a firmness in putting down riots with considerable sympathy for the rioters' cause. This latter attribute eventually led to his removal in 1842. Shaw, who had married in 1841 and had one son, finally retired from the Army by sale of his half pay commission in 1844, but continued to take a keen interest in military matters until his death in 1871.

Chapter IV

Ensign William Thain

33rd (1st West Riding) Regiment of Foot

William Thain was only sixteen years old when he was commissioned into the 33rd Foot on 13 May 1813, but by that time he had already served for a year as a volunteer in the Northumberland Militia. His father, James Thain, had himself served in the British Army during the American Revolutionary War, and subsequently as a mercenary officer in the service of Sweden, before returning to England and taking employment as manager of a soda works on Tyneside.[1] One of the earliest entries in Thain's diary of his military service notes that his commission came as the result of a recommendation from 'Lord Loraine', although this seems in fact to be a misapprehension of his benefactor's title: the magnate in question apparently being Sir Charles Loraine of Kirkharle Hall. Thain joined the 33rd at Windsor on 24 June 1813, only a few days before the battalion received its orders to embark for service in the Baltic, but – perhaps because of his earlier Militia experience – was nevertheless included with the men going overseas for what proved to be some fairly intensive on-the-job training. The 33rd had been largely rebuilt following its return to Britain in 1812 after sixteen years in India, and the spell of Baltic garrison duty provided a useful opportunity for all ranks to improve their readiness for renewed active service.

From the start of his military career, William Thain kept a diary which recorded both his daily activities and his observations on the places he served. There are occasional gaps, one of which falls at the end of his time in the Baltic; the new section, covering his service under Graham, begins with the 33rd aboard transport ships at anchor off Yarmouth, along with the other four battalions that had been redeployed from the Baltic under the command of Major General Samuel Gibbs. Although the early stages of the account relate only to

---

1. Uglow, Jenny, *The Pinecone* (London: Faber & Faber, 2012), p. 56.

time spent on board ship, they are interesting nevertheless for their detail of the preparations – both material and theoretical – that the young officer chose to make for the coming campaign. They also serve to remind us that although Gibbs's contingent had acquired a degree of seasoning from their spell in the Baltic, they had not benefitted from their time cooped up on the transports and that both officers and men were somewhat jaded by the experience.

1 December:

The wind blew so fresh last night that some of the ships dragged their anchors; no boats can get off from the shore.

2 December:

At anchor. Weather still very rough.

3 December:

Went on shore this evening. Dined with several others at the Angel Inn. Felt extremely pleased to be in England again. Got into an excellent bed, which was so different to what I had been accustomed to that I could not sleep.

4 December:

Wind still contrary. Bought several necessaries that I wanted. Had breakfast, dinner and supper at the Angel Inn with others of our Regiment.

5 December:

The wind became favourable. General Gibbs gave an order that all officers were to be on board at 3 o'clock pm.

6 December:

We got under way this afternoon. It was quite calm towards midnight.

7 December:

At Sea. At 5 o'clock the wind became quite contrary and, at 8 o'clock, we were obliged to put back towards Yarmouth and anchored in the Roads once more. Wind blowing very fresh.

8 December:

Yarmouth. At anchor all day, wind blowing contrary.

9 December:

Reading Phillipart's *Northern Campaigns* from the time the French entered Russia down to the conclusion of the armistice in 1813.[1]

10 December:

Yarmouth. Still at anchor. Attempted to get out but did not succeed.

12 December:

Weighed anchor but could not get out.

13 December:

This morning we succeeded in getting off under a fine breeze and soon lost sight of land. The *Ariel* sloop of war,[2] our convoy, and also a brig of war, in company.

14 December:

At sea. This morning, when we got up, the Dutch coast was in sight. At 9 o'clock we were off the mouth of the Maese,[3] Briel Church in sight. All the ships made signal for pilots, but none came off. At 5 in the evening we anchored after tacking about for some time.

15 December:

At about 1 in the morning we weighed. At about noon we entered Goree Gat. At 4 pm we anchored at Helvoetsluys. It appears to have one principal street through which a canal runs, on each side of the entrance of which is a kind of fort, resembling a contregard.[4] On every house, etc, the Dutch flag was

1. John Philippart was a prolific author on contemporary military matters at the time of the Napoleonic Wars, and later produced a number of reference books on the British Army of the day. The title referenced by Thain was a two-volume account of Napoleon's invasion of Russia and of the 1813 spring campaign in Germany; see also Appendix II.
2. HMS *Ariel*, launched 1806, a *Merlin*-class sloop of war rated at 16 guns.
3. The Maas.
4. A counterguard – an outwork intended to cover a larger bastion or ravelin.

hoisted and everyone had ribbons in their hats. We found several gun brigs and other transports from Ramsgate, etc, at anchor, likewise two English packets. On our arrival we received orders to proceed in the morning for Willemstad and the masters of transports to get a pilot on board within an hour and to have two days' provisions cooked for landing.

Helvoetsluys is a maritime town on the south side of the island of Voorn, five miles south of the Briel and six from the island of Goree.

16 December:

We weighed this morning but, the wind being contrary, we were not able to advance far before the tide began to ebb, when we anchored. The tide flows eight hours here and ebbs only four. A large French frigate was in the dock at Helvoetsluys and two French schooners sailed-up, which the malicious rascals had sunk to obstruct the passage. This was a very cold, frosty day. After we anchored a party went ashore.

17 December:

We got up to Willemstad and were landed very soon after anchoring. The 25th having disembarked first, proceeded to Fynart and the 73rd to Klindvart.[1] Our men were put into barracks for the night and the officers billeted on the inhabitants. This is quite a small town but appears to be strongly fortified. It is fifteen miles NE of Bergen op Zoom and twelve miles SSW of Dort.

18 December:

Marched this morning at 9 o'clock for Steenbergen. The road, for about two miles from Willemstad, was good, being paved, but afterwards was terribly bad. After we got through a small, open town called Princeland,[2] we absolutely were wading far above ankle deep in mud. About three miles from Willemstad is a large redoubt at an angle of the road and, afterwards, we passed another on our right just before we came to the first ferry; they are both well supplied with cannon. Princeland is between the two ferries.

1. Fijnaart and Klundert, respectively six miles to the south and five miles to the south-east.
2. In fact Dinteloord; Thain himself explains the dual name in a later entry.

We found some of the Foot Guards at Steenbergen occupied the billets, so our men were obliged to lie in a house all night upon straw without any fires to dry their wet clothes (for it rained almost incessantly the whole way). The officers got billets, some of them seven in a room. Steenbergen is a strong town of Brabant in the Dutch Netherlands, six miles NE of Bergen op Zoom.

19 December:

Steenbergen. The Guards marched out today and our men went into their billets. Lt Col Elphinstone joined and took command of the Regiment.[1]

The account of the unpleasant march to Steenbergen is closely mirrored by that offered by Thomas Austin, who also comments on the superior conditions enjoyed by the Foot Guards, noting of the latter that they 'as a matter of course, secured to themselves the more comfortable quarters, and less disagreeable duties in the town!'[2] Considering the attitudes towards the rest of the Army encapsulated in Duncombe's diary, the resentment felt by the line officers is hardly to be wondered at.

Once he is established at Steenbergen, Thain's diary entries for the next few days are focused largely on administrative matters; although he mentions having taken his turn on picquet duty covering the road to Bergen-op-Zoom, he gives no further details of this. However, the battalion's stay in its new quarters would prove to be brief, with new orders coming in while Thain was still with the outposts.

22 December:

I withdrew the piquet at daybreak and found the Regiment was to march in an hour. We set off at half past 8 o'clock and took up a position about 1½ miles from the east of the town in two barns, from whence we kept up communication by double sentries along a dyke with the 25th Regiment

1. Lt Col William Keith Elphinstone, appointed to the 33rd in September 1813 having previously been major in the 6th Dragoon Guards, replaced the previous commanding officer, Arthur Gore, who had been appointed brigadier general to command the troops left behind in the Baltic.
2. Austin, Brigadier General H. H. (ed.), *Old Stick Leg: Extracts from the Diaries of Major Thomas Austin* (London: Geoffrey Bles, 1926), pp. 49–52.

at Kruisland.[1] Had strong piquets out all round. Today, had the pleasure of seeing Sir Thomas Graham, who passed us at full speed on his way to Willemstad, where he was going to hasten up the artillery. The 73rd, having been attached to the Light Brigade under the command of Major General Mackenzie, marched into Steenbergen from Princeland.

23 December:

Sir Thomas Graham passed us today again on his way back to Tholen, his Headquarters. At 2 o'clock we received an order to march to Princeland, where we arrived just as it was getting dark, after plunging through the worst road I ever saw. Princeland was formerly called Dinteloord; it received its present name from one of the Princes of Orange having been born in it. It is an unfortified town.

24 December:

Princeland. Received an order to march at 10 o'clock for Kluindaart;[2] the road was tolerable enough. We passed the remains of several redoubts. Reached the town about 4 o'clock. The 25th also marched in from Kruisland. We suppose our being sent here is to cover Willemstad from the operation of the enemy on the side of Breda. We are distant from the former place six miles and from the latter, twelve. The people here are extremely attached to the Prince of Orange and showed us great hospitality.

25 December:

Kluindaart. The Regiments were, as usual, under arms an hour before daylight, guards mounted at 10, paraded for muster at 2. Sir Thomas Graham and his Staff passed through to Willemstad. General Gibbs arrived today. Sam Pagan[3] spent the evening and supped with me.

26 December:

Under arms at 6 o'clock, marched at 10 for Zevenbergen, where we arrived at 12.

1. Situated five miles to the east of Steenbergen.
2. Klundert.
3. Ensign Samuel Alexander Pagan, 33rd Foot. Promoted lieutenant, 7 April 1814; wounded at Waterloo.

27 December:

Zevenbergen is situated on the highest ground that I have seen in Holland. It is, however, unfortified. The 54th marched in today. Guards mounted at 11 o'clock and we paraded at half past, having strong piquets both without and within the town.

28 December:

A detachment of 200 men, under command of Major Harty,[1] was sent out. The 3rd Battalion of the 56th marched in today, as did the Depots of the 54th and our Regiment.

The troop movements and reinforcements described by Thain served largely to complete the initial organisation of Graham's forces, with the arrival of depot detachments for the battalions that had come from the Baltic serving to give these units a useful increment in strength. For the remainder of the year, Thain had little else to report beyond more administrative concerns and a false alarm that had the battalion ready to march only for no such orders to be received. The first day of the New Year, however, found him in a reflective mood.

1 January:

I have to thank my Maker that He has been pleased to let me see the beginning of another year and to pray that it may be a still more important one to me than the last, although in it I have had a great many changes, first of all volunteering into the Line and seeing my sister for the first time, then going on two expeditions and others of minor importance, such as seeing London, Windsor, Oxford, Cheltenham, etc, for the first time. The people at this place make a great holiday of this day and seem to welcome it with more than usual joy having been liberated from tyranny.

We were ordered, this evening, to march tomorrow morning at 6 o'clock.

Spent the evening at my quarter with Mr Graham and Mr Burrow of the 56th[2] who are billeted with me.

1. Maj. John Lockington Harty, 33rd Foot.
2. Lt L. Graham and Ensign William Burrow, both of the 3/56th Foot.

2 January

At 7 o'clock the three regiments marched. It was a cold, frosty morning, in consequence of which the roads were very good, the country was more agreeable than any I have seen before in Holland being more wooded and the fields laid out with greater taste. It is about twelve miles from Zevenbergen to Breda. We formed on the side of the road while the Russian Army marched out of the place, I never in my life saw such fine men, or men better equipped. There were three regiments of infantry, each a thousand strong, and several pieces of artillery and some troops of Cossacks, well armed, clothed and mounted. Altogether I never saw such a Brigade which excited my admiration so much – each Regiment had a very good band and the soldiers marched remarkably steadily and in good time, they looked down with an eye of contempt on our poor fellows as they passed.[1] On entering Breda, I was struck with the magnitude of the fortifications, all the shrubs, trees, etc, are levelled with the ground. I and [name illegible] got a billet in the same house where the people were very glad to see us. At 2 o'clock we were shown our alarm posts and, on our return, an excellent dinner was ready for us.

3 January:

On our posts at 6 o'clock, at 10 the alarm drums were beat through the whole town in consequence of the French making a forward movement, our Breda men turned out very well, we remained in the covered way until 3 o'clock when we were marched off.

I went today with Colonel Elphinstone to visit the Cossack stables, the horses were all standing saddled, which they always are and the men scarce ever take off any part of their dress, they always laugh when the French are mentioned and shewed us several fine gold repeating watches with chains and seals which they had taken from the French officers, besides daggers, swords, pistols, etc, all mounted with silver. There was an officer who, having an Italian servant who spoke French, acted as an interpreter. The officer lived with the men and horses and was only distinguished in dress by a little embroidery on his collar and a silver sash – there were three Calmucs who are a more savage race, their countenances exactly resemble the Chinese, they have some little boys with them which we were told were their sons, it was very entertaining to see their fathers teach them to ride and the use

1. See Appendix III for details of these troops.

of the sabre and lance. One of the Calmucs wore a cross hanging on his breast by a blue ribbon, this, we were informed, was a mark of distinction conferred upon him for having, in one day, slain three of the enemy. Ralph Gore[1] spent the evening and suppered with us.

4 January:

A wet day. Went to see the palace built by King William III, which is truly magnificent, even now, although it is converted into a kind of citadel, there being barracks for the soldiers, hospitals, stores of every description, etc, in it. Went in the evening to a public coffee room which was filled with officers and others of every nation, some Cossacks played very well at billiards, their dress is black, consisting of a short, tight vest with a kind of overall almost all covered with leather buttoning, down to the soles of their shoes. The collar and cuffs of the vest are sky blue and embroidered with silver, a black belt crosses their body, resembling that worn by the 95th, upon which is fixed a small cartridge box of black leather with a large silver star on the lid. The part next to the body, being concave, fits quite close on the side under the left arm. On the front part of the belt is a large letter A, in silver, from which are suspended several long chains of silver with a cartridge, ramrod, etc. Besides this belt they have another round the waist with slings for the sabre (which has a steel scabbard) and for the pistols and dagger. They have, also, round their waist a sash of a kind of cloth of silver, they generally wear an immense black or brown cloak, with a red collar, over everything and a little cap of the same.

5 January:

A Regiment of Cossacks passed through this morning. They were preceded by a band of singers. Was on the main guard with Captain Campbell of the 54th.[2]

6 January:

Was relieved at 10 o'clock, the Regiment paraded at half past 2 for punishment. The Brigade was ordered to be in readiness to march at daybreak tomorrow.

1. Lt Ralph Gore, 33rd Foot. Promoted captain 28 July 1814.
2. Capt. Duncan Campbell, 54th Foot.

7 January:

We did not march but were under arms from 12 o'clock until 4. A corps of Uhlans came in having lost some men and an officer in an affair with outposts of the enemy.

8 January:

Marched at 8 o'clock and entered Zevenbergen by the same road that we had left it. A Detachment of the Hussars of the King's German Legion and some artillerymen were with the Brigade today. 8,000 Prussians, under General Bulow, entered Breda after we left it.

9 January:

Zevenbergen. The Brigade marched to Oudenbosch, where the 25th Regiment joined us from Klundert – this is a small, open town.

10 January:

Oudenbosch. The Brigade, having the 25th on the right, the 33rd on the left and the 54th and 55th in the centre, set out this morning at daybreak for Roosendaal, six miles. The 33rd was, however, left at the village of Kalfsdour,[1] 1½ miles from the place. All day, troops, artillery, wagons, etc, have passed, the 55th and 69th Regiments went past, as did the Hussars of the King's German Legion, several pieces of heavy artillery, with wagon train, hospital troop train, etc, all in the highest order. The Light Brigade is at Roosendaal and neighbourhood, consisting of the 52nd, 35th and 73rd Regiments, all under General Mackenzie, who went through this place, as did General Graham and General Taylor with all their staff, baggage, etc. The forces are now concentrated on this spot. We expect to go to Antwerp before we go to Bergen. The Light Brigade is ordered to advance on Wouw and we to be in readiness at a moment.

11 January:

Kalfsdour. Having set off at 12 o'clock last night we marched to Kalmthout,[2] 16 miles, where we arrived about 8 o'clock and halted for the day. This is a most miserable village, without any inland navigation which is the great

1. Kalsdonk.
2. Calmthout.

source of wealth to the Dutch towns. We were billeted in farms and were not able to purchase anything, not even white bread. We were almost frozen during the march, it was so excessively cold and I could scarce keep myself awake.

12 January:

Kalmthout. The whole Brigade marched on to Capelle,[1] an open village where we halted for the night. I ought to have mentioned yesterday that we were drawn out in a large common expecting the French, who was expected, would have retired that way having previously been beaten by the Prussian force, but we were disappointed. We were also today marched to another part of the common when General Graham reconnoitred the enemy position.

13 January:

Capelle. Marched on towards Antwerp and, in a smart affair, drove the enemy from their position in the village of Merxem. The 78th Regt (Highlanders) lost a great many men. They charged the French three times down the street, killed hundreds, and pursued them to the very gates of the town, we and the 25th supported them, for which we were thanked in General Orders. The Prussians kept possession of the village and we retired to another village from whence, at 10 o'clock pm, the whole Brigade retired towards Capelle which we passed through.

14 January:

Kalmthout. Arrived early in the morning at Kalmthout. The country in the south of Roosendaal is quite different from any we have seen, being covered with large forests, though still very flat. Around Capelle it is beautifully cultivated and the neighbourhood of Antwerp is very fine.

15 January:

We marched to Nispen, a poor village, where we interred Lt Mackenzie of the 78th Regt,[2] who died of the wounds he received at the taking of Merxem.

1. Cappellen.
2. Lt William Mackenzie, 2/78th Highlanders.

16 January:

Nr. Kalamthout. The whole Brigade marched to Roosendaal and the Head-quarters are established at Oudenbosch. The 54th are at Nispen, some regiments are also at Wouw

17 January:

Roosendaal. Was in a Regimental Court Martial all day. Ten of us are billeted in one room and there are only two beds so that even here where we have come to refresh ourselves we cannot put off our clothes. I have not slept undressed since I was at Oudenbosche on the 9th.

Since the 33rd played only a supporting role in the First Battle of Merxem, Thain's account has little to add to our knowledge of that action. His relation of the two-day approach march, including the freezing conditions and the false alarm of French movements, tallies perfectly with other accounts of these operations. Until the end of January, the 33rd remained in garrison along with the rest of Graham's forces, with Thain having little of note to report other than a review of the whole brigade by the Duke of Clarence on 21 January, and his own posting to the battalion's grenadier company shortly afterwards. This was at the request of that company's captain, James Guthrie, who had evidently identified a promising young officer, but was against Thain's own preference: given the choice, he would have wished to join the light company. Only as the month drew to an end was there a return to activity.

30 January:

The Division, together with all the artillery, marched this morning for Kalmthout. It was excessively stormy and thawing rapidly so that the roads were very much flooded. I, being Orderly Officer of the Regiment, was obliged to accompany the baggage, which is a most troublesome employ-ment. The 54th Regt joined us at Nispen, a village three or four miles south of Roosendaal. The 52nd Regt and two field pieces formed the advance guard. We marched through Essen and, indeed, precisely the same route that we advance last time by. It continued to snow almost the whole day. We arrived about 10 o'clock. Roosendaal is a town in which three or four regiments might be very comfortably quartered, but it is too small to contain so many troops as were in it without being very much crowded. It contains three tolerable streets but has no good public buildings. The country round about it is very uninteresting, being quite flat, though pretty well cultivated, it is an entirely open place. One very material difference between the towns of this country and those in the north of Germany, is that the former never have any market days so that a stranger is at some loss to get things. Now, in the latter, you had large and plentiful markets for poultry, vegetables and even large cattle twice every week and large fairs very frequently. Dutch Brabant is, in every respect, as inferior to the north of Germany as the inhabitants of the former are to those of the latter.

In these towns, with the exception of Breda, you have no inns or public rooms and the people seem to be all of the same order or class, low, without literature, but full of cunning, which they exercise on all occasions to make money to the prejudice of their fellow creatures. Out of the great number of officers who bought carts and horses at Roosendaal, which they were obliged to do in consequence of a general order, there were not above two or three that were not cheated. There is no navigable river or canal at Roosendaal but there is a small canal at Oudenbosch, six miles off.

31 January:

Kalmpthout.[1] Marched in at 9 o'clock through West Wesel[2] to Brecht, a distance of twelve to fourteen miles, the country is barren almost all the way. West Wesel is a poor village close by the fine high road that Bonaparte laid, at great expense, from Antwerp to Breda and, I believe, is carried on from the former place to Paris, the distance from Antwerp to Breda is 35 or 40 miles by the new road. Before it was made it was almost double that. West Wesel is almost surrounded by a large heath or marsh. After we passed through it we had to wade up to the knees across three rivulets that were swollen by the melting snow, and marched on heath almost all the way to Brecht. This is a small, dirty town with a good-looking church. I mounted on an outlying piquet the moment that we got in, which was on the road to Hoogstraaten[3] where the Prussian General Bulow's Headquarters were.

1. Calmthout.
2. Wuustwezel.
3. Hoogstraten.

1 February:

Brecht. The Brigades proceeded by different routes to the village of Braxgatten.[1] It snowed most bitterly for a length of time. After passing over one large common we came into a very wooded country and marched several miles along the Breda road, passed through Greven Wesel[2] and, about a mile further, we reached Braxgatten, which is nothing more than a few farm houses on each side of the high road. The country here is entirely covered with wood and rows of fine elm trees grow on each side of the road.

Tomorrow we expect to be early engaged, all are in the highest spirits.

2 February:

Braxgatten. We fell in at day-break. Major General Gibbs commanded the Division, Major General Mackenzie having last night been thrown from his horse and lamed. Soon after we had passed a turn in the road, our Light troops became engaged, we met with great obstacles, the enemy having cut down all the large trees and laid them across the roads, but our brave soldiers, assisting the pioneers, soon threw them aside and pressed on, our right wing was detached to drive a French piquet out of the wood on the left. The enemy took up a strong position by a windmill and it was necessary to bring two field pieces up to drive them from it. Our Brigade entered Merxem by the main road. Our right wing entered it with part of General Skerret's [sic] Brigade on the left. All pressed on and the enemy flew into the gates of Antwerp.

The action lasted about three hours. When we returned through the streets it was astonishing to see the difficulties we had overcome. The enemy had high breastworks across the street at the distance of twenty to thirty paces and the walls of the houses at the entrance to the village were pierced with loop-holes. We stopped to breathe a little then our Brigade (the 2nd) retired to a large Gentleman's seat. The Brigade of Guards furnished the working parties for the night, which were immediately set on by the chief engineer, Lt. Col. Smith [Carmichael Smyth], in erecting batteries against the famous Scheldt Fleet. They were not molested during the night.

Our loss this day was not inconsiderable, though scarce to be compared to that of the enemy. We made our attacks on the village to the left of the

1. Brasschaat.
2. 's Gravenwezel.

place that we entered it last time. Thus we are again in possession of the village of Merxem.

3 February:

Merxem. At 4 o'clock pm our Batteries opened up on the fleet and continued till midnight with great fury but with little effect. Sir Thomas Graham and Sir George Wood, commanding the artillery, were both quite confident that the ships would have been on fire before that time. Our Regiment was in a large house exactly in rear of the batteries, ready to support the men in the trenches should the enemy have made a sortie. From it we have a fine view of the firing, which was beautiful after it became dark. No rockets were made use of but the shells were filled with the same combustible matter that they used.

4 February:

The firing having ceased on both sides for some hours, commenced again at about 8 in the morning. Our Regiment was removed from the large house in rear of the batteries and marched more to the rear, where we remained for the night. No flames or even smoke from the fleet. Weather beautiful.

5 February:

Paraded an hour before daylight and again at 11 o'clock, soon after which we were marched into the village of Merxem, where the 78th also were. The firing this day was excessively hot on both sides and we were soon obliged to quit the village and fall back. After dark our Brigade went into the trenches, when our Grenadiers were employed in dragging the guns and mortars out. General Taylor gave us an excellent supper afterwards.

6 February:

Merxem. At daybreak the troops were brought out of the trenches and, at noon, the forces all retired to the village of Braxgatten or Breshaar, three miles from Merxem, where we remained unmolested all night.

7 February:

Our Brigade marched all along the famous Breda road to West Wesel, where the 35th remained, we went to Loenhout, a village to the east of West Wesel and off the road, and the 56th were with us in Loenhout.

8 February:

Loenhout. Our necessaries were inspected, as an order was issued for all regiments to be completed with everything for the field.

The Second Battle of Merxem, unlike the First, saw a large number of Graham's regiments heavily engaged. Both brigades of the Second Division attacked straight down the main Breda–Antwerp *chaussée*, but this attack stalled and Graham was obliged to extemporise a flank attack by drawing off the left-hand regiments of both brigades. Overall direction of this attack was given to Major General Taylor, who ultimately made a success of it but at some cost in casualties both in the flank attack itself and in the renewed offensive by the remaining troops along the *chaussée*. The division of the 33rd into two wings, as described by Thain, is a new detail to be added to the narrative of this action presented in *A Bold and Ambitious Enterprise*, and reflects a further element of confusion to add to that already engendered by the breaking up of brigade organisations.

Taylor was evidently in the habit of giving dinners for his officers; Thomas Austin was the beneficiary of a similar meal the night prior to the attack on Merxem.[1] A popular and capable commander, Taylor was obliged to return to England shortly after the failure of the second operation against Antwerp, due to a longstanding commitment to resume his duties as Private Secretary to Queen Charlotte.

9 February:

I delivered the accounts of the 1st Company over to Mr Macquarie.[2] Orderly Officers of Companies are to report every morning an hour before daylight to the Captain of the Day that their men are accoutred and ready to turn out.

14 February:

Parades, etc, as usual. This village is very small and yet has such a large church which in the inside is beautiful. A large painting of the Descent from the Cross is by Rubens. Loenhout is three miles from West Wesel,

---

1. Austin, *Stick-Leg*, p. 127.
2. Lt Lachlan Macquarie, 33rd Foot. This was due to Thain's transfer to the Grenadier Company.

seven from Hoogstraten and about equidistant from Breda and Antwerp, ie fifteen or sixteen miles.

15 February:

Archbold[1] and I walked over, after morning parade, to the village of Hoog-straten, about eight miles to the west of this. It contains a nunnery with a small chapel; there were, however, none but some old nuns and very few even of these. I was not surprised at this when I perceived that every part of it had been numbered off by the French for the reception of soldiers, like the other houses of the place. The great church is magnificent and its steeple very high. Several of the works of Rubens still are remaining to adorn the walls. The painted windows must once have been beautiful, but are now very much mutilated. This church was built in 1600. The principal monuments are that of Antoine de la Laingen [de Lalaing], Premier Comte de Cette Terre, and that of the Prince of Salm, both of the most beautiful polished marble; the latter is by van Dael.[2]

17 February:

The 33rd was reviewed by Major General Taylor, prior to his returning to England, who was pleased to express his entire approbation of our appearance.

19 February:

Was on advanced piquet at the Windmill.

20 February:

Colonel Elphinstone was so good as to lend me one of his horses and we rode over to Brecht together. This village has nothing to particularise it. The inhabitants are poor and employ themselves in the manufacture of lace which, however, is of a quality much inferior to that made at Brussels. The prices they put upon it was for the broadest kind, two guilders per ell, that is, supposing the guilder at 1s 10d, to be 3s 8d English. But the fine Brussels lace is twenty, thirty and forty guilders per ell. The ell is about threequarters of an English yard.

1. Ensign John Archbald, 33rd Foot. Promoted lieutenant 27 October 1814.
2. Cornelis van Dael, noted eighteenth-century sculptor.

21 February:

The 33rd marched today to Groot Zundert, which was then the Head-quarters of the Army. Groot Zundert is a village on the Antwerp and Breda road, nine miles from the latter and six miles from Loenhout. It contained nothing remarkable.

It will already be observed that the above entries are for irregular intervals, with some days omitted, and such entries as there are consist largely of accounts of sightseeing. For the whole of the fortnight following the arrival of the 33rd at Groot Zundert, this lack of military activity became even more pronounced; so far as his diary is concerned, Thain made only a handful of brief entries, all of them dealing with aspects of the internal economy of his company and regiment. With so little to report in the interim, his detailed coverage of events only picks up again with the onset of preparations for the attack on Bergen-op-Zoom.

8 March:

Bergen op Zoom

We marched at 12 o'clock in light order to Huybergen[1] where we halted a couple of hours. Most of us were billeted in a large monastery, which is the only thing remarkable in the village. The 55th, under Major Hogg, and 69th, under the immediate command of Major Mutlebury, came in and we then got an unexpected order to march under the orders of Colonel Morris, of the 69th.[2] It was just dusk and we had already marched ten miles when we now set out on the Bergen op Zoom road. This was a thing which we never once thought at all probable. Some snow was on the ground, otherwise it was very dark and we had a very bad road over some sand hills. After marching six or eight miles we were halted and the Commander of the Forces ordered Officers Commanding Corps to make known [to] their officers and men that we were within a five minute walk of Bergen, which we were going to attempt to take by surprise.

1. Huijbergen; a march of fourteen miles from Groot Zundert.
2. Maj. Alexander Hogg, 55th Foot; Maj. George Muttlebury and Lt Col Charles Morrice, both of the 2/69th Foot. The latter battalion was under Muttlebury's immediate command as Morrice had command of the whole Centre Attack.

The Grenadiers were called to the head of the column; ours, being senior, took the lead. Ladders, supported by our 7th and 8th Companies, were placed four deep in front of the Grenadiers, a Sergeant and six of our Grenadiers preceded the whole.

As Lt. Col. Elphinstone was Second in Command, it was necessary that someone of our Officers should attend Colonel Morris to take any message to Colonel Elphinstone which the former might think necessary. Colonel Elphinstone honoured me with this appointment. In the meantime, the feint attack commenced on our right. Colonel Morris was ordered not to move until he heard firing from the attack on our left. As soon as he heard this, which was to commence precisely at ½ past 10, he was then to advance and surprise a subaltern's piquet of fifteen men which was in the covert way; which done he was to scale where the guide would show him and direct that the 55th and 69th should move along the rampart, one to the right, the other to the left. If they met any armed body they were to challenge by 'Orange Boven' and, if answered by 'God save the King' they were to be considered as friends. It was some minutes more than ½ past 10 o'clock when Colonel Morris gave the word to advance, but we had not heard a single shot on the left.[1] As we went up the glacis, the sentries fired at us and retired. We darted across the palisades. After this I am unable to tell what part of the fortification we passed, for it was as dark as possible. However, we ran to our left then turned at right angle to the right when we met with high palisades. It was in getting over these that our Grenadiers, in their ardour, would not wait long enough for the ladders to move over before them, as they ought to have done, but rushed on. In consequence, some confusion ensued and the ladders were deserted and left. Colonel Morris, Captain Mitchell,[2] the guide and myself got over these palisades first and, running on, we were challenged by the French sentries on the rampart above us by 'Qui vive la?' when the foolish fellow of a guide,[3] instead of being as still as death, roared out 'Orange Boven! Orange Boven!' which made the troops in our rear give a cheer of three times three! After this, of course, our intentions were no longer concealed and the enemy threw up an abundance of blue lights

1. For more on this delay, see Appendix V.
2. Capt. Edward Mitchell, RA, attached to the Centre Attack as acting engineer officer.
3. The guide to the Centre Attack was Capt. de Bère of the Engineer Corps of the Netherlands Army.

to discover exactly where we were, which were followed by a tremendous fire of grape and musketry on the spot. Colonel Morris, Captain Mitchell, the guide and myself pressed on to the piquet house, followed by the 33rd Grenadiers who had so imprudently left the ladders in the rear. But the piquet had retired within the works. In fact, it would be absurd to expect that they would be there, after the noise we had just been making, and we kept pressing forward to our right. We met with another row of palisades, having passed which we came to the place where we ought to scale. Here we discovered that there was not a single ladder with us and only one Company of Grenadiers!

I was instantly despatched to the rear to bring them up. The firing was now dreadful from the rampart. I found the ladders at the palisades where they had been left, some on one side and some on the other, and the head of the column had moved down into the outer ditch on the right, where they were stopping. I collected as many men as I could and made them to follow me with some ladders. When I got back to the place I had left Colonel Morris, I found that he had been wounded and carried off, as had Captain Guthrie, commanding our Grenadier Company, the whole of which had been obliged to fall back for shelter. Whilst I was telling Captain Mitchell that I had brought up some of the ladders he received a second, severe, wound which obliged him to be carried off also. It now became my duty to tell Colonel Elphinstone what had happened, but he no sooner assumed command than he was wounded and taken off. Major Muttlebury was the next senior Officer but he, having no orders and not knowing of whom to get any, ordered the whole to retire, but it was in such a direction that we were entirely enfiladed by a heavy fire of every description which threw the troops into confusion. We were, however, soon formed again on the road from which we had advanced.

9 March:

At about 1 o'clock this morning we were ordered round to the left to support the Guards who had effected an entrance. We got in by the ladders which they had planted. Here, instead of pushing forward and taking possession we were ordered to lie down on the snow, where we remained for two hours, exposed to occasional shot from the town. The Guards met with no opposition, for Brigadier General Gore, with a handful of men, had taken possession of all that part of the rampart, so that they were received at the top of the ladders by their friends. General Gore was killed and his small force driven back by superior numbers on the head of the column of Guards who, however, did not advance in the same direction to support them. It was past 3 o'clock am when General Cooke ordered the 33rd to proceed to the left and support the Royals, under Colonel Muller,[1] at the Water Port Gate. We, accordingly, left the 69th and Guards in the bastion, where we had entered, and took up a position on the inside of the gate, where we remained until daybreak.

At daybreak, I could perceive that we were behind a house which was filled with wounded Officers and men. In our front was a kind of canal which ran up into the heart of the town. Over this, to the right, was a stone bridge, beyond which was an arsenal from the windows of which we were a good deal assayed. On the east end of this arsenal was a work in possession of the enemy, with a ditch round it, from this they fired two guns all last night upon some of our artillery in the place. On our left was the Water Port Gate in the gorge of which was the head of the column of the Royals. The Flank Companies were, however, in the town and under the bridge. When daylight appeared the 91st came scrambling over one end of the work in our front pursued by the enemy at the point of the bayonet.[2] We were ordered first of all to charge and save them, upon which the Grenadiers and the 1st Company darted through the enemy's fire and along the bridge, where we were surprised to find that the Regiment had been counter-ordered and were again in their former position. We were now close under the windows of the arsenal but screened from fire by some heaps of wood, past the end of which we kept up a smart fire on the enemy at the guns. For want of support our flanks were threatened, we therefore thought it prudent to retire, which we did through showers of shot, with the loss of only two men wounded. We, however, did not join the Regiment, but kept behind a house on their right and rather to the rear. It was a most provident thing that we did so, for this house would have prevented the Regiment from seeing the force which came to turn our right flank, which became unsupported by the retreat of

1. Lt Col Frederick Muller, 4/1st Foot; see also account of 2nd Lt Moodie in this volume, and discussion in Appendix V.
2. This is a mystery, as the 2/91st were supposed to be part of the False Attack and should not have got into this part of the town; it is, however, possible that their flank companies were attached to the Right Attack along with those of the 2/21st and 2/37th.

the Guards from the position in which we had left them. We, by being there, gave timely notice to Major Parkinson,[1] who immediately fell back behind the parapet, having previously ascertained that the Royals had quitted their position, without Colonel Muller having given the slightest intimation of his intention, although we were placed under his orders. Now the Guards had left our right, as the Royals had our left unprotected, consequently both were in imminent danger.

We, notwithstanding, kept up a smart fire for more than half an hour. Then, seeing that the enemy were turning their guns upon us, Major Parkinson withdrew the men, by degree, from behind the parapet across the ditch. We then got upon an inundated country which, luckily, as the tide had ebbed, had not much water upon it, but was covered with large sheets of ice. We had to walk over this for almost a mile and a half before we were at all sheltered from a cross fire and we had to wade through several streams up to the shoulders. We were soon formed and, dispositions having been made for the retreat of the force, we were ordered to take up our old quarters in Kalmthout, where we arrived about 5 o'clock in the evening, quite faint with fatigue and hunger. I could not swallow anything but tea, which revived me immediately and created an appetite.

10 March:

Kalmthout. I could scarce move this morning, every bone of my body was so sore by bruises and the extreme exertion which I had made yesterday. Our loss was dreadful, one battalion of Guards came out of the place commanded by the Sergeant Major. The Royals all laid down their arms and General Cooke was taken prisoner. The loss of our Regiment was trifling compared with that of others. We had only two Sergeants and twenty six rank and file killed, eight Officers and 30 wounded, and two Officers and 53 taken.

13 March:

Was Garrison Subaltern of the Day.

1. Maj. Edward Parkinson, 33rd Foot. Later severely wounded at Quatre Bras but survived to reach the rank of lieutenant general.

14 March:

The Commanding Officer appointed me to do duty as Adjutant of the Regiment, Mr Priestly[1] having been wounded.

15 March:

Wrote to Captain Davison, by Captain Colclough, who, having been released on his parole, was sent to bear the melancholy tidings to poor Mrs Gore, who was at Hanover.[2] He also took despatches from Sir Thomas Graham to HRH The Duke of Cambridge.

For the next few days, entries are again sparse, as Thain was evidently extremely busy getting to grips with his new duties as Adjutant. As such, one of his responsibilities was the battalion's drill, the improvement of which was complicated, as Thain recorded, due to the recent influx of a large number of German recruits who had been obtained by the late Brigadier General Gore during his command on the Baltic.[3] Nevertheless, Thain must have made a good job of things, as his next entry makes clear.

22 March:

Major Parkinson ordered me today to put the Regiment through the platoon exercise as Light Infantry and told me afterwards that he was satisfied with the manner in which I did it.

23 March:

Busy in Orderly Room almost all day. Priestly still remains very ill. Major Parkinson and Stoddart[4] live together. As I am obliged to report personally every night at 8 o'clock whether the Regiment is all present, I generally spend the rest of the evening with them. Without this, I should scarce know what to do with myself after tattoo except sit down and drink gin and smoke tobacco, for my baggage is so light that I cannot carry any books.

1. Lt and Adjutant Edward Jonathan Priestly, 33rd Foot.
2. The identity of Capt. Davison is not clear; Colclough was Capt. George Colclough, 33rd Foot.
3. For which see Bamford, *Sickness, Suffering, and the Sword*, p. 165.
4. Paymaster Edward Stoddart, 33rd Foot.

24 March:

Post day. Muster of the Regiment at 4 o'clock. Headquarters of the Army remains here.

25 March:

Were inspected by Lieutenant Colonel Brown, 3rd Bn, 56th Regiment (Pompadours),[1] who commands the Brigade. He was very minute with the men's necessaries but, as there is not at present in the neighbourhood ground enough, he did not put us through any manoeuvres. Spent the evening as normal at Major Parkinson's. Arthur Gore[2] and I still live in the same room together and are better lodged than almost every other officer, some of whom are miserably off indeed.

26 March:

We were very suddenly today all in a hustle. In the afternoon an Hussar came galloping over with an order that we were to get under arms immediately and to remain so until ordered to advance. We did remain until nearly dark, when an Officer of the Quarter Master General's Department came to lead us to the place where we were destined for and, at the same time, told us that the enemy had sallied in great force both from Antwerp and Fort Lillo and were advancing on our lines. It was dark, beginning to rain and we had turned out in such haste that most of the men and Officers had eaten nothing. When we began this march, through roads almost impassable, God knows in what condition we should have brought up before the French, but luckily we had scarce moved off the ground when another Officer arrived to say we might return to our quarters, it having been found out that the whole alarm had been raised by a young Hussar Officer on piquet. He got all our curses for having kept us standing out in the cold so long, but otherwise we returned to our miserable hamlet very well contented that it was no worse. Dined with Major Parkinson and Stoddart.

27 March:

Prayers in the morning by Mr James, the Chaplain.[3]

1. Lt Col John Frederick Brown, 3/56th Foot.
2. Lt Arthur Gore, 33rd Foot; later killed at Waterloo.
3. The Rev. Maurice James, Chaplain to the Forces.

28 March:

This day, to the astonishment of us all, the charges, which Lieutenant Beauclerk preferred against Captain Haigh and Lieutenant Fitzpatrick,[1] and which had been forwarded to Headquarters, were sent back and these Officers warned to prepare for trial. Spent the evening at Major Parkinson's.

29 March:

Weather getting much finer. Parades at 11 o'clock and at 5 in the evening.

30 March:

A General Court of Inquiry sat at Kalmthout today on the charges above mentioned. Lieutenant Colonel Vigoureux, 30th Regiment, President.[2] The evidence that was called on gave everyone reason to think that the charges were preferred through sheer malice to Captain Haigh and not through zeal for the service. Lieutenant Beauclerk had been *in Coventry*, as it is called, for more than three years, in consequence of some circumstances that took place while the Regiment was in India and when they returned and were quartered at Hull in Yorkshire it was proposed by some Officers that he should again be noticed, at which time Haigh spoke against it very strongly and was the great means of the measures not being adopted. Many suppose that this was the reason of Beauclerk's bringing this forward.

31 March:

Kalmthout. Lieutenants Oliver and Oddie joined today, having volunteered from the Militia according to the new Act of Parliament so much detested by all the subalterns in the Army.[3]

For more on the enquiry, which led to Fitzpatrick being tried by court martial for drunkenness on duty during the operations against Antwerp, see Appendix II. The record of the trial shows that no charges were brought against Haigh, although he was implicated in the

1. Lt Thomas Beauclerk, Capt. John Haigh, Capt. Edward Fitzpatrick, all of the 33rd.
2. Lt Col Charles Vigoureux, 2/30th Foot.
3. Lieutenants John Oliver and E. W. Oddie both joined the 33rd from the Militia at this time. The former is also given as Olivier and Ollivier in some sources. For more on this, see Appendix II.

case; evidently the court of enquiry found nothing sufficient to bring charges against him. The fact that the case was brought at all, some time after the fact and as a result of a personal quarrel, does indicate the difficulties that could arise from differences amongst the officers of a regiment; it evidently did Beauclerk little good, however, since he was no longer present with the regiment by the time of the Hundred Days campaign, during the course of which Haigh was killed at Waterloo. The objection to the arrival of Lieutenants Oliver and Oddie was due to their having obtained their places through an act of Parliament designed to encourage the volunteering of men from the Militia into regiments of the line, which allowed Militia officers to transfer and retain their existing ranks. Such officers would serve as supernumeraries until a regular vacancy opened up, to the discomfiture of those within the regiment who would otherwise have benefited by stepping up to fill the vacancy. Thankfully, neither quarrels nor new arrivals seem to have had a long-lasting effect amongst the officers of the 33rd, for there is no further mention of dissent, and Thain's diary begins in April with a return to relative tranquillity.

1 April:

Priestly still unwell. Fine, warm, showers of rain.

2 April:

A *Feu de Joie* fired by the whole Army for one of Blucher's victories in France.

5 April:

Very rainy weather. Headquarters of the Army still at Kalmthout, which makes us better off than we would otherwise should be for we take care to catch all the sutlers, etc, that are bringing up wine and, if Headquarters were not here, would never find us out. An Englishwoman brought up a cart load of very fine old port from Brussels which she sold instantly, for it was by far the best thing we had seen since we came into Holland.

6 April:

Change of quarters in the village.

7 April:

I forgot to mention that on the 31st ult. a General Court of Enquiry, ordered by the Prince Regent, sat at General Gibbs' quarters, at a chateau between Loenhout and West Wesel, on the conduct of Lieutenant Colonel Muller of the Royals in having abandoned the Water Port Gate at Bergen op Zoom on the morning of 10th March, without orders. It was here clearly shewn that the 33rd did not follow the Royals when they retired from that gate and also that the latter took themselves off without our knowing anything of their having thus left our left flank quite exposed.

8 April:

At last we got an order to quit this miserable hole, which I do not care if I never see again as long as I live, and marched today through Putte, where the 30th Regiment were quartered, to the pleasant little village of Starbroeck,[1] six miles from Kalmthout, where we found the 25th and 52nd Regiments.

12th April

Starbroek. We hear very often the firing of cannon at different points, but they do not give us much alarm as everyone is now thinking of peace and of our entry into Antwerp. They are like the dying groans of the vanquished enemy which only calls to our recollection what they once were. I went to have a look at Fort Lillo today and was really surprised by its strength. The country around it is entirely inundated with the exception of a dyke which leads up to it and this is enfiladed by the broad side of a two-decker lying in the river besides the works and other preparations from the fort itself. It is in this dyke that we have a temporary work (Fort Frederick) with a piquet of 100 men.

16 April:

We marched to Putte this evening, which is only two miles from Starbroek. This was on account of the Army being divided into different Brigades.[2]

1. Stabroek.
2. There was a substantial reorganisation of Graham's army at this time, to allow for the losses suffered at Bergen-op-Zoom; for details of the new order of battle, see Appendix I.

17 April:

Marched from Putte, across a heath, passing Kalmthout close on our left, to West Wesel, a distance of about twelve English miles. Here we joined the 54th, the provisional battalion of the 21st and the 37th Regiments and were presented to our new Brigadier, Lieutenant Colonel Crawford, 73rd Regt.[1] Priestly resumed his duties again.

18 April:

West Wesel. Marched at 6 o'clock, passed through the village of Brecht and arrived at West Maal[2] at about 1 o'clock. The provisional battalion of the 21st, the 37th and the 54th marched with us today. Weather very warm. The whole of the country that we crossed this day was very deep sand, not all cultivated, with here and there a plantation of fir trees which did not appear to thrive well. Both in Brecht and West Maal some kind of pestilential disorder was raging with great violence amongst its inhabitants. At the latter place we did not enter a house without finding either dead or dying people in. It was today that I met my old friend Costly of the 37th,[3] whom I had known at Kilkenny in Ireland when he was recruiting there last year. He introduced me to Colonel Hart.[4]

19 April

West Maal. The Brigade marched again this morning at 4 o'clock. We had some rain today, roads horrible and must certainly be impassable in winter. Country richly cultivated, sandy soil, some good looking country houses and villages with, here and there, a plantation of fir trees. The provisional battalion and 54th Regiment occupied Broeschem and adjacent hamlets and the 33rd marched about two miles further south to Viersel.[5] All these

1. Capt. Robert Crawford, 2/73rd Foot, had held the brevet rank of lieutenant colonel in the Army since 1810. He was thus one of Graham's most senior field officers, and therefore eligible for a brigade command. The brigade whose formation Thain details was numbered as the First, and formed part of the First Division; see also Appendix I.
2. Westmalle.
3. Lt John Costly, 2/37th Foot.
4. Lt Col Simon Hart, who commanded the 2/37th throughout its service in the Low Countries.
5. Broechem and Viersel, situated immediately to the south of Zandhoven.

little places are in the midst of a most fruitful country but very flat. The Grenadiers occupied a water mill which is turned by a branch of the river Nethe from which the department derives its name.

20 April:

The poor inhabitants have all suffered extremely by the Cossacks and Prussians who think they are revenging themselves for the cruelties committed by the French in their countries. They are entirely ignorant of the great events that have taken place in France and don't know whether they ought to be sorry or glad for the abdication of Bonaparte and the restoration of the Bourbons. How different from the people of England, where every man is a politician! There in every, even the poorest, village you can find a newspaper, because every peasant who reads or hears the news is at liberty to give his opinion freely on every part of it, but here no one durst say one word against any public transaction or against any public character for, if he did, information would soon be given against him and he would be seized, thrown into prison and his goods confiscated.

This village, being extremely small, and our men, in consequence, too much scattered, Major Parkinson ordered three Companies to occupy a very fine chateau, the property of the mayor of this place (Mr L. E. Brun) who is, at present, in Antwerp. Here we made ourselves very comfortable, although there was scarce any furniture in the house and the Cossacks had been in it before to ravage every corner. They found out a hidden cellar filled with valuable old wine and drank or destroyed the whole of it. Upstairs, finding that one of the walls sounded hollow, they had broken through into a most beautiful private chapel and destroyed the altar and everything in it except a very valuable painting which was not touched. The war being now ended we have no outlying piquets, which would not be so unpleasant now the weather is fine as they were when the ground was covered with snow.

Viersel is six English miles east of Lire,[1] which is at present occupied by the Brigade of Guards. The Headquarters of the Army is now at St Greven Wesel and the Heads of Department at St Job and Ghoer,[2] both near Antwerp, on the Breda Road. Malines and Brussels are still filled with

1. Lier.
2. 's Gravenwezel and Sint-Job-in-'t-Goor.

Prussians, who live entirely on the inhabitants without paying them a single sou, from the General right down to the Private soldier. It may, therefore, be imagined how anxious they are for the arrival of the British who have left every town richer than when they entered it. The gates of Antwerp are now permitted to be open for the inhabitants, but no officer or soldier can go in or come out.

21 April:

We were surprised today with an order to hold ourselves in readiness to march at a moment's notice back to Willemstad to embark for Cork and, as the 54th and us both got the order, and we being the only single battalion Regiments in the army, we had no doubt but we were to be sent from Cork to America. None of us liked this much.

22 April

Parade at 6 o'clock in the morning for punishment. The Court Martial on Haigh and Fitzpatrick sat today for the first time at Schilde in the chateau of the baron of that name.[1]

23 April:

There are a great number of country houses in this neighbourhood which are surrounded by woods of large oak timber. The German recruits brought by force by General Gore are deserting very fast.

24 April:

Today the white flag was hoisted throughout the fleet and on the works of Antwerp and, in consequence, a *feu-de-joie* was fired at noon by all the British Line. The Regiment was mustered immediately afterwards.

25 April:

Lieutenant General Ferguson, who has lately arrived from England and taken command of the 2nd Division,[2] inspected our Regiment this morning

1. See Appendix II for commentary; Thain was in error in believing that Haigh was also being tried.
2. Ferguson was in fact in command of the First Division, of which the 33rd was now part. However, the battalion had spent most of the campaign in the Second Division which no doubt accounts for this slip.

'Lieutt. Genl. Lord Lyndock K.C.B' [*sic*: General Graham]. Print by Fry after Wright, 1815.

Sir James Carmichael Smyth, 1st Baronet. Mezzotint by Thomas Hodgetts, after Eugenio H. Latilla.

Thomas Slingsby Duncombe. Pencil and watercolour by James Warren Childe, 1836.

1813.

Sappers & Miners.
Working dress.

Sappers & Miners, in working dress, 1813. Watercolour by Charles Lyall.

field officer of Royal
ngineers and a private
pper. Pen and wash drawing
Charles Hamilton-Smith.

n officer and private of the
nd Ryl. Lt. Infantry'. Pen
d wash drawing by Charles
amilton-Smith.

Above left: Junior officer, Coldstream Guards, *c.* 1814. Living history re-creation by The Coldstream Regiment of Foot Guards, 1815.

Above: Junior officer, 33rd Foot, *c.* 1814. Living history re-creation by His Majesty's 33rd Regiment of Foot.

Left: Junior NCO, 1st Foot Guards, *c.* 1814. Living history re-creation by 1st Foot Guards (1815).

oldstream Guards, 1814.
atercolour by Orlando
orrie, showing a corporal
d a pioneer.

1814

ngraving of the attack on
ergen-op-Zoom.

The 1st Foot Guards *c.* 1813–15, detail from a depiction of Grenadier Guards uniforms at various dates; ink and watercolour by P. W. Reynolds.

at six o'clock and was pleased to express his entire satisfaction with their appearance. Immediately after the inspection Reid and I set off to Lire, where we breakfasted at the inn, in company with Captain Knight,[1] and, having hired a cabriolet, we all three drove over to Malines. Here we saw everything that was curious, dined and returned to Viersel the same night.

Lire, or Lierre, as it is sometimes spelt, is a neat little town situated in the Department of the two Nethes, twelve miles east of Antwerp and the same distance north of Malines. It has formerly been fortified, the ditch and remains of a fortification round the town are still remaining. It contains one or two decent streets, a good market place and neat church.

We were perhaps better pleased with its appearance, because we have not lately been accustomed to seeing towns, than we would coming direct from England. The drive to Malines is beautiful, the country on each side of the road being very rich and in the highest state of cultivation, it is watered by a branch of the Nethe.

The first thing that strikes your attention on approaching Malines is the height of the church steeple, which is an immense square tower without any spire and, therefore, has a heavy appearance. The church is very handsome and contains still some good pictures, but the best were taken away by the French.

The inhabitants appear most miserable and we were surrounded by flocks of beggars who all knew English already. We had a good dinner at the Stork Inn but paid dear, indeed they tell you always that they expect when we come in to make up all that has been lost by the Prussians. The French made an excellent promenade on the ruins of the old fortifications.

This town is in the Department of the Dyle which divides it and is famous for the manufacture of lace and for bacon hams. Another thing is always noticed by our countrymen, which is the numerous parties of fiddling girls which frequent the streets and hotels.

26 April:

Rainy weather. Archibald and I walked to the neat little interesting village of Polderloos[2] and returned to dinner to our chateau. The gardens round this

---

1. Capt. Charles Knight and Lt Thomas Reid, 33rd Foot. Both would be wounded at Waterloo; Knight would later go on to command the battalion in the 1830s.
2. Pulderbos; a round trip of five miles.

house are rather in ancient Dutch style, a great many canals divide them and one washes the front of the house, which is a most ugly, disagreeable thing.

28 April:

Archibald and I, as usual, took advantage of this fine day and walked over to Herentals, distant about nine English miles. We were surprised to find it a very considerable place. It is situated in the midst of barren country with scarce anything but heath and fir wood about it; indeed, I am told that the country continues the same flat, barren waste all the way to the Rhine.

When the French first came into this country they had a great deal of trouble keeping the people quiet, considerable bodies were constantly forming and harassing them. One of these, after causing the French great loss in several actions, were at last forced to seek shelter at Herentals, which was then well fortified, and the French, finding they would not surrender, set fire to the town when most of them perished in the flames. It contains a good church and a deserted nunnery. The inhabitants are all farmers and lace makers.

2 May:

At last we began to approach Antwerp, this day having joined the 54th and Provisional Battalion at Broechem, we marched through a beautiful country to Borsbecke[1] which, however, could only contain our Regiment, the others were quartered in other villages close by. Priestly back again.

3 May:

Borsbecke. Large parties of officers from every direction go to visit the princely house and grounds of M. Smit, a banker in Antwerp and Swedish Consul. The gardens by far exceed any that I have seen before, in beauty and extent, the Queen's garden at Frogmore is not to be compared to them. In there is everything to be found to please the eye and satiate the appetite of the greatest epicure. The most skilful botanist would find amusement in them for weeks. I did not know which to admire most, the beautiful water filled with fishes and the park behind with all sorts of water fowl, and bridges, both Chinese and grotesque, the statues, the immense hot houses,

1. Borsbeek.

the beautiful groves and curious grottos, some of which are most fancifully cut in the rock even under the water, the flower garden or the magnificent Indian Pagoda, from the top of which we saw all over Antwerp. None of these things are in the miserable little style that you often see in the gardens in England, but in the style of princely munificence. Strangers coming to Antwerp, I am told, always make a point of visiting this truly delightful spot. The country all round is beautiful.

The Dutch, having relieved the French garrison of Bergen op Zoom, the latter have come to Antwerp. The men took care to show off the British firelocks that they had taken on the night of our unsuccessful attack to some of the English officers, who had ventured into the town, although contrary to orders, and even the officers had the barefaced impudence to carry English swords. The Governor of Bergen had positively ordered that every British officer would have his sword returned to him, as he highly deserved it!! The French sold several of them in Antwerp and our fellows had an opportunity of buying them again.

4 May:

We marched through Schoten to Merxem where we all busied making ourselves as smart as possible to enter Antwerp in the morning, we being ordered to parade at 4 o'clock in the morning for that purpose. At best we were very shabby, as might be expected after lying out all the winter, and we were not a little glad to get into a town at last where we could get some necessaries.

5 May:

Merxem. The Grenadier Company of the 25th Regiment, having previously taken possession of Port Rouge, the other Regiments, at 4 o'clock, paraded in the following order:

> Squadron of the 2nd Hussars in full uniform.
> Advance Guard.
> General Cooke and Staff.
> 25th Regiment
> 54th Regiment
> 73rd Regiment
> 33rd Regiment

Several other regiments marched in during the day. We formed line on the Place de Meir, opposite the Hotel du Grand Laboureur, and there had to wait several hours for the arrival of the Austrian General, Count Künigl, Commissaire de Hautes Puissances Alliés, into whose hands the keys of the town were delivered in great ceremony by the Mayor and municipality.

Whilst we were thus waiting, Major Parkinson came up to see me and said he had been applied to recommend an officer for the situation of Town Adjutant and that he proposed giving my name if I had no objection. I felt very diffident at first, not being at all acquainted with the duties of such a situation, but resolved to try it and the Major consequently introduced me to the Town Major, thus fulfilling his kind promise to be of service to me whenever he could, and this over the heads of about thirty subalterns, many of whom could speak French better than I.

On entering Antwerp I could not help but admiring the beauty of the fortification, the streets appeared well built, but dirty, and looked deserted. From the neighbouring country we had long admired the beautiful spire of Notre Dame, which is the finest I have seen. The people appeared to welcome our arrival with sincerity. Some of the troops were put into barracks and others into billets, the officers were all billeted on the inhabitants. I could not much admire that which I got.

6 May:

Antwerp. Today I got a billet for the Town Major's Office, and myself, in the house of Mr Stappaerts Diercks, 117 Place de Malines, where I got a most friendly reception from Madame Stappaerts. I was occupied all day long in writing Garrison Orders, laying in stationery, etc, signing passports and attending Guard mounting.

7 May:

The French are still in possession of the Dockyards and Basin. Town Major and myself are fully occupied in making arrangements for the Garrison.

8 May:

So busy from 6 o'clock in the morning until 10 at night that I had not time to think of anything else, obliged to rub up my French for I must speak it all day long.

9 May:

Four hundred men mount guard every morning at 10 o'clock on the Esplanade under the works of the Citadel.

10 May:

Great deal of trouble with the billets. The Brigade of Guards marched in yesterday. The 33rd are in the Citadel with the 35th, 37th and 21st Regiments. Headquarters of the Army established at Brussels, where the 52nd, 78th, 81st and 95th Regiments are.

Dined at General Cooke's today, he commands the Garrison. A ball in the theatre in the evening.

11 May:

A grand dinner was given by the municipality to the Garrison in the Stadthouse.

12 May:

After working all day in the office, I dined at home and went to the theatre in the evening. It is pretty good but the actors are generally allowed to be bad. I do not pay for any place, having succeeded to the French Town Adjutants in this privilege.

13 May:

Begin now to get into a more regular system, but I certainly never was so busily employed in my life before. The correspondence with the heads of the civil departments of the Army and with the municipality is very great. I have, however, two clerks under me.

18 May:

There are several hundred galley slaves in the Citadel who, loaded with chains, are employed continually in the most laborious work. We have got one poor, unfortunate Sergeant Major out. He was condemned to serve in them for fifteen years, having been caught in Hanover recruiting for the King's German Legion; an ample subscription was made for him in the Garrison.

I was this day in General Orders for Town Adjutant. No French soldier is allowed to appear in the streets either night or day.

Although this portion of Thain's diary runs on into June, his subsequent entries deal largely with the minutiae of occupation duties in Antwerp which, though fascinating in themselves, have little bearing on the focus of this work. A major part of Thain's work was to issue and check the paperwork of the demobilised French soldiers who were passing through the city in great numbers as men from outlying garrisons returned to France, along with others who had been held as prisoners of the allies. Relations between the former enemies were frosty, and Thain noted that even in late May the river batteries were still mounted to cover the Scheldt estuary, no British were permitted into the dockyard, and 'the French ships of war are still lying with their broadsides against any attempt to come up to the place'. A few days later, Thain recorded that 'A Garrison Court of Enquiry is sitting on the conduct of Ensign Ryan, 69th Regiment, and Ensign Staunton, 37th Regiment, who thrashed some French officers in a coffee house the other evening.'[1]

At length, however, things began to settle down and work steadily progressed towards turning Antwerp into the main depot for the British forces remaining on the continent, in which work Thain was occupied until 16 May 1815, when he was invited to assume permanently the post of adjutant of the 33rd in place of Priestly, who had resigned that post so as to serve as a company officer. As a result, Thain re-joined his battalion just in time to see action in the Waterloo campaign, where the 33rd were heavily engaged at both Quatre Bras and at Waterloo itself. Thain was amongst those wounded at Waterloo, recording in his diary that 'It was about 8 o'clock that a musket shot pierced through my left arm close by the shoulder, which obliged me to fall to the rear and, having met with a Dragoon of the Enniskillen Regiment, I borrowed his wounded horse and rode into Brussels, where I got my wound dressed at the General Hospital and was glad to find that the bone was not broken.' Losses in the action did, however, ensure Thain his lieutenancy as he

1. Ensigns William Ryan and George Staunton; Ryan had been taken prisoner at Bergen-op-Zoom, which may account for his pugnacious behaviour.

was sufficiently senior amongst the regiment's ensigns to be carried upwards by the process of filling dead men's shoes. Thereafter he had to wait another ten years for his captaincy, in the meantime serving with the 33rd in the West Indies.

Thain maintained his connection with his old commanding officer, Elphinstone, and when the latter was promoted to major general and given a command in India he took Thain with him as an aide de camp. To facilitate this, Thain exchanged from the 33rd into the 21st Fusiliers, who were serving in India, and the appointment also brought him a brevet promotion to major. Ultimately, however, this posting would prove a fatal one, for Elphinstone was in 1841 appointed to lead the British occupation force in Afghanistan, garrisoned at Kabul. After bungling by his political masters, Elphinstone – ageing and ill – was compelled to try and evacuate his army and its sizeable train of camp followers back to India. The retreat turned into a disaster, in which the whole force was destroyed. A handful of men made it to safety at Jalalabad, whilst others – including Elphinstone, who died in captivity – were taken prisoner. William Thain, already wounded once in the skirmishing around the Afghan capital, nevertheless stuck with the retreating forces to the very end, being killed in action at Jugdulluk on 12 January 1842 when the British survivors made their last stand.

Thain never married, but maintained a friendship with the architect Sarah Losh, whose family owned the soda works where his father had been employed. In one of his last letters home he had sent Sarah a pinecone, from which a tree was raised that she planted as a monument to him in the grounds of the chapel at Wreay, Cumbria. Next to it was placed a memorial stone, bearing the inscription:

> This Khelat pine is planted in the memory of Wm. Thain, major of the 33rd, and was raised from seed transmitted by him to England. He perished in the fatal pass of Coord Kabul, esteemed and lamented by all who knew him.[1]

1. Uglow, *Pinecone*, pp. 243–6. On Thain's death, see also Lewis, Stephen, 'Officers Killed – Afghanistan 1838–42', at http://glosters.tripod.com/FAfghan.htm.

Chapter V

Corporal Alexander Frederic Meuller

2nd Battalion, 1st Foot Guards

Unlike the commissioned officers whose accounts form the remainder of this work, little is known about Alexander Frederick Meuller, the author of this short series of letters. Evidently he was a man of some learning, for his letters home are lively, informed, and well-written. Then again, however, it is quite possible – indeed, quite probable – that they were tidied up for eventual publication, for they did not appear in print until 1822 when they were added as an appendix to the third edition of the ever-popular *Journal of a Soldier of the 71st Regiment*. The letters printed in that work were by no means Meuller's complete account of the campaign, being advertised as a selection, and, indeed, an 1829 catalogue of manuscripts tantalizingly records the existence of a full handwritten manuscript with the note that:

> The author of these Letters appears to have received an education superior to that which is common to persons in his station, and he has given an amusing account of the campaign in the Netherlands under Sir Thomas Graham, (Lord Lynedoch). It includes a personal narrative of the failure of the British attack on Bergen-op Zoom, where the author was taken prisoner. The volume is unpublished, except two or three letters which were appended to a little work entitled, 'The Journal of a Soldier of the 71st regiment.'[1]

It is, alas, only the short 1822 selection that is reproduced here.

Evidently this first selection of letters was well received, albeit not sufficiently for the remainder to make it into print, for Meuller went on the following year to publish a stand-alone account of his earlier service

---

1. Cochran, John, *A Catalogue of Manuscripts, in Different Languages on Theology, English and Foreign History, of Various Dates, from the Twelfth to the Eighteenth Century* (London: Ibotson & Palmer, 1829), pp. 46–7.

under Graham at Cadiz and Barossa, entitled *Letters from Spain*.[1] When this was published in 1823, its frontispiece listed Meuller as also being the author of '*Anecdotes of Illustrious Characters; Letters from the Netherlands; An Abridgement of Geography; Catechism of English Grammar*, &c &c', so he was evidently beginning to become established as a jobbing author by this time. Beyond this, however, little information seems to be available as to his background, the circumstances that took him into the Army – where, even in the Guards, he must have been an educated anomaly in the ranks – or, indeed, his eventual fate. What is apparent from the letters that follow, however, is that his education does not seem to have prevented him being accepted by his fellows, nor from striking up several close friendships. When it is considered that other educated men in the ranks were objects of fun and even derision, this may speak something for the attitudes prevalent within the Foot Guards regiments, or, perhaps, to the fact that all three Guards 2nd Battalions were composed to a far greater extent than was typical of older, mature men. Meuller himself, however, may perhaps have been amongst the younger element of the battalion, since in his first letter he refers to those who had seen previous service in the Low Countries as being 'old men'.

Hague, December 7, 1814.

You may remember the sudden order we received to go on Foreign Service; in Obedience to which we embarked at Greenwich on the 24th ult. on board of some small craft, which carried us down the river into Ously Bay,[2] where we were again transferred to ships of war. It fell to our lot to go on board of the *Freya*, an old Danish frigate, said to have been taken at Copenhagen.[3] We were put in the lower tier, which was every way in good order, except the want of bedding.

We kept cruising in the North Sea till the 5th inst. when we beheld the sandhills on the coast of Holland, rising, as it were, out of the sea. Upon sight of which, every countenance brightened up; no doubt, it was the hope

1. Meuller, A. F., *Letters from Spain* (Dundee: J. Chalmers, 1823).
2. Hollesley Bay (also spelt Hoseley), off the Suffolk coast to the north of Felixstowe.
3. HMS *Freya* was formerly the Danish frigate *Freja*, captured at Copenhagen in 1807 as Meuller notes. Initially added to the fleet as a 38-gun frigate, she was in 1811 re-rated as a troopship and her armament reduced to 22 guns only.

of getting from our wooden prison, of which all seemed to be heartily tired; and no wonder. We had not been able to undress since we left England; so a deliverance from such a place was acceptable, whatever the consequences were to have been upon our landing. It was uncertain if the French were in possession of the coast, and if they were, we might expect a warm reception; but all difficulties were preferable to our present state.

Several of the old men, who knew the coast from former experience, reasoned upon the subject, and plainly demonstrated the difficulty of making the landing good with the small force we had. After a great deal of debate amongst us, night came on, and orders were issued to prepare to disembark in the morning.

The watch being set, the rest retired to sleep, little heeding what might follow in the morning, or whether they should behold another setting sun, (as we were as yet partly ignorant of the general revolution that had taken place.) But to proceed:- Morning came; nothing but bustle; every one being employed in doing something or other: here a group parting their bread, another their meat, a third measuring their grog with the minutest exactness, a fourth busy in packing their own or their comrade's knapsack, who were engaged in looking after their provisions during the distribution. In short, I cannot compare this scene to any thing else than the day after a country fair, when the merchants and traders are engaged in packing up their unsold goods, eatable and uneatable.

No sooner were we on land than the crowd overwhelmed us with congratulations; but, what was better, numbers brought liquors, apples, and others, again, would give us a warm at their small portable wooden stoves, which the women carried about with them.

After having got firm footing we formed into sections, then marched over the sand-hills and passed through the village of Scheveling,[1] along the high road leading to the Hague, a multitude of the inhabitants of which accompanied us on our way.

Upon our arrival in this elegant place, we could not but with admiration behold the exhibition of flags in all directions; the doors and windows filled with plump merry faces, shouting, at intervals, *Orange Boven*.

At length, after passing through several streets, we found ourselves in the great Mall, facing the late French Prefecture, where the Prince of

1. Scheveningen.

Orange, and several other distinguished personages, reviewed us. His Highness, together with almost every person we saw, had a cockade, or a piece of orange-coloured ribbon, in some conspicuous part of their dress. I likewise noticed a Russian Officer of rank, attended by two Cossacks; he wore several *orders*, but his name or title I did not learn.

After this inspection we were marched to our respective cantonments. Poor H------ begged of me to join with him for a billet, which I did, and, after searching about a long time, we found it in Rue ------, near the French Protestant Church. It was at a spirit-dealer's, and we presented our paper to the mistress of the house; but she, not being certain whether it was for her, called in a gentleman to look at it, (as her husband was not at home,) who immediately convinced her of our right to her hospitality. During the suspense, you would have smiled to have heard H------ observing, with a significant look, that such a cold reception foreboded nothing that was good; but he was soon deceived when she turned about, and frankly requested us to follow her into the parlour, which we did; and although it was so late in the year, yet the fire was out, but she soon lighted one, and made ready coffee. This, you may be sure, was no small luxury; in addition to this, the prospect of enjoying a night of undisturbed repose exhilarated our spirits, and made us forget the late dis-agreeable way on ship-board.

Coffee being ready, and no sugar making its appearance, I inadvertently spoke about it, at which the good woman expressed her surprise, by saying, that it was an article they did not use, on account of its enormous price; but, without saying any more, she went and brought some of the best, at the same time remarking, that nothing was too good for the English.

Our host came home soon after, and treated us liberally with what his shop afforded. Poor old H------ was quite in his own element now, and, soldier-like, was for paying as long as he had money; but knowing the state of our affairs, I persuaded him past it, by representing the difference between Continental and British quartering. About ten o'clock we went to bed, felicitating ourselves on being able to close our eyes in sleep, far from the noise of the roaring waters.

There is little in this first letter that adds much to our understanding of the course of the campaign, but the description of life on the lower decks of the *Freya* stands in sharp contrast to the experience of passage described by the various officers whose accounts make up the rest of this volume. As British military commitments overseas grew, so too did the need for troop ships. However, whilst conditions on the *Freya* were clearly not pleasant, she was at least a commissioned warship, and a recently refitted one at that, and a rather better prospect than some of the requisitioned merchant transports which were smaller, more crowded, and not unfrequently unsafe. It is a shame that the next letters in this sequence were not deemed of sufficient interest to make it into the 1822 selection, for even the closing paragraphs of this first one help give a useful idea of the experiences and attitudes of the ordinary British soldier on campaign. That Meuller, as a Peninsular veteran, was able to capitalise on that past experience in, for example, securing a free meal, does however set him in contrast to the majority of Graham's rank and file, many of whom were on active service for the first time.

In the weeks immediately after landing the three Guards battalions covered a substantial amount of ground as Graham first concentrated his army and then set it in motion for the first attempt against Antwerp. For a record of these movements, however, it is necessary to turn back in this volume to the diary of Ensign Duncombe, for Meuller's letters only picked up the story as preparations got under way for the second advance on Antwerp in the first week of February 1814.

Rosendahl,[1] *February 17, 1814.*

We left Steenbergen on the 30th ult. and slept at the village of Essen that night; next day we arrived at a village about thirteen miles from Antwerp, on the Breda road. As this place lay so contiguous to the line of march of the French and Allied armies, it, of course, was ransacked, and partly deserted. We only slept here a night, and on Tuesday the 1st inst. we left it, and advanced to the village of Breschat,[2] about two leagues from Antwerp.

We now began to think that the commander-in-chief was in earnest with regard to that city. We met a number of fugitives, some of them driven out by fear of the dangers of a siege, others were said to have been sent out by the French.

February 2 – The army advanced left in front; we had hardly left the village before a thick snow came on, and about two miles or better from Breschat,

1. Roosendaal.
2. Brasschaat.

we fell in with the enemy's picquet, who disputed every foot of ground with us, till they were driven back upon the village of Marksam,[1] when suddenly a panic seized them, and they retreated with great precipitation to Antwerp. We took a few prisoners, apparently of a late levy.

As they had expected us, they had felled a number of trees and barricaded the road, so that it was no small difficulty for our pioneers to remove them for the passage of the army.

Upon our arrival in Marksam, the doors and window-shutters were closed, and we, of course, thought the place had been deserted; but no sooner did the wary inhabitants know who were masters, than they came out with liquors to treat the victors. Some of our soldiers looked upon the poor creatures with contempt, calling them deceitful; but the more reflecting rather pitied them, having the misfortune to be so near the seat of war. I forgot to mention, that about the time we entered the village, the Duke of Clarence, Sir Thomas Graham, and a Prussian officer, came up, no doubt eager to see the termination of the conflict. The commander-in-chief gave immediate orders for constructing batteries; those that were not for any kind of duty were marched to cantonments in the neighbouring hamlets and farm houses.

I was on picquet during this short siege; and it was by no means an enviable duty, (which no, winter campaign can be.) We lay in holes dug out in the dyke that runs nearly parallel from Marksam to the Scheldt. The mortar batteries were behind, on the low ground; so by that means, you see, we lay between both fires. We could very distinctly hear the French drums; and the balls from their batteries went, in general, above half a mile beyond us; yet we had but few killed or wounded! Our company lost two.

That I should not want a *memento* concerning the uncertainty of things, I had no more to do than to look out of my hole, where lay a dead horse, which had been shockingly mangled by a ball, or shell; but what was worse, the cold was intense, and we were ordered not to stir for fear of drawing the fire of the enemy upon the spot near where he could see any of us.

This kind of warfare was rather galling to some of our high bloods, who thought they had no chance of signalizing themselves; and, as I observed before, the frost was so severe, that numbers lost either fingers or toes. But in the midst of these inconveniences, I reflected with pleasure, that we

1. Merxem.

were in no want of plenty of provisions and liquors; by the latter you must understand me as alluding to a moderate drinker.

You will smile, when I inform you that we relieved picquet in the morning! The enemy, of course, could see, and gave us plenty of metal during that time. Whether the commander-in-chief was aware of this, I know not. Another thing nearly as strange, was that of no sortie being made on our side of the town.

The village of Marksam was deserted, and part of it in ruins; the enemy being determined that this place should not afford any shelter to us. The church, although nearly in the middle of the street, remained untouched, although a certain cannon on one of the enemy's batteries swept at intervals, in so much, that the guards and picquets going to the advanced post, must range on either side, and leave the middle of the street vacant. It is related, that two British Officers walking in the street, had each of them a leg shot off by the same ball!![1]

It is generally thought that there has been considerable damage done to the enemy, as we could see several places on fire near the arsenal and great bason. There is a large fleet here; and the capture of it would be of no small advantage to the British nation.

Whatever Sir Thomas Graham expected, I know not; but, after all this ado, we received orders on Sunday the 6th for retreating, which we did about dusk, and took up our old quarters in Breschat, from whence we marched for Grot-Sundert,[2] and Essen, where we staid [sic] a few days, and then passed on to this place, where we shall probably remain for some time.

It must be reiterated, thanks to the omission of the preceding letter or letters covering earlier operations, that this description relates to the second advance on Antwerp, the Second Battle of Merxem, and the ensuing bombardment. Again, a fine opportunity for contrast is presented here between the science of bombardment as described by Carmichael Smyth, and the reality of service in the front-line trenches and other siege emplacements. That said, it was not just the rank and file who suffered, and a number of other accounts mention the fluke

1. The unfortunate officers were Lt Robert Stowers and Ensign George Chapman of the 2/37th; see Return of Casualties, 3–5 February 1814, TNA, WO1/199, p. 589.
2. Groot Zundert.

shot that carried the legs from beneath two officers of the 2/37th. A third, unidentified, individual was apparently walking between the two injured men, but, having fallen out of step, was unharmed.[1]

Rosendahl, March 11, 1814.

Before this comes to hand, you will probably have read in the public papers, of the sad calamity that has befallen the British army here.

You will remember, that my last letter was dated from Put.[2] In it I mentioned a rumour of an intended attack upon Fort-Lillo; and it was the prevailing opinion amongst us; but it has since appeared that Sir Thomas Graham had another and more important object in view.

On the morning of the 7th instant, the day after I wrote you, I was ordered to go on the working party engaged in building batteries on the banks of the Scheldt. Nothing of importance happened. A vessel, supposed to have troops on board, sailed up the river evidently bound for Antwerp, or some of its forts. The commanding officer of the party ordered the guns to bear on her, which compelled her to desist for that time: some, on board got into the boat; others leaped overboard, and swam to the opposite shore; but whether there were any lives lost I know not.

Towards night, Colonel Clifton[3] came to visit us. I suppose he was field-officer of the day. He ordered us back to our cantonments in Put, the distance being little short of nine or ten miles; and, had it not been for the kind assistance of my worthy friend P------, I fear I should not have reached my home that night; but when I at length arrived at my corner of our straw-covered mansion, I dropped down, scarcely able to undress myself; but, when down, I certainly enjoyed my blanket.

In the course of the night, an order came for me to prepare to go as guide to the fresh working party in the morning; but upon my declaring my inability, another was ordered, at which I was not a little pleased, especially at the expectation of having some rest the next day. But, oh! the uncertainty of things; for a little after day-break, an aid-de-camp came with orders; and serjeants of companies being called, the brigade was ordered to get ready in

1. Austin, *Stick Leg*, pp. 155–6.
2. Putte. This letter was not included in the 1822 selection.
3. Capt. and Lt Col George Clifton, 1st Foot Guards. Served with the regiment's 3rd Battalion during the Corunna campaign, at Cadiz where he was for a time brigade major, and with Wellington's main field army.

full marching order, when we were sent by companies to the church, for the purpose of depositing our knapsacks and blankets.

We now began to suspect that something of note would follow, and we were not deceived; for after having left bag and baggage, we marched in the direction of Bergen-op-Zoom, and halted at a village near the angle of the great road, about half-way betwixt our old cantonments and that town, till after dark, when we again paraded, and put on our great coats over our accoutrements. Something dark and mysterious was in all appearance going on, as we were ordered not to speak, except in whispers; and truly the orders were strictly attended to. The march had more the appearance of a funeral than any thing else. Fancy to yourself a fine clear night; the country around covered with snow; a column of men marching at a very slow pace, great-coats and cap-cases on, arms secured; nothing heard but the bark of dogs at the farm houses adjacent to the road.

Such was this nocturnal scene, that M. M------ observed to a comrade, that such as this, meaning the barking of the dogs, when he was on the Continent before, was the prelude to some sanguinary conflict. He was in the right so far; for a few hours after this his observation, he was numbered with the dead! I have since thought that this man had a presentiment of his fate.

Meanwhile we approached till within a mile and a half of the out-works, when we turned to our left, into a field, where we halted, and were ordered to pull off our great-coats; which were left in heaps, under the charge of some drummers.

Volunteers, together with the men for duty, were called upon to place scaling ladders. Orders were likewise issued; not to take any notice of the French picquet, even though it should fire upon us; but simply to follow the guides, and when we should once get into the town, and should hear the inhabitants shouting *Orange Boven*, we should answer with [God save the King].[1] We passed the enemy's picquet, when some cannon went off, together with a number of blue-lights, informing us that the garrison were upon the alert, and ready to receive us; however, nothing daunted us, and we moved on at a pretty quick pace, and, in the midst of the enemy's shot, got into the ditch, which was frozen; and at length got on the ladders, and mounted the ramparts. Owing to the enemy being engaged elsewhere,

1. For some reason, the countersign is replaced by an ellipsis in the 1822 text but can be confirmed from multiple other sources.

we did not meet so much opposition as we expected, and there were but few killed in crossing the ditch. After all had gotten up, we formed right in front, near the Antwerp gate. All was silence for a little; the French drums had just before that beat a *chamade*, or, as some of our men said, to cease firing.

During this interval the moon shone from behind a cloud; the clock struck twelve; it was the knell for many a spirit that then was going to make its exit, and, ere it struck one, had passed into the unknown world.

In this momentary suspense, we congratulated each other upon our easy victory in taking a place deemed impregnable, with so little loss; never suspecting that the enemy would make any further resistance, since we had gotten into the town. But we were soon undeceived. The enemy having breathed a little, all of a sudden threw up some blue lights, and recommenced a heavy fire in different quarters. The street at the end of which we stood, the enemy kept sweeping with shot; an order, at the same time, came for the two companies on the right to advance: they crossed the street with but little loss, and advanced along the ramparts on the other side of the gate. They had not been long gone, when W------, one of the men belonging to them, came back, requesting immediate assistance, as there was a terrible slaughter among them, and that the whole would be cut off, unless prompt aid were rendered. Accordingly our company, together with another, followed the same route with the greatest rapidity; but what number we left in crossing the above mentioned street I know not.

We had not gone far before a scene truly appalling presented itself, the ground being literally covered with killed and wounded, a heavy fire, at the same time, kept sweeping all before it. The enemy, emboldened, advanced; the few that remained, perhaps from forty to fifty, with Lieutenant Colonel J[ones][1] at our head, descended from the ramparts into a vacant space at the end of a narrow street, there to make a stand, if possible, as by this time the French drums in the direction of the Antwerp gate were heard. Now, that being the place we had left our other two companies, plainly intimated to us our situation; however, Lieutenant Colonel J[ones], not daunted, formed the few of us that he had still by him; but no sooner was this done, than the enemy's column appeared, and seeing that it was in vain to resist, our

---

1. Given only as 'J------' in the original text; this was Capt. and Lt Col Leslie Grove Jones, 1st Foot Guards: see also above p. 40.

little band dispersed, and flew to such places for shelter as the impulse of the moment directed them. Some that could not get into the houses were killed or wounded. I, along with some more, got into a house where we found Colonel Clifton mortally wounded, lying in a corner, attended by two serjeants; round the stove were the afflicted family sitting. I had time to notice no more, before a French marine came in, blustering, and ordering us to throw down our arms and accoutrements. He then turned us out of doors into the street, which was found covered with broken muskets, accoutrements, and ammunition. There were some killed or wounded lying, but, to the honour of the enemy, there were none of our party killed but such as were obstinate, and would not lay down their arms quickly, when ordered to do so.

The noise and confusion around, and the indignation I felt at being a prisoner, when thinking upon nothing but victory, hindered me from noticing things as I ought to have done.

I had not looked long about me before I was hurried into a large room on the opposite side of the street, apparently a back kitchen; here we were left till the place was nearly filled with British prisoners. In the mean time we could hear the work of destruction going on in other parts of the town, and we hoped to be rescued, but our hope soon vanished upon the French ordering us into the street, where they commanded us to *form*, and then marched us to the guard-house in the great square, where we were lodged, and put under the care of some *gens d'armes*. It was some time before I could persuade myself that I actually was a prisoner; but, finding it to be a reality, and that it would be of no use to take it to heart, I sat down, and had some discourse with one of them who seemed to be a good-natured fellow. He told me he was an Italian by birth, and had been for some time in the French service, which he liked well. Shortly after, Lieutenant Colonel J[ones] came in, accompanied by a French officer, apparently of rank, requesting all that were wounded to follow him, on purpose to have their wounds dressed. I noticed the Lieutenant Colonel's epaulettes were gone, probably torn off when taken prisoner. There likewise came into the place women with provisions for sale, at which we were not a little astonished, having previously understood that they were in a starving condition.

In this state we continued till morning, when we were sent to the church; where we found several hundreds of British prisoners already lodged. The French soldiers, as we marched along, generally felt our pockets, and took out what best pleased them! Some of our men, indignant at such usage, appealed to the French officers that happened to be near, who shrugged up their shoulders, significantly meaning, that they could not do any thing for the poor fellows thus robbed. I escaped without the loss of any thing; what silver I had with me, I had previously put in my shoes or secret pockets; neither took they any thing out of my canteen or haversack. As an individual, I have nothing to lay to their charge, but certainly received the best of such usage as they were able to give. But, after all, I felt such curious sensations, when I reflected that yesterday's sun had witnessed me a free, but to-day a bond-man; however, finding this reflection to be of no avail, and seeing that I could not mend the matter, I reconciled myself to my lot, and therefore put on an air of cheerfulness, as I found the rest had done.

During this time the French were busy in marching prisoners from all quarters to the church, – a mortifying sight truly. Here we continued until the afternoon of the 10th, when we understood a convention had been entered into between the governor and Sir Thomas Graham. You may be sure these [sic] news were received with joy, and the excess of it was such, that the French imagined it to be insurrection. They sent cannon to the principal avenues of the church, declaring, at the same time, if there should be any more noise heard, they would blow down the building about us; but luckily by the persuasion, (for I need not say command,) of their non-commissioned officer, they desisted, and became quiet

I must not omit observing that the clerk of the church, who was of Scotch descent, a reverend looking man, showed us the greatest kindness and attention that his means would allow.[1] I both ate and drank in his house without being charged any thing; his family were continually on the alert to help the prisoners. I am sure there is many a grateful heart panting to return this worthy family's kindness in some shape or other; but one consolation is, 'that virtue is its own reward,' and such, I fear, it must be, for any thing we can do.

But I must return to my subject. We were marched out by regiments into the square, where we formed double files, faced to the right, and marched out, under the command of Colonel Muller of the Royals,[2] he

---

1. Perhaps this individual was the 'Scotchman named Stewart' identified by Shaw as acting as a guide to sightseers after the peace; see above p. 82.
2. Lt Col Frederick Muller, commanding officer of the 4/1st Foot.

being the senior field officer not wounded. The streets through which we passed were lined with French infantry. They gave us some sarcastic nods and smiles as we passed. Coming to the gates, we observed the dead bodies of our comrades lying on the ramparts, some of them seemingly laid in such a posture as to mortify and disgust us. Passing over the draw-bridge, it was the wonder of all discerning persons how we had been able to get up such a height as the glacis was from the moat, and my astonishment has not subsided to this hour concerning this matter, when I reflect how many things a soldier is encumbered with! A little from the town we met some *gens d'armes* who had been out in the neighbouring country. I believe they received no insult from any of our soldiers as they passed; it would have been dishonourable, and even dangerous, thus to have treated defenceless individuals; – by saying dangerous, you will remark that we were not then out of the reach of the enemy's cannon, but no sooner were we removed to a respectable distance, than the tongue-strings of our men were loosed; a few gave some cheers, but it was by no means general; after which we separated for the night. The prisoners of our brigade slept in the barns of some farm-houses. As we had neither blankets nor great-coats, we found it very cold, but creeping a foot or two below the straw and lying still, we found that partly answer our purpose. Getting up in the morning, we had nothing to do but shake off the straw with which we had been enveloped, and we were soon in condition for our march for Rosendahl. I had some bread and honey for breakfast! I fancy I see you smiling and asking, how I came by it in such a place? Well! it was in the apiary, from the bee-hives. I thought it strange that they should have been so long unmolested, as this place had been alternately visited both by British and French, as well as by the Russian Cossacks; and you are not ignorant of their mode of ransacking the neighbourhood of their quarters; but, luckily for us, we did not overlook this treasure.

As we had nothing to carry, we soon arrived here; but, believe me, I felt ashamed to look the people in the face, when I thought upon the state we were in. But upon my arrival at my quarters, which was at a tailor's, the good woman received us most kindly; told us she was happy to find we had escaped with life, got ready our dinner, which was seasoned with a good deal of judicious and sensible discourse, in which the master of the house joined; but he wanted some of the loquacity of his wife.

Having completed his narrative of his own adventures during the attack and its aftermath, Meuller saved his reflections on proceedings for a second missive some days later. Whilst all the letters seem to some extent to have been tidied up for publication, this one, in particular, has benefitted from some after-the-fact additions, at least so far as the history of the fortress is concerned.

Rosendahl, March 17, 1814.

Bergen-op-Zoom, as you must know, is the *chef d'oeuvre* of the celebrated Coehorn.[1] The town is small and neat, almost hid from the view of the traveller, (except the steeple, which is none of the finest,) by the huge ramparts and outworks surrounding it. It lies in Dutch Brabant, on the eastern shore of the Scheldt, six miles from Steenbergen, and about twenty from Antwerp. As you are so well acquainted with the military history of this place, I shall therefore confine myself to the recent attack. I have spoken to several individuals who were prisoners as well as myself, and the result of my inquiries are, that there were four different points of attack; the commanders were, Generals Skerret[t] and Gore; Colonels Lord Proby and Carleton; Major-General Cook[e] having the supreme command; – each of these columns being provided with an experienced guide. It is said that the garrison were almost panic-struck, and their amazement was beyond any thing, when the column at the Water-Port Gate first began the attack, which was too soon, it not being altogether low water; but notwithstanding their disagreeable situation from the wet and cold, they soon drove the enemy before them, and possessed themselves of the arsenal, which they kept for some time.

The other two columns met with more serious opposition at their respective points, and with great loss at length established themselves on the ramparts. The enemy not finding the assailants in such formidable numbers as they had expected, cheered up their spirits, made a desperate charge on that column which had possessed themselves of the arsenal, and with great loss retook it.

1. Menno van Coehoorn (1641–1704), Dutch soldier and engineer famous, along with the Frenchman Vauban, for developing many of the characteristic features of eighteenth-century fortification.

This exploit, of course, elated them; and their next step was to cut off the communication of the British from each other, and from coming into the town, by placing cannon at the streets and avenues leading to the great square. In all this they succeeded. The slaughter of our soldiers in endeavouring to gain the wished-for points was dreadful.

About this time of night the superior officers, together with some of the guides, must have fallen. The heads of the principal streets were in general occupied by the French; the lower end by the British. It was no uncommon thing for one side of a street to be occupied by the soldiers of one nation, and the other side by those of the other; even the passages and rooms of some great houses were the scenes of slaughter and confusion. Much blood was shed in apartments where, only a few hours before, the gay company had been assembled round the festive board, little thinking what the morning sun should witness in the same place! Another thing that frequently occurred, was escorts of both nations meeting each other in the streets, or on the ramparts, with prisoners, which occasioned serious, but at the same time ludicrous *fracas*, in the act of each party rescuing their own, and keeping those from escaping that they had with them. Many prisoners on both sides were unexpectedly released in this manner.

But, as I observed before, all our efforts to reach the great square were abortive, on account of the heavy fire thrown down the streets leading to it. It is reported of the governor, General Besanet,[1] that soon after the British had possessed themselves of the ramparts and adjoining streets, and had driven the French into the bastions, or the interior of the town, he, thinking it in vain to resist any longer, sent an officer with terms of surrender; but that the officer was killed before he could reach the British General. The governor, of course, impatiently waited for the return of his messenger, but as that did not happen, and, in the interim, hearing favourable reports from his troops, resolved to prolong the contest. I should suppose this was about twelve o'clock, when, as I mentioned in my last, a general silence prevailed every where. The heavy firing that commenced soon after was probably when M. le Général had altered his mind. They say that this brave veteran stood the greatest part of the night in the square, giving orders, and receiving reports. The reward of his perseverance was victory. I am sometimes at a

1. Général de Brigade Guilin-Laurent Bizanet, commander of the Bergen-op-Zoom garrison.

loss whom to admire, the brave defender of Bergen-op-Zoom, or the hero of Barossa, who could conceive a project so bold, and so unparalleled an attempt; which certainly, as far as human prudence and foresight were concerned, was accomplished.

The placing of the scaling-ladders was the most arduous work; and if these troops did not meet with the most serious opposition, little else was to be feared. In all this the general-in-chief was concerned. After getting into the town, it was natural to think that every one would know his duty. Every obstacle in the plan itself was surmounted; for who could ever think, after having possession of the works, that the garrison would not submit? But as every one is willing to account for it in some way or other, the loss of one or two of the guides, together with most of the superior officers, may be considered as the greatest evil. Secondly, the soldiers, of course, being unacquainted with the topography of the place, the enemy knowing this, often led our detachments into ambuscades. There being numbers in the French ranks natives of Ireland, who by their knowledge of their nominal countrymen; and by getting our countersign. All these, as you plainly see, proved useful auxiliaries to the enemy, after having given over all thoughts of surrendering.[1]

Besides, the garrison is thought to have been little inferior in numbers to the British, who are said to have amounted to about four thousand; but, on the other hand, had Sir Thomas Graham kept pouring in troops, after the attacking columns had got footing, there would have been no doubt but the town would have been taken; but, as they were not at hand, or probably could not be spared, hindered him from meeting with that applause which success would have insured him. It is likewise thought that the commander-in-chief had been misinformed as to the numerical strength of the garrison; but there can be no blame attached to him, or any other person; and all parties seem filled with astonishment and admiration at this unprecedented act of modern tactics.

It is related of one of the guides, who was a native of the place, being mortally wounded, was taken by the enemy, and when they found what he was, they resolved to execute him as a traitor. But on Sir Thomas Graham's

1. The common belief amongst the British that the garrison included the 3e Régiment Étranger, formerly the Légion Irlandois, was in fact false, although a battalion of that unit was in Antwerp at the time. Possibly ruses were being employed by English-speaking Frenchmen.

protest, which declared him to be in the British service, they permitted him to retire to his own house, where he died. I cannot get an account of the number of killed, but there must have been many. The hospitals, and other places in the town, were filled with soldiers of both nations alike; no distinction was paid, from the general to the drummer, only the former had the mortification to behold with his last breath a French sentinel over him. Another petty mark of respect these noble persons received, was the privilege of having a corner bed, which, you know, is of no small consequence in such a place. H------, together with others who were ordered to stop in the hospital after we left the place, relate many strange and melancholy facts respecting the transactions carried on there; among others, they say there lay two large heaps of dead bodies in the hospital-yard, as well those whose shoulders had once been graced by epaulettes as the private; and, as they were naked, and their faces disfigured, it was difficult to find the bodies that were searched for, either to be sent home to England, or buried elsewhere. W------ of our company had the superintendence of the interment of several of the principal officers in the church-yard of Wow.[1] Some of them have since been disinterred and conveyed to England.

There have fallen in this conflict two generals, and four colonels, besides a great number of other officers. Colonel M'D[onald][2] was killed a little previous to Lieutenant Colonel J[ones], and the detachment that I belonged to were repulsed. Our adjutant, Captain B[ulteel], was mortally wounded; about the same time, his brother, belonging to another regiment, was killed. I feel for their unhappy family, thus to lose two such promising youths. The former you know was in Spain with us, and at Barossa gave proofs of what he in time would be; but death, the great leveller, has laid poor B[ulteel]'s prospects low in the dust, along with himself.[3]

1. Wouw.
2. With the name partially disguised by an ellipsis in the original, this was Capt. and Lt Col Hon. James MacDonald, another veteran of service with 3/1st Foot Guards at Cadiz and in the Peninsula.
3. Lt and Capt. John Bulteel, serving as Adjutant of 2/1st Foot Guards, was killed as Meuller reports. He had previously served with the same battalion at Cadiz and Barossa, and then transferred to the regiment's 3rd Battalion for a further two years' Peninsular service. His brother, rather peculiarly also listed as John, was a 2nd lieutenant in the 2/21st and died of wounds received in the same action: see also the account of 2nd Lt Moodie of that regiment, in this volume. Again, the names are disguised by ellipses in the original.

I am sorry to inform you of the loss of my good friend C------ P------, to whom I was under so many obligations.

There is a daily intercourse between Bergen-op-Zoom and this place. Numerous waggons, both military and country, are employed in removing the wounded from the former place; and the other night, one of the principal streets in Rosendahl was choked up with them. The inhabitants, while they halted, administered what relief they could to the unhappy sufferers, numbers of whom died by the way.

Colonel J[ones], who understands French, is the principal channel through which every thing is transacted. It was he who had the mortification to go along with the French officer who summoned Major General Cook[e] to surrender, and he has likewise been (if I am right informed) of the party who had the drawing up of the articles of the convention for our exchange, which, I understand, is to take place as soon as the same number of French prisoners can be sent from England; but the article which appears rather mortifying is, that one of the enemy's officers is to have safe conduct from Bergen-op-Zoom to Antwerp, for the express purpose of informing the governor thereof of the result of our attack upon the former place.

The French picquets, whom, as I observed before, we were not to fire upon, were taken, and an immediate exchange has taken place. The pay-sergeant of our company being on the *staff*, availed himself of this, and is gone along with those that are exchanged, to the army.

As a mark of the humanity of the enemy, it ought not to be forgotten that numbers of our soldiers, in the act of escaping from that scene of slaughter in the morning, were called upon in the English tongue to make the best of their way, as they did not wish to fire upon fugitives who were not in the act of resistance. Admirable generosity, indeed, and worthy of our highest praise!

This is all I have to send you; if there is any misstatement it is not my fault. There are many strange reports current; but as they are for the most part foreign to this subject, I shall say no more, but wish you health and happiness.

With this abrupt summary, reflective though it is of the confusion and uncertainty that came after the failure of the attack on Bergen-op-Zoom, this selection of Meuller's letters comes to an end. There is little more that can be added by way of commentary, nor any further details about the writer and his life. He did not participate in the Waterloo campaign; he does not figure on the roll for the Waterloo Medal, and, in any case, his letters from that campaign would surely have followed his others into print had he been a participant. Nor did he receive the retroactive Military General Service Medal of 1848, which would suggest that he was no longer living at that date. Lastly, it may be inferred, judging by the place of publication of his books, that his home upon leaving the Army was, for a time at least, in Scotland. Beyond that, we have nothing.

Chapter VI

2nd Lieutenant Dunbar Moodie

2nd Battalion, 21st (Royal North British) Fusiliers

John Wedderburn Dunbar Moodie, who seems to have used the third of his Christian names for preference, was born on 7 October 1797 at Melsetter in the Orkneys. He was the fourth son of Major James Moodie, 9th Laird of Melsetter, but, judging by the varied means in which the brothers were forced to seek their fortunes across the globe, this status came with little attached to it by way of wealth. Two of his brothers entered the Royal Navy, but for Dunbar Moodie it was to be the Army instead and he was duly gazetted a 2nd lieutenant in the 21st Fusiliers on 24 February 1813.[1] All three fusilier regiments eschewed the rank of ensign, but that, in effect, is what Moodie's commission equated to: in all other respects, except for sporting bearskin caps in full dress uniform, the wearing of flank company wings by all companies, and a certain self-assumed superiority, there was no practical distinction between the fusiliers and ordinary line infantry. The 1st Battalion of the 21st was at this time serving in the Mediterranean, subsequently redeploying to North America in the summer of 1814, but as a newly joined and junior officer, Moodie remained with the understrength 2nd Battalion at Fort George, Inverness. So weak, indeed, was the 2/21st that the battalion was not initially earmarked for service under Graham; only a shortfall in the numbers fit for service in those units first deployed to the Netherlands caused it to be called upon and ordered to march down to Leith to embark. The following is Moodie's account of his service with the battalion during its – and his – only spell of active service, and was first printed in the *United Service Journal* and

---

1. Biographical information from Ballstadt, Carl P., 'Moodie, John Wedderburn Dunbar', in *Dictionary of Canadian Biography* (Toronto: University of Toronto/ Université Laval, 2003), Vol. 9; available online at http://www.biographi.ca/en/ bio/moodie_john_wedderburn_dunbar_9E.html.

then included in a compendium of accounts assembled under the aegis of that journal and published in 1833.[1]

There are certain events in the life of every man on which the memory dwells with peculiar pleasure; and the impressions they leave, from being interwoven with his earliest and most agreeable associations are not easily effaced from his mind. Sixteen years have now elapsed since the short campaign in Holland, and the ill-fated attack on Bergen-op-Zoom; but almost every circumstance that passed under my notice at that period, still remains as vividly pictured in my mind as if it had occurred but yesterday.

Our regiment, the 21st, or Royal North British Fusileers, was stationed at Fort-George when the order came for our embarkation for Holland. Whoever has experienced the dull monotony of garrison duty, may easily conceive the joy with which the intelligence was hailed. The eve of our embarkation was spent in all the hilarity inspired by the occasion, and, as may be supposed, the bottle circulated with more than ordinary rapidity. Our convoy, Captain Nixon, R.N. in return for some kindness he had met with from my family, while on the Orkney Station, insisted on my taking my passage to Helvoet Sluys [sic], along with our commanding officer and acting-adjutant, on board his own vessel, the Nightingale.[2] The scene that was exhibited next day, as we were embarking, must be familiar to most military men. The beach presented a spectacle I shall never forget. While the boats, crowded with soldiers, with their arms glittering in the sun, were pushing off, women were to be seen up to their middles in the water, bidding, perhaps, a last farewell to their husbands; while others were sitting disconsolate on the rocks, stupefied with grief, and almost insensible of what was going forward. Many of the poor creatures were pouring out blessings on the officers, and begging us to be kind to their husbands. At last, when we had got the soldiers fairly seated in their places, which was no easy task, we pulled off, while the shouts of our men were echoed back in wailings and lamentations, mixed with benedictions, from the unhappy

1. Cooke, Captain, et al., Memoirs of the Late War (London: Henry Colburn & Richard Bentley, 1833), Vol. II, pp. 259–314.
2. HMS Nightingale was a 16-gun brig-sloop, launched in 1805. Her captain was Commander Christopher Nixon, RN. The Nightingale had been serving extensively in North Sea waters off Scotland and had just completed a refit at Leith when assigned to convoy duty.

women left behind us. As for the officers, most of us being young fellows, and single, we had little to damp our joy at going on foreign service. For my own part, I confess I felt some tender regrets in parting with a fair damsel in the neighbourhood, with whom I was not a little smitten; but I was not of an age to take these matters long to heart, being scarcely sixteen at the time. Poor A------ R------ has since been consigned, by a calculating mother, to an old officer, who had nearly lost his sight, but accumulated a few thousand pounds in the West Indies.

We soon got under way, with a fair wind, for Holland. Instead of being crammed into a transport, with every circumstance which could render a sea-voyage disagreeable, we felt ourselves lucky in being in most comfortable quarters, with a most excellent gentlemanly fellow for our entertainer in Captain Nixon. To add to our comforts, we had the regimental band with us, who were generally playing through the day, when the weather or sea-sickness would allow them. On arriving off Goeree, we were overtaken by one of the most tremendous gales I have ever experienced, and I have had some experience of the element since. We had come to anchor, expecting a pilot from the shore, between two sandbanks, one on each side of us, while another extended between us and the land. The gale commenced towards night, blowing right on shore; our awful situation may well be conceived when the wind increased almost to a hurricane, with no hope of procuring a pilot. The sea, which had begun to rise before the commencement of the gale, was now running mountains high, and we could see the white foam, and hear the tremendous roar of the breakers on the sandbank astern of us. Of the two transports which accompanied us with the troops on board, one had anchored outside of us, and the other had been so fortunate as to get out to sea before the gale had reached its greatest violence. We had two anchors a-head, but the sea was so high, that we had but little expectation of holding-on during the night. About midnight, the transport which had come to anchor to windward, drifted past us, having carried away her cables.

The sea every now and then broke over us from stem to stern, and we continued through a great part of the night to fire signals of distress. It is curious to observe on these occasions the different effects of danger on the minds of men: the nervous, alarmed too soon, and preparing themselves for the worst that may happen; the stupid and insensible, without forethought of danger, until they are in the very jaws of destruction, when they are taken quite unprepared, and resign themselves up to despair; and the thoughtless, whose levity inclines them to catch the external expression of the confidence or fear in the countenances of those around them. About one o'clock in the morning, the captain got into bed, and we followed his example, but had hardly lain down, when the alarm was given that one of the cables was gone. We immediately ran on deck, but it was soon discovered that the wind had shifted a few points, and that the cable had only slackened a little. As the day dawned, the wind gradually abated, and at length fell off to a dead calm. A light haze hid the low land from our view, and hung over the sea, which still rolled in huge billows, as if to conceal the horrors of our situation during the preceding night. In an hour or two, the fog cleared away sufficiently to enable us to see a few miles in all directions. Every eye was strained in search of the two transports, with our regiment on board, but seeing nothing, we all gave them up for lost; for we could hardly conceive the possibility of the transport, which drifted past us in the night escaping shipwreck on this low and dangerous coast, or of the other being able to get out to sea. By the help of our sweeps and a light breeze, we were getting more in with the land when at last we observed a pilot-boat coming out to us. Our little Dutch pilot, when he got along-side of us, soon relieved our minds from anxiety as to the fate of one of the transports, which fortunately escaped the sandbanks, and was safe in Helvoet Sluys.

A Dutchman being an animal quite new to many of us, we were not a little diverted with his dress and demeanour. Diederick was a little, thick-set, round-built fellow, about five feet three inches in height, bearing a considerable resemblance in shape to his boat: he was so cased up in clothes, that no particular form was to be traced about him, excepting an extraordinary roundness and projection 'a posteriori,' which he owed as much, I believe, to nature as to his habiliments. He wore a tight, coarse, blue jerkin, or peajacket, on his body, and reaching half-way down his legs, gathered up in folds tight round his waist, and bunching out amply below. His jacket had no collar, but he had a handkerchief tied round his neck like a rope, which with his protruding glassy eyes, gave him the appearance of strangulation. On his legs he wore so many pairs of breeches and trowsers, that I verily believe we might have pulled off three or four pairs without being a whit the wiser as to his natural conformation. On his feet he wore a pair of shoes with huge buckles, and his head was crowned with a high-topped red nightcap. Thus equipped, with the addition of a short pipe stuck in his mouth, 'ecce' Diederick, our worthy pilot, who stumping manfully up to the Captain, with his hand thrust out like a bowsprit, and a familiar nod of his head, wished him *'goeden dag'* and welcomed him cordially to Holland. I observed that our Captain seemed a little 'taken aback' with the pilot's republican manners; however, he did not refuse honest Diederick a shake of his hand, for the latter had evidently no conception of a difference in rank requiring any difference in the mode of salutation. After paying his respects to the captain, he proceeded to shake us all by the hand in turn, with many expressions of goodwill to the English, whom he was pleased to say had *always* been the Dutchmen's best friends. Having completed the ceremonial of our reception, he returned to the binnacle, and, hearing the leadsman sing out 'by the mark three,' clapping his fat fists to his sides, and looking up to see if the sails were 'clean full,' exclaimed with great energy, *'Bout Skipp'*. The captain was anxious to procure some information regarding the channels between the sandbanks, and depth of the water, but all the satisfaction our friend Diederick would vouchsafe him was, *'Ja, Mynheer, wanneer wij ni beter kan maaken dan moeten wij naar de anker komen.'*[1] We soon reached Helvoet Sluys, and came to anchor for the night.

On landing next day, we found the half of the regiment which had so fortunately escaped ship wreck, with the transport which had drifted past us in the night of the gale. Here we took leave of our kind friends the captain and officers of the *Nightingale*, and next day marched to Buitensluys,[2] a little town nearly opposite to Willemstadt. Here we were detained for several days, it not being possible to cross the intervening branch of the sea, in consequence of the quantities of ice which were floating down from the rivers. We soon got ourselves billeted, out in the town and neighbouring country, and established a temporary mess at the principal inn of the place, where we began to practise the Dutch accomplishments of drinking gin and smoking, for which we had a convenient excuse in the humidity and coldness of the climate. Our hard drinkers, of course, did not fail to inculcate the doctrine,

1. Moodie's own footnote here offers the translation, 'When we can't do better we must come to anchor,' which he states to be 'a common Dutch saying'. In modern Dutch, this would be expressed as, *'Wanneer wij het niet beter kunnen maken, dan moet we naar het anker komen'*, which suggests either that Moodie is recording archaic dialect or that his memory is at fault.
2. Buytensluys, across the water from Willemstad on the north bank of the Hollands Diep. Now no longer on the map, it was once the crossing point for a ferry to Willemstad.

that wine and spirits were the 'sovereignest remedy' in the world for the ague, of which disease they seemed to live in constant dread, particularly after dinner. During our sojourn at Buitensluys, our great amusement through the day was skaiting [sic] on the ice with the country girls, who were nothing shy, and played all manners of tricks with us, by upsetting us, &c. &c. thus affording rather a dangerous precedent, which was sometimes returned on themselves with interest.

We are accustomed to hear of the Dutch phlegm, which certainly forms a distinguishing feature in their 'physical character;' they are dull and slow in being excited to the strong emotions, but it is a great mistake to suppose that this constitutional sluggishness implies any deficiency in the milder moral virtues. The Dutch, I generally found to possess, in a high degree, the kindly, charitable feelings of human nature, which show themselves to the greater advantage from the native simplicity of their manners. I had got a comfortable billet at a miller's house, a little out of the village. The good folks finding that I was a Scotchman, for which people they have a particular liking from some similarity in their manners, began to treat me with great cordiality, and threw off that reserve, which is so natural with people who have soldiers forced into their houses whether they will or not. The miller and his cheerful 'frow' never tired of showing me every kindness in their power while I remained with them, and to such a degree did they carry this, that it quite distressed me. On leaving Buitensluys, neither my landlord nor his wife would accept of any remuneration, though I urgently pressed it on them. When the avarice of the Dutch character is taken into account, they certainly deserve no small praise for this disinterested kind-heartedness.

The ice having broken up a little, we were enabled to get ferried over to Willemstadt, and proceed on our march to Tholen, where we arrived in two or three days. The cold in Holland this winter was excessive, and Tholen, being within four miles of Bergen-op-Zoom, a great part of the inhabitants, as well as the garrison, were every day employed in breaking the ice in the ditches of the fortifications. The frost, however, was so intense, that before the circuit was completed, which was towards evening, we were often skaiting on the places, which had been broken in the morning; we could not, with all our exertions, break more than nine feet in width, which was but an ineffectual protection against the enemy, had they felt any inclination to attack us in this half dilapidated fortress, with our small garrison.

After we had been here some days, the remainder of our regiment, who had been saved by the transport getting out to sea, joined us. They had sprung a leak, and were near perishing, when it was fortunately stopped, and the gale abated. The first thing we all thought of on coming to Tholen was procuring snug billets, as we might remain some time in garrison. With this view, I employed a German corporal, who acted as our interpreter. He volunteered from the Veteran Battalion at Fort George to accompany us.[1] After looking about for some time, he found out a quarter which he guessed would suit my taste. The house was inhabited by a respectable burgher, who had been at sea, and still retained the title of Skipper. His son, as I afterwards learned, had died a few months before, leaving a very pretty young widow, who resided with her father-in-law. I had not seen her long before I became interested in her.

Johanna M------ was innocence and simplicity itself; tender, soft, and affectionate; her eyes did not possess that brightness which bespeaks lively passions, and too often inconsistency, but they were soft, dark, and liquid, beaming with affection and goodness of heart. On coming home one day, I found her with her head resting on her hands and in tears; her father and mother-in-law, with their glistening eyes resting on her, with an expression of sympathy and sorrow, apparently more for her loss than their own; as if they would have said 'Poor girl! we have lost a son, but you have lost a husband'. Johanna, however, was young, and her spirit naturally buoyant: of course it cannot be supposed that this intensity of feeling could exist but at intervals. As usual, I soon made myself quite at home with the Skipper and his family, and became, moreover, a considerable favourite, from the interest I took in Johanna, and a talent at making punch, which was always put in requisition when they had a visit from the '*Predikaant*' or priest of the parish; on these occasions I was always one of the party at supper, which is their principal meal. It usually consisted of a large tureen, with bits of meat floating in fat or butter, for which we had to dive with our forks; we had also forcemeat-balls and sour-crout. The priest who was the very picture of good-nature and good-living, wore a three-cornered cocked-hat, which, according to the fashion of the middle classes, never quitted his head, excepting when he said grace. When supper was over and the punch made, which always drew

1. This would have been the 6th Royal Veteran Battalion, but it has proved impossible to identify the corporal by name.

forth the most unqualified praises of the '*Predikaant*' , he would lug out a heap of papers from his breeches-pocket, inscribed with favourite Dutch ditties, which, so far as I could understand the language, contained political allusions to the state of matters in Europe at the time. The burden of one of the songs I still remember, from the constant recurrence of the words, '*Well mag het Ue bekoomen*' at the end of each stanza.[1] The jolly priest being no singer, always read these overflowings of the Dutch muse with the most energetic gestures and accent. At the end of each verse, which seemed by its rhyme to have something of the titillating effect of a feather on the sober features of the 'Skipper,' the reader would break out into a Stentorian laugh, enough to have shaken down the walls of Jericho, or the Stadt-huis itself. The good 'vrow,' whose attention was almost entirely occupied with her household concerns, and who had still more prose in her composition than her mate, would now and then, like a good wife, exhibit some feeble tokens of pleasure, when she observed his features to relax in a more than ordinary degree.

Soon after I had taken up abode in the house, I observed that Johanna had got a Dutch and English grammar, which she had begun to study with great assiduity, and as I was anxious to acquire Dutch, this naturally enough brought us often together. She would frequently come into my room to ask the pronunciation of some word, for she was particularly scrupulous on that head. On these occasions, I would make her sit down beside me, and endeavour to make her perfect in each word in succession; but she found so much difficulty in bringing her pretty lips into the proper form, that I was under the necessity of enforcing my instructions by punishing her with a kiss for every failure. But so far was this from quickening her apprehension, that the difficulties seemed to increase at every step. Poor Johanna, notwithstanding this little innocent occupation, could not, however, be entirely weaned from her affection for the memory of her departed husband, for her grief would often break out in torrents of tears; when this was the case, we had no lesson for that day.

Garrison duty is always dull and irksome, and soldiers are always glad of any thing to break the monotony of a life where there is no activity or excitement. One day, while we lay at Tholen, a letter was brought from head-

1. 'May it sit well with you', a phrase – now verging on obsolete – used as a form of grace before a meal.

quarters which was to be forwarded from town to town to Admiral Young,[1] who was lying in the Scheldt at the time. A couple of horses and a guide were procured, and I was sent with the letter, much to my own satisfaction, as I was glad of an opportunity to see more of the country. I was ordered to proceed to a certain town, the name of which I forget, where another officer should relieve me. It was late when I got to the town, and not being aware that it was occupied by a Russian regiment, I was not a little surprised in being challenged by a sentry in a foreign language. I could not make out from the soldier what they were, until the officer of the guard came up, who understood a little English. He informed me that they were on their march to Tholen, where they were to do garrison duty.[2] On desiring to be conducted to his commanding officer, he brought me to the principal house in the town, at the door of which two sentries were posted. The scene in the interior was singular enough. The first object that met my eyes on entering the Colonel's apartment was a knot of soldiers in their green jackets and trowsers, lying in a heap, one above another, in the corner of the room, (with their bonnets pulled over their eyes,) like a litter of puppies, and snoring like bull-frogs. These were the Colonel's body-guard.

The room with its furniture exhibited a scene of the most outrageous, debauchery. Chairs overturned, broken decanters and bottles, fragments of tumblers and wine glasses lay scattered over the floor and table. Two or three candles were still burning on the table, and others had been broken in the conflict of bottles and other missiles. Taking a rapid glance at the state of matters in passing, we approached the Colonel's bed, which stood in one corner of the room. My conductor drew the curtains when I saw two people lying in their flannel-shirts; the elder was a huge broad faced man with a ferocious expression of countenance, who I was informed was the Colonel; the other was a young man about seventeen years of age, exceedingly handsome and with so delicate a complexion, that I actually thought at the time he must be the Colonel's wife. With this impression I drew back for a moment when he spoke to me in good English and told me he was the Adjutant and begged I would state what I had to communicate to the Colonel, which he would interpret to him, as the latter did not understand

---

1. Admiral Sir William Young, commanding the North Sea Fleet and having overall responsibility for naval operations off the Dutch coast.
2. For details of these Russian troops, see Appendix III.

English. The Colonel said he should forward the letter by one of his officers, and as I could then return to Tholen, we should proceed to that place next morning. We proceeded accordingly next morning on our march to Tholen. The Colonel had sent on his light company as an advanced-guard, some time before us, with orders to halt at a village on the road, until the regiment came up. Whether they had mistaken his orders I know not, but on coming to the village, no Light Company was to be found; and on inquiry, we learned that they had marched on. The rage of the Colonel knew no bounds, and produced a most ridiculous and childish scene betwixt himself and the officers. With the tears running down his cheeks, and stamping with rage, he went among them; first accusing one, and then the other, as if they were to blame for the mistake of the advanced-guard. Each of them, however, answered him in a petulant snappish manner, like enraged pug-dogs, at the same time clapping their hands to their swords, and some of them drawing them half out of the scabbards, when he would turn away from them, weeping bitterly like a great blubbering boy all the while. The officers, however, began to pity the poor Colonel, and at last succeeded in appeasing his wrath and drying his tears. He proceeded forthwith to order an enormous breakfast to be prepared for us immediately. It was of no use for the innkeeper to say that he had not any of the articles they desired, he was compelled by threats and curses to procure them, come where they would. As our landlord knew well whom he had to deal with, our table soon groaned under a load of dishes, enough apparently to have dined four times our number. In a trice we had everything that could be procured for love or money, and it was wonderful to observe with what alacrity the landlord waited on us, and obeyed the orders he received. He appeared, in fact, to have thrown off his native sluggishness and two or three pairs of breeches for the occasion. Before proceeding on the march, I wished to pay my share of the entertainment, but my proposal was treated with perfect ridicule. At first, I imagined that the Russians considered me as their guest, but I could not discover that the innkeeper received any remuneration for the entertainment prepared for us. The Russians had many odd customs during their meals, such as drinking out of each other's glasses, and eating from each other's plates; a compliment, which in England, we could willingly dispense with. They seemed to have a great liking to the English, and every day our men and theirs were seen walking arm-in-arm about the streets together. The gin, which was rather too cheap in this country, seemed to be a great bond of union between them; and strange to say I do not recollect a single instance of their quarrelling. Notwithstanding the snapping between the commanding officer and the other officers, they seemed on the whole to be in excellent discipline in other respects. The manner in which they went through their exercise was admirable, particularly when we consider that they were only sailors acting on shore. There was one custom, however, which never failed to excite our disgust and indignation; hardly a day passed but we saw some of their officers boxing the ears of their men in the ranks, who seemed to bear this treatment with the greatest patience, and without turning their eyes to the right or left during the operation; but such is the effect of early habits and custom, that the very men who bore this degrading treatment, seemed to feel the same disgust for our military punishment of flogging; which, however degrading in its effects on the character of the sufferer, could not at least be inflicted at the caprice of the individual. We may here observe the different effects produced on the character of men by a free and a despotic system of Government: it was evidently not the *nature*, but the *degree* of punishment in our service which shocked the Russian prejudices.

We had all become thoroughly sick of the monotony and sameness of our duties and occupations at Tholen, when we received orders to march the next day, (8th March, 1814). As the attack on Bergen-op-Zoom, which took place on that evening, was of course kept a profound secret, the common opinion was that we were destined for Antwerp, where the other division of the army had already had some fighting. Though elated, in common with my brother officers, with the prospect of coming to closer quarters with the enemy, it was not without tears on both sides that I parted with poor Johanna, who had somehow taken a hold of my affections that I was hardly aware of till this moment. The time left us to prepare for our march I devoted to her, and she did not even seek the pretext of her English grammar to remain in my room for the few hours we could yet enjoy together. We had marched some miles before I could think of any thing but her, for the recollection of her tears still thrilled to my very heart, and occasioned a stifling sensation that almost deprived me of utterance. But we were soon thrown into a situation where the excitement was too powerful and engrossing to leave room for other thoughts than of what we were immediately engaged in.

It was nearly dark when we arrived at the village of Halteren,[1] which is only three or four miles from Bergen-op-Zoom, where we took up our

1. Halsteren.

quarters for the night. On the distribution of the billets to the officers for the night, I received one upon a farm house about a mile in the country. I had not been long at my new lodging, when I was joined by four or five officers of the 4th Battalion Royal Scots,[1] who had just arrived by long marches from Stralsund, and were billeted about the country. They had heard that an attempt to surprise Bergen-op-Zoom would be made that same night. It is not easy to describe the sensations occasioned in my mind by this intelligence; it certainly partook but little of fear, but the novelty (to me at least) of the situation in which we were about to be placed, excited a feeling of anxiety, as to the result of an attempt, in which, from the known strength of the place we dared hardly expect to be successful. There is also a degree of melancholy which takes hold of the mind at these moments of serious reflection which precede the conflict. My comrades evidently shared this feeling with me. One of them remarked, as we were preparing to march, 'My boys, we'el see something like service to-night,' and added, 'we'el not all meet again in this world.' Poor Mac Nicol,[2] who made the remark, fell that night, which was the first and the last of my acquaintance with him. I believe every one of us were wounded. Learning from my new acquaintances that the grenadier company of their regiment, (Royal Scots), which was commanded by an old friend of mine, (Lieutenant Allan Robertson,) and whom I had not seen for some years, was only about a mile farther off, I thought I should have time to see him and join my regiment before they marched, should they be sent to the attack.[3] However, the party of the Royals whom I accompanied lost their way, from their ignorance of the road, and we in consequence made a long circuit, during which I heard from an aid-de-camp who passed us, that the 21st were on their march to attack the place on another quarter from us. In these circumstances I was exceedingly puzzled what course to take; if I went in search of my regiment,

1. This battalion formed part of the reinforcing brigade under Brigadier General Arthur Gore; see also Appendix I.
2. Capt. Donald McNichol, 4/1st Foot. A veteran of the Corunna campaign, McNichol left a wife and child who were later the recipients of a compassionate pension.
3. Evidently some years older than Moodie, Robertson had obtained his ensigncy in the 1st in 1810, seeing action with the regiment's 3rd Battalion at Fuentes de Onoro; he seems to have transferred to the 4th Battalion after obtaining his lieutenancy in 1810.

I had every chance of missing them in the night, being quite ignorant of the roads. Knowing that the Royals would be likely to head one of the columns from the number of the regiment, I took what I thought the surest plan, by attaching myself to the grenadier company under my gallant friend. There is something awfully impressive in the mustering of soldiers before going into action; many of those names, which the Serjeants were now calling in an under tone of voice, would never be repeated but in the tales of their comrades who saw them fall.

After mustering the men, we proceeded to the general 'rendez-vous' of the regiments forming the column; the Royals led the column followed by the other regiments according to their numbers. As every thing depended on our taking the enemy by surprise, the strictest orders were given to observe a profound silence on the march.

While we are proceeding to the attack, it will not be amiss to give the reader a slight sketch of the situation of Bergen-op-Zoom, and the plan of the operations of the different columns, to render my relation of the proceedings of the column I served with the more intelligible.

Bergen-op-Zoom is situated on the right bank of the Scheldt, and takes its name from the little river Zoom, which, after supplying the defences with water, discharges itself into the Scheldt. The old channel of the Zoom, into which the tide flows towards the centre of the town, forms the harbour, which is nearly dry at low-water. The mouth of the harbour was the point fixed upon for the attack of the right column, under Major-General Skerret, and Brig.-Gen. Gore. This column consisted of 1,100 men of the 1st Regiment, or Royal Scots, the 37th, 44th, and 91st, (as far as I can recollect). Lieut.-Col. Henry, with 650 men of the 21st, or Royal Scot's Fusileers [sic], was sent on a false attack near the Steenbergen-gate, to the left of the harbour, (I suppose the reader to be standing at the entrance of the harbour facing the town). Another column, consisting of 1,200 men of the 33rd, 55th, and 69th regiments, under Lieut. Col. Maurice [Morrice], were to attack the place near the Bredagate, and endeavour to enter by escalade. A third column, under Col. Lord Proby, consisting of 1,000 men of the 1st and Coldstream Guards, was to make nearly a complete circuit of the place, and enter the enemy's works by crossing the ice, some distance to the right of the entrance of the harbour and the Waterport-gate. This slight account of the plan of attack I have borrowed in some degree from Col. Jones' Narrative, who must have procured his information on these points from the best sources.[1] However, as I only pretend to speak with certainty of what fell under my own immediate observation, I shall return to the right column, with which I served on this occasion.

When we had proceeded some way we fell in with a picket, commanded by Capt. Darrah, of the 21st Fusileers,[2] who was mustering his men to proceed to the attack. Thinking that our regiment (the 21st), must pass his post on their way to the false attack, he told me to remain with him until they came up. I, in consequence, waited some time, but hearing nothing of the regiment, and losing patience, I gave him the slip in the dark, and ran on until I regained my place with the grenadier company of the Royals. On approaching the place of attack, we crossed the Tholen-dike, and immediately entered the bed of the Zoom, through which we had to push our way before we entered the wet ditch. It is not easy to convey an idea of the toil we experienced in getting through the deep mud of the river; we immediately sank nearly to our middles, and when, with great difficulty, we succeeded in freeing one leg from the mire, we sank nearly to the shoulder on the other side before we could get one pace forwards As might be expected, we got into some confusion in labouring through this horrible slough, which was like bird-lime about our legs; regiments got intermixed in the darkness, while some stuck fast, and some unlucky wretches got trodden down and smothered in the mud. Notwithstanding this obstruction, a considerable portion of the column had got through, when those behind us, discouraged by this unexpected difficulty, raised a shout to encourage themselves. Gen. Skerret, who was at the head of the column, was furious with rage, but the mischief was already done. The sluices were opened, and a torrent of waters poured down on us through the channel of the river, by which the progress of those behind was effectively stopped for some time. Immediately after the sluices were opened, a brilliant firework was displayed on the ramparts, which showed every object as clearly as daylight. Several cannon and some musketry opened on us, but did us little harm, as they seemed to be

1. This refers to Jones, Maj. Gen. Sir John T., *Journal of Sieges Carried on by the Army under the Duke of Wellington*, first published in 1818. Like most accounts of this operation, Jones's version errs in the belief that the False Attack was under Lt Col Henry; it was in fact led by Lt Col Benjamin Ottley of the 2/91st. Moodie himself errs in placing Ottley's battalion and the 2/37th with the Right Attack; for a full order of battle, see Appendix I.

2. Capt. Nicholas Lawson Darrah, 2/21st Fusiliers.

discharged at random. At the moment the water came down, I had just cleared the deepest part of the channel, and making a great effort, I gained a flat piece of ice which was sticking edgeways in the mud. To this I clung till the strength of the torrent had passed after which I soon gained the firm land, and pushed on with the others to the ditch. The point at which we entered was a bastion to the right of the harbour, from one of the angles of which a row of high palisades was carried through the ditch. To enable us to pass the water, some scaling-ladders had been sunk to support us in proceeding along the palisade, over which we had first to climb with each other's assistance, our soldiers performing the office of ladders for those who preceded them. So great were the obstacles we met with, that had not the attention of the enemy fortunately (or rather most judiciously), been distracted by the false attack under Col. Henry, it appeared quite impossible for us to have affected an entrance at this point. While we were proceeding forward in this manner, Col. Muller of the Royals[1] was clambering along the tops of the palisade, calling to those who had got the start of him, to endeavour to open the Waterport-gate, and let down the drawbridge to our right; but no-one in the hurry of the moment seemed to hear him. On getting near him, I told him that I should effect it if it was possible.

We met with but trifling resistance on gaining the rampart; the enemy being panic struck, fled to the streets and houses of the town, from which they kept up a pretty sharp fire on us for some time. I got about twenty soldiers of different regiments to follow me to the Waterport-gate, which we found closed. It was constructed of thin paling, with an iron bar across it about three inches in breadth. Being without tools of any kind, we made several ineffectual attempts to open it. At last, retiring a few paces, we made a rush at it in a body, when the iron bar snapped in the middle like a bit of glass. Some of my people got killed and wounded during this part of the work, but when we got to the drawbridge, we were a little more sheltered from the firing. The bridge was up, and secured by a lock in the right hand post of the two which supported it. I was simple enough to attempt to pick the lock with a soldier's bayonet, but after breaking two or three, we at last had an axe brought us from the bastion where the troops were entering.

1. An original footnote by Moodie here notes that Muller was 'Now of the Ceylon Regiment'. This transfer took place in 1825, Muller having previously been on half pay as a result of the peacetime reduction of the Army.

With the assistance of this instrument we soon succeeded in cutting the lock out of the post, and taking hold of the chain, I had the satisfaction to pull down the drawbridge with my own hands.

While I was engaged in this business, Col. Muller was forming the Royals on the rampart where we entered; but a party of about 150 men of different regiments, under General Skerret, who must have entered to the left of the harbour, were clearing the ramparts towards the Steinbergen-gate, where the false attack had been made under Col. Henry; and a party, also, under Col. Carleton, of the 44th regiment, was proceeding in the opposite direction along the ramparts to the right, without meeting with much resistance. Hearing the firing on the opposite side of the town from Gen. Skerret's party, and supposing that they had marched through the town, I ran on through the streets to overtake them, accompanied by only one or two soldiers, for the rest had left me and returned to the bastion after we had opened the gate. In proceeding along the canal or harbour, which divided this part of the town, I came to a loop-holed wall, which was continued from the houses down to the water's edge. I observed a party of soldiers within a gate in this wall, and was going up to them, taking them for our own people, when I was challenged in French, and had two or three shots fired at me. Seeing no other way of crossing the harbour but by a little bridge, which was nearly in a line with the wall, I returned to the Waterport-gate, which I found Col. Muller had taken possession of with two or three companies of his regiment. I went up to him, and told him that I had opened the gate according to his desire, and of the interruption I had met with in the town. Not knowing me, he asked my name, which he said he would remember, and sent one of the companies up with me to the wall, already mentioned, and ordered the officer who commanded the company, after he should have driven the enemy away, to keep possession of it until farther [sic] orders. On coming to the gate, we met with a sharp resistance, but after firing a few rounds, and preparing to charge they gave way, leaving us in possession of the gate and bridge.

Leaving the company here, and crossing the little bridge, I again set forward alone to overtake Gen. Skerret's party, guided by the firing on the ramparts. Avoiding any little parties of the enemy, I had reached the inside of the ramparts where the firing was, without its occurring to me that I might get into the wrong box and be taken prisoner. Fortunately I observed a woman looking over a shop door, on one side of the street; the poor creature, who must have been under the influence of some strong passion to remain in her present exposed situation, was pale and trembling. She was a Frenchwoman, young, and not bad-looking. I asked her where the British soldiers were, which she told me without hesitation, pointing at the same time in the direction. I shook hands with her, and bade her good night, not entertaining the smallest suspicion of her deceiving me; following her directions, I clambered up the inside of the rampart, and rejoined Gen. Skerret's party.

The moon had now risen, and though the sky was cloudy, we could see pretty well what was doing. I found my friend Robertson here, with the grenadier company of the Royals; I learned from him that the party, which was now commanded by Capt. Guthrie of the 33rd regiment,[1] had been compelled by numbers to retire from the bastion which the enemy now occupied, and should endeavour to maintain the one which they now possessed, until they could procure a reinforcement. He also told me of Gen. Skerret's being dangerously wounded and taken prisoner, an irreparable loss to our party, as Capt. Guthrie was ignorant of the General's intentions. In the mean time the enemy continued a sharp firing on us, which we returned as fast as our men could load their firelocks. Several of the enemy who had fallen, as well as of our own men, were lying on the ramparts; one of our officers, who had been wounded in the arm, was walking about, saying occasionally, in rather a discontented manner, 'This is what is called honour;' though I could readily sympathise with him in the pain he suffered, I could not exactly understand how, if there is any honour in getting wounded, any bodily suffering can detract from it.

We found a large pile of logs of wood on the rampart; these we immediately disposed across the gorge of the bastion, so as to form a kind of parapet, over which our people could fire, leaving, however, about half the distance open towards the parapet of the rampart. On the opposite side of the bastion were two twenty-four-pounders of the enemy's, which being raised on high platforms, we turned upon them, firing along the ramparts over the heads of our own party. However valuable this resource might be to us, we were still far from being on equal terms with the French, who besides greatly exceeding us in numbers, had also brought up two or three field-pieces, which annoyed us much during the night. There was also a windmill on

1. Capt. John Guthrie, 33rd Foot.

the bastion they occupied, from the top of which their musketry did great execution among us. In the course of the night they made several ineffectual attempts to drive us from our position: on these occasions, which we always were aware of from the shouts they raised to encourage each other, as soon as they made their appearance on the rampart, we gave them a good dose of grape from our twenty-four-pounders, and had a party ready to charge them back. I observed our soldiers were always disposed to meet the enemy half-way, and the latter were soon so well aware of our humour, that they invariably turned tail before we could get within forty or fifty paces of them. The firing was kept up almost continually on both sides until about two o'clock in the morning, when it would sometimes cease for more than half-an-hour together. During one of these intervals of stillness, exhausted with our exertions, and the cold we felt in our drenched clothes, some of the officers and I lay down along the parapet together, in hopes of borrowing a little heat from each other. I fell insensibly into a troubled dozing state, in which my imagination still revelled in the scenes of night. While I yet lay the firing had recommenced, which, with the shouts of the enemy, and the words of those about me, seemed to form but the ground work of my fitful dream, which continued to link imaginary circumstances to reality. How long I might have lain in this stupor, between sleeping and waking, I know not, when suddenly I felt the ground shaken under me, and heard at the same time a crash as if the whole town had been overwhelmed by an earthquake; a bright glare of light burst on my eyes at the same instant and almost blinded me. A shot from the enemy had blown up our small magazine, on the ramparts, on which we depended for the supply of the two twenty-four-pounders which had been of such material use to us during the night. This broke our slumbers most effectually; and we had now nothing for it but to maintain our ground in the best way we were able until we could receive a reinforcement from some of the other parties. Immediately after this disaster, raising a tremendous shout or rather yell, the enemy again attempted to come to close quarters with us, in hopes of our being utterly disheartened; but our charging party, which we had always in readiness, made them wheel round as usual. In the course of the night, we had sent several small parties of men to represent the state of our detachment, and endeavour to procure assistance, but none of them returned, having, we supposed, been intercepted by the enemy. Discouraged as we were by this circumstance, we still continued to hold our ground until break of day.

By this time the firing had entirely ceased in the other part of the town, naturally leading us, in the absence of all communication, to conclude that the other parties had been driven from the place. However this may have been, the first dawn of day showed us in but too plain colours the hopelessness of our situation. The enemy now brought an overwhelming force against us; but still we expected, from the narrowness of the rampart, that they would not be able to derive the full advantage of their superiority; but in this we were deceived. The bastion we occupied was extensive, but only that portion of it near the gorge was furnished with a parapet. At this spot, and behind the logs which we had thrown up, our now diminished force was collected. Keeping up an incessant fire to divert our attention, the French (who now outnumbered us, at least three to one,) detached a part of their force, which skirting the outside of the ramparts, and ascending the face of the bastion we occupied, suddenly opened a most destructive fire on our flank and rear. From this latter party we were totally unprotected, while they were sheltered by the top of the rampart: we were thus left to defend ourselves from both [parties] at once as we best could. But still they would not venture to charge us, and it would have been of little use for us to charge them, for the moment we quitted the parapet, we would have been exposed to a cross fire from the other bastion.

The slaughter was now dreadful, and our poor fellows, who had done all that soldiers could in our trying situation, now fell thick and fast. Just at this moment, my friend Robertson, under whose command I had put myself at the beginning of the attack, fell. I had just time to run up to him, and found him stunned from a wound in the head; when our gallant commander, seeing the inutility of continuing the unequal contest, gave the order to retreat. We had retired in good order about three hundred yards, when poor Guthrie received a wound in the head, which I have since been informed deprived him of his sight. The enemy, when they saw us retreating, hung upon our rear, keeping up a sharp fire all the time, but they still seemed to have some respect for us from the trouble we had already given them. We had indulged the hope, that by continuing our course along the ramparts, we should be able to effect our retreat by the Waterport-gate,[1] not being aware that we should be intercepted by the mouth of the harbour. We were already at the

1. An original footnote by Moodie here reminds the reader that 'this was the only gate which was opened during the night'.

very margin before we discovered our mistake and completely hemmed in by the French. We had therefore no alternative left to us but to surrender ourselves prisoners of war, or to attempt to effect our escape across the harbour, by means of the floating pieces of ice with which the water was covered. Not one of us seemed to entertain the idea of surrender, however, and in the despair which had now taken possession of every heart, we threw ourselves into the water, or leaped for the broken pieces of ice which were floating about. The scene that ensued was shocking beyond description – the canal or harbour was faced on both sides by high brick walls; in the middle of the channel lay a small Dutch decked vessel, which was secured by a rope to the opposite side of the harbour. Our only hope of preserving our lives or effecting our escape, depended on our being able to gain this little vessel. Already, many had, by leaping first on one piece of ice and then on another, succeeded in getting on board the vessel, which they drew to the opposite side of the canal by the rope, and thus freed one obstruction: but immediately afterwards, being intercepted by the Waterport redoubt, they were compelled to surrender. The soldiers in particular, when they found themselves inclosed [sic] by the enemy, seemed to lose the power of reflection, and leaped madly into the water, with their arms in their hands, without even waiting until a piece of ice should float within their reach. The air was rent with vain cries for help from the drowning soldiers, mixed with the exulting shouts of the enemy, who seemed determined to make us drain the bitter cup of defeat to the very dregs. Among the rest I had scrambled down the face of the canal to a beam running horizontally along the brick-work, from which other beams descended perpendicularly into the water, to prevent the sides from being injured by shipping. After sticking my sword into my belt, (for I had thrown the scabbard away the previous night,) I leaped from this beam, which was nine or ten feet above the water, for a piece of ice, but not judging my distance very well, it tilted up with me, and I sunk to the bottom of the water. However, I soon came up again, and after swimming to the other side of the canal and to the vessel, I found nothing to catch hold of. I had therefore nothing for it but to hold on by the piece of ice I had at first leaped on, and swinging my body under it, I managed to keep my face out of the water. I had just caught hold of the ice in time, for encumbered as I was with a heavy great coat, now thoroughly soaked, I was in a fair way to share the fate of many a poor fellow now lying at the bottom of the water. I did not, however, retain my slippery hold undisturbed. I was several times dragged under water by the convulsive grasp of the drowning soldiers, but by desperate efforts I managed to free myself and regain my hold. Even at this moment, I cannot think without horror of the means which the instinct of self-preservation suggested to save my own life, while some poor fellow clung to my clothes: I think I still see his agonized look, and hear his imploring cry, as he sank for ever.

After a little time I remained undisturbed tenant of the piece of ice, I was not, however, the only survivor of those who had got into the water; several of them were still hanging on to other pieces of ice, but they one by one let go their hold, and sank as their strength failed. At length only three or four besides myself remained. All this time some of the enemy continued firing at us, and I saw one or two shot in the water near me. So intent was every one on effecting his escape, that though they sometimes cast a look of commiseration at their drowning comrades, no one thought for a moment of giving us any assistance. The very hope of it had at length so completely faded in our minds, that we had ceased to ask the aid of those that passed us on the fragments of ice. But Providence had reserved one individual who possessed a heart to feel for the distress of his fellow-creatures more than for his own personal safety. The very last person that reached the vessel in the manner I have already described, was Lieut. M'Dougal, of the 91st Regiment.[1] I had attracted his attention in passing me, and he had promised his assistance when he should reach the vessel. He soon threw me a rope, but I was now so weak, and benumbed with the intense cold, that it slipped through my fingers alongside of the vessel; he then gave me another, doubled, which I got under my arms, and he thus succeeded, with the assistance of a wounded man, in getting me on board. I feel that it is quite out of my power to do justice to the humanity and contempt of danger

1. Ensign Hugh MacDougall (also given in some sources as M'Dougald and McDugald), 2/91st Highlanders. This officer was returned as killed at Bergen-op-Zoom, but in fact survived the action and remained with the regiment until placed on half pay in 1816. If, as the regimental history theorises, he was wounded and left for dead on the field, he must have been hit very late in the action, after helping aid Moodie; on the other hand, considering his activities in the water, it may well be that he was falsely assumed to have drowned. See Goff, Gerald Lionel Joseph, *Historical records of the 91st Argyllshire Highlanders, now the 1st Battalion Princess Louise's Argyll and Sutherland Highlanders, containing an account of the Regiment in 1794, and of its subsequent services to 1881* (London: R. Bentley, 1891), p. 345.

displayed by our generous deliverer on this occasion. While I was assisting him in saving the two or three soldiers who still clung to pieces of ice, I got a musket-ball through my wrist; for all this time several of the enemy continued deliberately firing at us from the opposite rampart, which was not above sixty yards from the vessel. Not content with what he had already done for me, my kind-hearted friend insisted on helping me out of the vessel; but I could not consent to his remaining longer exposed to the fire of the enemy, who had already covered the deck with killed and wounded, and M'Dougal fortunately still remained unhurt.

Finding that I would not encumber him, he left the vessel, and I went down to the cabin, where I found Lieut. Briggs, of the 91st, sitting on one side, with a severe wound through his shoulder-blade.[1] The floor of the cabin was covered with water, for the vessel had become leaky from the firing. I took my station on the opposite side, and taking off my neckcloth, with the assistance of my teeth, I managed to bind up my wound, so as to stop the bleeding in some measure. My companion suffered so much from his wound that little conversation passed betwixt us.

I fell naturally into gloomy reflections on the events of the night. I need hardly say how bitter and mortifying they were: after all our toils and sanguine anticipations of ultimate success, to be thus robbed of the prize which we already grasped, as we thought, with a firm hand. Absorbed in these melancholy ruminations, accompanied from time to time by a groan from my companion, several hours passed away, during which the water continued rising higher and higher in the cabin, until it reached my middle, and I was obliged to hold my arm above it, for the salt water made it smart. Fortunately the vessel grounded from the receding of the tide. Escape in our state being now quite out of the question, my companion and I were glad on the whole to be relieved from our present disagreeable situation by surrendering ourselves prisoners.

The firing had now entirely ceased, and the French seemed satiated with the ample vengeance they had taken on us. As there was no gate near us, we were hoisted with ropes over the ramparts, which were here faced with brick to the top. A French soldier was ordered to show me the way to the hospital in the town. As we proceeded however, my guide took a fancy to my canteen

1. Ensign James Briggs, 2/91st Highlanders, who was returned as severely wounded and taken prisoner at Bergen-op-Zoom.

which still hung by my side, and laying hold of it without ceremony, was proceeding to empty its contents into his own throat. Though suffering with a burning thirst from loss of blood, I did not recollect till this moment that there was about two-thirds of a bottle of gin remaining in it. I immediately snatched it from the fellow's hand and clapping it to my mouth, finished every drop of it at a draught, while he vented his rage in oaths. I found it exceedingly refreshing, but it had no more effect on my nerves than small beer in my present state of exhaustion.

The scene as we passed through the streets, strewed here and there with the bodies of our fallen soldiers, intermixed with those of the enemy, was, indeed, melancholy; even could I have forgotten for a moment how the account stood between the enemy and us, I was continually reminded of our failure, by the bodies of many of our people being already stripped of their upper garments. When we arrived at the hospital, I found one of the officers of my regiment, who had been taken prisoner, standing at the door. My face was so plastered with blood from a prick of a bayonet I had got in the temple from one of our soldiers, that it was some time before he knew me. In passing along the beds in the hospital, the first face I recognised was that of my friend Robertson, whom I had left for dead when our party retreated. Besides the wound he received in the head, he had received one in the wrist, after he fell.

On lying down on the bed prepared for me, I was guilty of a piece of simplicity, which I had ample occasion to repent before I left the place. I took all my clothes off, and sent them to be dried by the people of the hospital, but they were never returned to me. I was in consequence forced to keep my bed for the three days I remained prisoner in Bergen-op-Zoom.

The hospital was crowded with the wounded on both sides. On my right hand lay Ensign Martial of the 55th regiment, with a grapeshot wound in his shoulder, of which, and ague together, he afterwards died at Klundert.[1] On my left, in an adjoining room, lay poor General Skerret, with a desperate wound through the body, of which he died next night. It was said that he might have recovered, had it not been for the bruises he had received from the muskets of the enemy after he fell. This story I can hardly credit. However that may be, there is no doubt we lost in him a most gallant, zealous, and active

1. Ensign Walter Marshal, 55th Foot; died of wounds, 6 April 1814; see notes to battalion return in TNA, WO17/278.

officer, and at a most unfortunate time for the success of the enterprise. On the opposite side of the hospital lay Capt. Campbell, of the 55th regiment.[1] He had a dreadful wound from a grape which entered at his shoulder and went out near the back-bone. He was gifted with the most extraordinary flow of spirits of any man I have ever met with. He never ceased talking from sun-rise till night, and afforded all of us who were in a condition to relish any thing, an infinite deal of amusement. I had told Campbell of the trick they had played me with my clothes, and it immediately became with him a constant theme for rating every Frenchman that passed him.

In the course of the next day a French Serjeant came swaggering into the hospital with an officer's sash tied round him, and stretched out to its utmost breadth. He boasted that he had killed the officer by whom it had been worn. Twice a day two of the intendants of the hospital went about with buckets in their hands, one containing small pieces of boiled meat, which was discovered to be horseflesh by the medical people, while another contained a miserable kind of stuff, which they called soup, and a third contained bits of bread. One of the pieces of meat was tossed on each bed with a fork in passing; but the patient had always to make his choice between flesh and bread, and soup and bread, it being thought too much to allow them soup and meat at the same time. I was never so much puzzled in my life as by this alternative. Constantly tormented with thirst, I usually asked for soup, but my hunger, with which I was no less tormented, made me as often repent my choice. While we lay here we were attended by our own surgeons, and had every attention paid to us in this respect that we could desire.

In the mean time arrangements were entered into with Gen. Bizanet, the French commander, for an exchange of prisoners, and in consequence the last of the wounded prisoners were removed in waggons to Rozendaal,[2] on the third day after we had been taken. On this occasion I was obliged to borrow a pair of trowsers from one of the soldiers, and a coat from my neighbour Martial, of the 55th, who being a tall man and I rather little, it reached half-way down my legs. Altogether I cut rather an odd figure as I started from the hospital. My regimental cap and shoes had, however, escaped the fate of my other habiliments, so, considering circumstances, matters might

1. Capt. John Campbell, 55th Foot.
2. Roosendaal.

have been worse. But, one trial to my temper still remained which I did not expect: the old rascal, to whom I delivered my clothes when I sent them to be dried, had the unparalleled impudence to make a demand on me for the hospital shirt, with which, in place of my own wet one, I had been supplied on entering the hospital. I was so provoked at this unconscionable request, that I believe I should have answered him with a box on the ear, but my only available hand was too well employed at the time in supporting my trowsers. There was still another reason for my objecting to his demand: before I was taken prisoner, while lying in the vessel, I had managed to conceal some money which happened to be in my pockets on going to the attack; this I had carefully transferred, with due secrecy, to the inferior margin of the hospital shirt in which it was tied with a garter, when we were preparing to leave the place. This treasure, though not large, was of some importance to me, and I determined that nothing short of brute force should deprive me of it. My gentleman, however, pertinaciously urged his claim to the aforesaid garment, and a violent altercation ensued between us, in which I had an opportunity of showing a proficiency in Dutch swearing, that I was not aware of myself till this moment. My friend Campbell came up at last to my assistance, and discharged such a volley of oaths at the old vampire, that he was fairly beaten out of the field, and I carried away the shirt in triumph.

We were marched out of the town by the Breda-gate to Rozendaal, a distance of about fifteen miles, where we arrived the same night. The French soldiers who had fallen in the conflict had all been removed by this time, but, as we proceeded, escorted by the victors, many a ghastly corpse of our countrymen met our half-averted eyes. They had all been more or less stripped of their clothing, and some had only their shirts left for a covering, and were turned on their faces. My heart rose at this humiliating spectacle, nor could I breathe freely until we reached the open fields beyond the fortifications. All who were unable to march were crowded into the waggons which had been prepared for them, while those who were less disabled straggled along the road the best way they could. As may be supposed, there were no needless competitors for the waggon conveyance, for the roads were rough, and every jolt of the vehicles produced groans of agony from the wretched passengers.

On arriving at Wouw, which I took in my way, I explained my absence from the regiment to the satisfaction of the commanding officer. I soon heard of the fate of poor Bulteel, (2nd Lieutenant 21st Regiment,) who fell during this ill-starred enterprise, by a cannon-ball, which carried off the top of his head. Never was a comrade more sincerely lamented by his messmates than this most amiable young man. His brother, an officer in the Guards, whom he had met only a few days before, fell the same night.[1] The captain of my company, and kind friend, M'Kenzie,[2] had his leg shattered by a shot on the same occasion, and I was informed that he bore the amputation without suffering a groan to escape from him. Four others were more slightly wounded. The dead had all been collected in the church, and a long trench being dug by the soldiers, they were all next day deposited in the earth without parade, and in silence. In a few days I proceeded to Rozendaal, where, for the present, the prisoners were to remain.

At this place I had more cause than ever to feel grateful for the kindness of my Dutch landladies and landlords; the surgeon who attended me finding it necessary to put me on low diet and to keep my bed, the sympathy of the good people of the house knew no bounds; not an hour passed but they came to inquire how I was. So disinterested was their unwearied attention, that on leaving them I could not induce them to accept the smallest remuneration. After some time we went to Klundert, where we were to remain until our exchange should be effected.

Before concluding my narrative of the unfortunate attack on Bergen-op-Zoom, the reader may expect some observations relative to the plan of attack, and the causes of its ultimate failure; but it should be remembered, before venturing to give my opinions on the subject, that nothing is more difficult for an individual, attached to any one of the different columns which composed the attacking force, than to assign causes for such an unexpected result, particularly when the communication between them has been interrupted. In a battle in the open field, where every occurrence either takes place under the immediate observation of the General, or is speedily communicated to him, faults can be soon remedied, or at least it may be afterwards determined with some degree of accuracy where they existed. But in a night-attack on a fortified place, the case is very different. As the General of the army cannot be personally present in the attack, any blame which may attach to the undertaking, can only affect him in so far

1. The officer of the 2/21st was 2nd Lt John Bulteel; as noted above his brother, a captain and lieutenant in the 1st Foot Guards, is also listed as John.
2. Capt. Donald McKenzie, 2/21st Fusiliers; his wound is confirmed by the casualty return for the action.

as the original plan is concerned; and if this plan succeeds so far that the place is actually surprised, and the attacking force has effected a lodgment within it, and even been in possession of the greater part of the place, with a force equal to that of the enemy, no candid observer can attribute the failure to any defect in the arrangements of the General. Nothing certainly can be easier than, after the event, to point out certain omissions which, had the General been gifted with the spirit of prophecy, *might possibly*, in the existing state of matters, have led to a happier result; but nothing, in my humble opinion, can be more unfair or more uncandid, than to blame the unsuccessful commander, when every possible turn which things might take was not provided against, and while it still remains a doubt how far the remedies proposed by such critics would have succeeded in the execution.

According to the plan of operations, as stated in Sir Thomas Graham's dispatch, it was directed that the right column, under Major-General Skerret, and Brig.-General Gore, which entered at the mouth of the harbour, and the left column under Lord Proby, which Major-General Cooke accompanied in person, and which attacked between the Waterport and Antwerp gates, should move along the ramparts and form a junction. This junction, however, did not take place, as General Cooke had been obliged to change the point of attack, which prevented his gaining the ramparts until half-past eleven o'clock, an hour after General Skerret entered with the right column; a large detachment of which, under Colonel the Hon. George Carleton, and General Gore, had, unknown to him, (General Cooke), as it would appear, penetrated along the ramparts far beyond the point where he entered. The centre column, under Lieut.-Colonel Morrice, which had attacked near the Steenbergen lines, being repulsed with great loss, and a still longer delay occurring before they entered by the scaling-ladders of General Cooke's column, the enemy had ample opportunities to concentrate their force, near the points in most danger. However, notwithstanding all these delays and obstructions, we succeeded (as already stated) in establishing a force equal to that of the enemy along the ramparts. But still, without taking into account the advantage which the attacking force always possesses in the alarm and distraction of the enemy, (which, however, was more than counterbalanced by our entire ignorance of the place,) we could not, in fact, be said to have gained any decided superiority over our adversaries; on the contrary, the chances were evidently against our being able to maintain our position through the night, or until reinforcements could come up.

'But why,' I have heard it often urged, 'were we not made better acquainted with the place?' In answer to this question, it may be observed, that though there can be no doubt that the leaders of the different columns, at least, had seen plans of the place, yet there is a great difference between a personal knowledge of a place, and that derived from the best plans, even by daylight; but in the *night* the enemy must possess a most decided advantage over their assailants, in their intimate knowledge of all the communications through, the town, as well as in their acquaintance with the bearings of the different works which surround it.

Another circumstance which must have tended most materially to the unfortunate result of the attack was, that the two parties, which had been detached from the right column, were deprived of their commanders in the very beginning of the night, by the fall of Generals Skerret and Gore, and Colonel Carleton. The reader, were I inclined to account for our failure by these early calamities alone, need not go far to find instances in history where the fate of an army has been decided by the fall of its leader. There are some statements, however, in the excellent account published by Colonel Jones, (who must have had the best means of information on these points), which irresistibly lead the mind to certain conclusions, which, while they tend most directly to exonerate Sir Thomas Graham, as well as the General entrusted with the command of the enterprise, from the blame which has so unfairly been heaped on them, at the same time seem to imply some degree of misconduct on the part of the battalion detached by General Cooke to support the reserve of 600 men under Lt. Col. Muller at the Waterport gate. This battalion, he (Colonel Jones), states, perceiving the enemy preparing to attack them after having got possession of the Waterport-gate, left the place, by crossing the ice. No reason is given why this battalion did not fall back on General Cooke's force at the Orange bastion.

The surrender of the reserve at the Waterport-gate seems to have arisen either from some mistake, or from ignorance of the practicability of effecting their escape in another direction, for it does not appear that they were aware of General Cooke's situation. The loss of these two parties seems, therefore, to have been the more immediate cause of the failure of the enterprise; for had both these parties been enabled to form a junction with General Cooke, we should still, notwithstanding former losses, have been nearly on an equality, in point of numbers at least with the enemy. As matters now stood, after these two losses, which reduced our force in the place to less than half that of the French, General Cooke appears to have done all that could be expected of a prudent and humane commander, in surrendering to prevent a useless expenditure of life, after withdrawing all he could from the place. It would appear, in consequence of the delay that occurred before General Cooke entered the place, and the repulse of Colonel Morrice's column, that the plan of the attack had been altered; otherwise it is difficult to account for the proceedings of General Skerret in his attempting to penetrate so far along the ramparts to the left of the entrance of the harbour, with so small a force.

In Sir Thomas Graham's dispatch, (as I have already noticed), it is stated that the right column under General Skerret, and the left under General Cooke, 'were directed to form a junction as soon as possible' and 'clear the rampart of opponents.' From the latter words it is evident that he meant by the nearest way along the ramparts; consequently, according to this arrangement, General Skerret's column, after entering at the mouth of the harbour, should have proceeded along the ramparts to its right. In this direction Colonel Carleton had proceeded with 150 men, while General Skerret pushed along the ramparts in the opposite direction; from these circumstances, it is fair to conclude that General Skerret despaired of being able to form a junction with the left column, and therefore wished to force the Steenbergen-gate, and admit the 21st Fusileers, under Colonel Henry, while Colonel Carleton should form a junction with Colonel Jones. It is stated in Col. Jones's account that General Skerret attempted to fall back on the reserve at the Waterport-gate, but was prevented by the rising of the tide at the entrance of the harbour. Though it would be rash at this distance of time to venture to contradict this statement, I cannot help thinking that he has been misinformed on this point; for, on my joining the party, after opening the Waterport-gate, I heard nothing of such an attempt having been made; and if they had still entertained the idea of retiring from their position, I could have easily shown them the way by the foot-bridge across the harbour, where Colonel Muller had sent a company of the Royals from the Waterport-gate. The party were, when I came to them, at bastion 14,[1] to which they had just retired from bastion 13, where General Skerret had been wounded and taken prisoner, and they were now commanded by

1. An original footnote by Moodie here refers readers to 'the plan at the end of the 2nd vol. of Colonel Jones Journals of Sieges, &c.'; readers of this work should instead consult Map 5, notes B and E.

Captain Guthrie of the 33rd Regiment: it was under the orders of the last mentioned officer that we threw up the log parapet, which was of such use to us during the night. The admirable judgment and coolness displayed by this gallant officer, upon whom the command so unexpectedly devolved, cannot be mentioned in too high terms of commendation.[1]

In concluding my narrative, it will, I trust, be admitted, that however much we may deplore the unfortunate issue of the enterprise, and the unforeseen difficulties which tended to frustrate the best concerted plan of operations, there have been few occasions during the war in which the courage and energies of British soldiers have been put to such a severe test, or have been met by a more gallant and successful resistance on the part of the enemy.

As a result of his wound at Bergen-op-Zoom, Moodie was for two years in receipt of a compensatory pension whilst completing his recovery. At about the same time that his pension ceased, his finances received a further blow by virtue of his being placed on half pay as part of the peacetime reduction of the Army. Accordingly, he elected to seek his fortune in the colonies, spending some years in southern Africa in the company of two of his brothers. Moodie was for a time a magistrate in Natal, but in 1829 he returned to Britain where he met and married the author Susanna Strickland. The couple settled for a time in Suffolk, but soon Moodie was again bound for the colonies, settling in Canada in 1832. The pioneer lifestyle, which Mrs Moodie later used as the basis for one of her own books, was not one to which they were suited, and they eventually took up residence in Belleville, Ontario, where he served as a sheriff and as an officer of militia during the suppression of the 1839 rebellion. Moodie also continued to write, producing an account of his time in Africa as well as a more general memoir of his life as whole, but it was always his wife who enjoyed the greater literary success. Frequently impecunious, and at times bitter over his lack of success in civilian life following the termination of his military career, Moodie eventually died, still at Belleville, on 22 October 1869.[2]

---

1. These points, along with other controversies arising from the failed attack, are discussed more fully in Appendix V.
2. Biographical details from Ballstadt, 'Moodie'.

Appendix I

Command and Order of Battle Under Graham

The primary purpose of this listing, which in part duplicates information provided in *A Bold and Ambitious Enterprise*, is to place the accounts in this volume in context inasmuch as it enables the reader to see where in the army's organisational structure the various eyewitnesses and their units were assigned. However, its presence here also allows a greater amount of detail to be included than was possible in *A Bold and Ambitious Enterprise*, and the opportunity has also been taken to correct a small number of errors that were made in the previous work.

Forming Graham's Army

In a memorandum of 21 November 1813, Secretary of State for War and the Colonies Lord Bathurst outlined the following proposed organisation for the force under Graham, with what he understood as the strengths of the units in question:[1]

3rd King's German Legion Hussars	480
Royal Artillery	615
Major General Cooke's Brigade	
Detachment 1st Foot Guards	800
Detachment Coldstream Guards	400
Detachment 3rd Foot Guards	400
Major General Mackenzie's Brigade	
2/35th (Sussex)	600
2/37th (North Hampshire)	500
2/44th (East Essex)	500
2/52nd (Oxfordshire) Light Infantry	300

1. Memorandum of 21 November 1813, TNA, WO6/16, pp. 18–19.

Major General Skerrett's Brigade

55th (Westmoreland)	400
3/56th (West Essex)	400
2/69th (South Lincolnshire)	500
3/95th Rifle Corps	250
1st Royal Veteran Battalion	500

Major General Gibbs's Brigade

2/25th (King's Own Borderers)	390
33rd (1st West Riding)	600
54th (West Norfolk)	510
2/73rd	560

This would give a total of 7,610 infantry, and 8,705 all arms. The staff was to comprise one deputy adjutant-general and one deputy quartermaster-general, with two deputy assistants in each department, medical staff sufficient for a force of 7,000, and a due proportion of officers from the commissary and paymaster's departments.

The brigades of Mackenzie and Skerrett were comprised of units drawn from the home station, split by seniority, whilst Gibbs's Brigade was to be created from four of the six battalions from Germany already serving under that officer. The 4/1st (Royal Scots) and 2/91st would remain in the Baltic; reports indicate that these were the least effective battalions under Gibbs's command.[1] The Foot Guards detachments were all to come from the standing Second Guards Brigade, which comprised the 2nd Battalions of the three Foot Guards regiments and functioned largely as a depot; nevertheless, the brigade had been called upon for active service before, sending its flank companies to Walcheren and providing troops for a provisional brigade at Cadiz in 1810–11. Mention of the 3rd King's German Legion (KGL) Hussars would seem to be in error for the 2nd Regiment, since the former was already in Germany whilst the latter was available in Britain; a subsequent proposal for shipping the force listed the 2nd KGL Hussars, and it was indeed this regiment that initially went out with Graham.[2]

1. Bamford, *Bold and Ambitious Enterprise*, pp. 18–19.
2. 'Return of the Officers, Non Commissioned Officers, Drummers and Private men who are ready, or who are expected to be prepared for embarkation for Holland', TNA, WO1/198, p. 3.

Unfortunately, Bathurst's conception of the strength of the available forces did not correspond with the reality: effective strength when the troops arrived in the Low Countries fell short of Bathurst's target by nearly a thousand men. Additionally, there were organisational changes with respect to the contingent provided by the Foot Guards even before the force set sail. Bathurst seems to have envisaged an organisation similar to that used at Cadiz in 1810-11, with a full battalion from the 1st Foot Guards and a provisional battalion formed out of men from the other two regiments. What happened in reality was that each regiment deployed the effective part of its 2nd Battalion, subsequently providing reinforcements over the course of the following months as more fit men became available. The three Guards battalions were initially prepared for service with a six-company organisation, with 2/1st Foot Guards adding a seventh company before departure.[1]

The Guards, however, were something of an exception in having more men available than Bathurst had assumed, emphasising the fact that the line battalions were for the most part particularly weak. Once the shortfall became apparent – albeit too late to do anything before the expedition sailed – the decision was taken to reinforce Graham's force with the following battalions.[2]

From Jersey:

2/30th (Cambridgeshire)	assumed strength about 600 rank and file.
2/81st	assumed strength about 490 rank and file.

From Leith:

2/21st (Royal North British Fusiliers)	assumed strength about 380 rank and file.
2/78th (Ross-shire Buffs Highland)	assumed strength about 400 rank and file.

Additionally, a reinforcement of 550 rank and file was prepared to go out to join the three Foot Guards battalions, followed later by another,

1. Hamilton, Lt Gen. Sir F. W., KCB, *The Origin and Service of the First or Grenadier Guards* (London: John Murray, 1874), Vol. II, pp. 484–5.
2. Torrens to Bunbury, 19 December 1813, TNA, WO1/198, p. 39.

smaller, draft.[1] It was further envisaged that the British and KGL units serving as part of Lieutenant General Wallmoden's corps in the allied Army of the North would be sent to reinforce Graham, these being the 3rd Hussars and 1st and 2nd Horse Batteries of the KGL, and the 2nd Rocket Troop, Royal Horse Artillery. Wallmoden wrote to Graham, however, explaining that some delay would be involved before these forces could be expected to arrive.[2]

Initial Organisation

Once they were fully disembarked, Graham organised his forces in the following fashion (it will be noted that this brigading, other than with respect the Guards, dispensed with Bathurst's proposals and deliberately created brigades with a mixture of veteran and inexperienced units):[3]

Commander of Forces: *General Sir Thomas Graham*

Guards Brigade: *Major General George Cooke*
    2nd Battalion, 1st Foot Guards
    2nd Battalion, Coldstream Guards
    2nd Battalion, 3rd Foot Guards

Light Brigade: *Major General Kenneth Mackenzie*
    2nd Battalion, 35th (Sussex) Regiment
    2nd Battalion, 52nd (Oxfordshire) Light Infantry
    2nd Battalion, 73rd Regiment
    Rifle Battalion[4]

First Brigade: *Major General John Skerrett*
    2nd Battalion, 37th (North Hampshire) Regiment
    2nd Battalion, 44th (East Essex) Regiment
    55th (Westmoreland) Regiment

1. Torrens to Bunbury, 30 December 1813, TNA, WO1/198, p. 55.
2. Wallmoden to Graham, 18 January 1814, TNA, WO1/199, p. 509.
3. See 'Cantonments of the Army under General Sir Thomas Graham', dated 27 December 1813, TNA, WO1/199, p. 245.
4. The Rifle Battalion comprised Fullarton's and Kent's companies 3/95th, Glass's company of the 1/95th, and Eeles's company 2/95th. It was commanded from January 1814 by Brevet Lt Col Cameron of the 1/95th. Cope, Sir William H., *The History of the Rifle Brigade (The Prince Consort's Own) Formerly the 95th* (London: Chatto & Windus, 1877), pp. 175–9.

2nd Battalion, 69th (South Lincolnshire) Regiment
1st Royal Veteran Battalion

Second Brigade: *Major General Samuel Gibbs*
2nd Battalion, 25th (King's Own Borderers)
33rd (1st West Riding) Regiment
54th (West Norfolk) Regiment
3rd Battalion, 56th (West Essex) Regiment

Royal Artillery: *Lieutenant Colonel Sir George Wood*
Rogers's Brigade (2nd Company, 3rd Battalion)
Truscot's Brigade (5th Company, 3rd Battalion)
Fyers's Brigade (9th Company, 3rd Battalion)
Tyler's Brigade (6th Company, 5th Battalion)
Hawker's Brigade (4th Company, 9th Battalion)[1]

In addition to these units, there were detachments of Royal Engineers and Royal Sappers and Miners – for details of which see the letters of Lieutenant Colonel Carmichael Smyth in this work – and of the Royal Waggon Train.

To some extent, this organisation was a product of circumstances, since the 2/73rd was found on landing to be in poor health and was therefore left to garrison Willemstad during the earliest operations. Meanwhile, the 2/37th and 3/56th had been misdirected to Scheveningen when the rest of the army entered the Scheldt, and took some time to re-join. When they did arrive, the 2/37th relieved the 2/73rd at Willemstad – making its assignment to Skerrett rather nominal – and the other battalions were assigned as above. Although still recovering its fitness, the 2/73rd had at least seen action at Göhrde earlier in the year: this baptism of fire may explain why it was ultimately posted to the Light

1. For individual units, see Duncan, Francis, *History of the Royal Regiment of Artillery* (London: John Murray, 1879). Service histories in these volumes do not list Fyers's Brigade as present in the Netherlands until 1815, but Graham explicitly mentions that unit in a dispatch of 14 January 1814 and Anon., *British Minor Expeditions 1746 to 1814* (London: HMSO, 1884), does state five companies as present in December 1813 whereas Duncan only gives four; it would therefore seem reasonable to conclude that Fyers's was the fifth company present from the outset.

Brigade, which seems to have been assigned the pick of Graham's line infantry to bulk up the small numbers of genuine 'light bobs' provided by the 52nd Light Infantry and 95th Rifles.

Reinforcements, Reorganisation, and the First Attack on Antwerp

The above organisation was almost immediately supplemented by the arrival of the 2nd KGL Hussars on 27 December, and subsequently by the reinforcements from Leith, the 2/21st and 2/78th, which joined on 10 January 1814. The 2/21st was nominally assigned to the First Brigade, displacing the 1st Royal Veteran Battalion, which went into garrison, and the 2/78th was posted as a reinforcement to the Second Brigade. In reality, however, the 2/21st also assumed a garrison role, so that the only actual reinforcement for the field force was the 2/78th. Concurrent with the arrival of these reinforcements, the army as a whole assumed a divisional organisation, with Cooke and Mackenzie commanding the First and Second Divisions respectively. Cooke was replaced at the head of the Guards Brigade by Captain and Lieutenant Colonel John, Lord Proby, of the 1st Foot Guards, who was appointed a colonel on the staff. To replace Mackenzie at the head of the Light Brigade, Gibbs was moved across from the Second Brigade, and was in turn scheduled to be replaced by Major General Herbert Taylor. However, before Taylor could take up this post Major General Skerrett was injured in a fall from his horse and could not take part in the initial advance on Antwerp. Taylor was therefore assigned temporary command of the First Brigade pending Skerrett's recovery. Once his battalion joined the field army, Colonel John Macleod of the 2/78th took command of the Second Brigade, with command of the 2/78th passing to Lieutenant Colonel Martin Lindsay. These changes creating the following order of battle, which was in force during the first series of operations against Antwerp.[1]

---

1. Unit strengths given are effective rank and file, using data for 25 December for those units present in the theatre on that date, and for 25 January for the late arrivals.

Commander of Forces:	*General Sir Thomas Graham*	
First Division:	*Major General George Cooke*	
Guards Brigade:	*Colonel Lord Proby*	
2nd Battalion, 1st Foot Guards		(696)
2nd Battalion, Coldstream Guards		(490)
2nd Battalion, 3rd Foot Guards		(509)
First Brigade:	*Major General Herbert Taylor*[1]	
2nd Battalion, 44th (East Essex) Regiment		(406)
55th (Westmoreland) Regiment		(340)
2nd Battalion, 69th (South Lincolnshire) Regiment		(487)
Divisional Artillery		
Rogers's Brigade		
Second Division:	*Major General Kenneth Mackenzie*	
Light Brigade:	*Major General Samuel Gibbs*	
2nd Battalion, 35th (Sussex) Regiment		(453)
2nd Battalion, 52nd (Oxfordshire) Light Infantry		(191)
2nd Battalion, 73rd Regiment		(402)
Rifle Battalion		(287)
Second Brigade:	*Colonel John Macleod*[2]	
2nd Battalion, 25th (King's Own Borderers)		(316)
33rd (1st West Riding) Regiment		(502)
54th (West Norfolk) Regiment		(395)
3rd Battalion, 56th (West Essex) Regiment		(262)
2nd Battalion, 78th (Highland) Regiment		(301)[3]
Divisional Artillery		
Fyers's Brigade[4]		

1. Replacing Maj. Gen. Skerrett, injured in a fall from his horse.
2. Of the 2/78th, replacing Taylor temporarily reassigned to the First Brigade.
3. Strength calculated by adding 25 January strength of 262 rank and file to the 39 casualties at suffered at First Merxem.
4. Duncan, *Royal Regiment of Artillery*, Vol. I, p. 223, only gives Rogers's Brigade as present at Merxem, Graham specifically notes that Fyers's was attached to the Second Division there, leading to the assignments conjectured as per this order of battle. For want of other information it is inferred that these divisional assignments remained in force for the rest of the campaign; certainly, these seem to have been the only batteries equipped for field service.

Cavalry: *Lieutenant Colonel Baron Linsingen*
          2nd King's German Legion Hussars   (451, with 517 horses)

Left in Garrison
          2nd Battalion, 21st (Royal North British) Fusiliers   (174)
          2nd Battalion, 37th (North Hampshire) Regiment   (279)
          1st Royal Veteran Battalion   (459)

Unassigned Artillery: *Lieutenant Colonel Sir George Wood*
          Truscot's Brigade
          Tyler's Brigade
          Hawker's Brigade

Colonel Macleod was wounded during the first attack on Merxem, 'but did not quit command of the brigade till he became weak from loss of blood'.[1] He was replaced by Lieutenant Colonel John Brown of the 3/56th. It is not clear whether Brown also commanded prior to Macleod's arrival, or if – as seems likely – Gibbs initially remained with his old brigade until the 2/78th joined, with Mackenzie retaining personal command of the Light Brigade in the early stages of the operations, whilst also commanding the Second Division as a whole.

Further Reorganisation, and the Second Attack on Antwerp

Although there was no reinforcement of Graham's army in the interval between the two Antwerp operations, a limited reorganisation nevertheless took place, with the 2/35th moving from the Light Brigade to the Second in exchange for the 2/25th and 54th. Two of the rifle companies may also have been attached to the Second Brigade during the advance on Antwerp, but all four were operating as a battalion again at Second Merxem. Skerrett, recovered from his fall, resumed command of the First Brigade, which was joined by the flank companies of the 2/21st and 2/37th; the 2/44th, which had temporarily been detached to reinforce the garrison at Tholen, also re-joined the brigade before the second advance on Antwerp. Skerrett's return to duty in turn released Taylor to command the Second Brigade as originally planned, replacing Brown. During the night immediately prior to the second attack on Merxem,

---

1. Graham to Bathurst, 14 January 1814, in Delavoye, Alex. M., *Life of Thomas Graham, Lord Lynedoch* (London: Richardson, 1880), pp. 703–5.

Mackenzie was injured after falling from his horse. He was relieved by Gibbs, with Lieutenant Colonel William George Harris of the 2/73rd stepping up to take temporary command of the Light Brigade.[1] This final set of changes produced the following order of battle for Second Merxem and the subsequent operations against Antwerp.[2]

Commander of Forces:	*General Sir Thomas Graham*	
First Division:	*Major General George Cooke*	
Guards Brigade:	*Colonel Lord Proby*	
2nd Battalion, 1st Foot Guards		(708)
2nd Battalion, Coldstream Guards		(479)
2nd Battalion, 3rd Foot Guards		(499)
First Brigade:	*Major General John Skerrett*	
2nd Battalion, 44th (East Essex) Regiment		(399)
55th (Westmoreland) Regiment		(295)
2nd Battalion, 69th (South Lincolnshire) Regiment		(433)
Flank Companies, 2/21st and 2/37th		(264)[3]
Divisional Artillery		
Rogers's Brigade		
Second Division:	*Major General Samuel Gibbs*[4]	
Light Brigade:	*Lieutenant Colonel W. G. Harris*[5]	
2nd Battalion, 25th (King's Own Borderers)		(319)
2nd Battalion, 52nd (Oxfordshire) Light Infantry		(185)
54th (West Norfolk) Regiment		(439)
2nd Battalion, 73rd Regiment		(474)
Rifle Battalion		(255)

1. Graham to Bathurst, 6 February 1814, in Delavoye, *Graham*, pp. 707–10.
2. Strengths are effective rank and file, from Monthly Return of 25 January 1814 in TNA, WO17/1773.
3. Calculated based on numbers of men returned as 'on command' by these two battalions; actual figure may have been lower if detached men from the centre companies were also listed under this heading. Whilst it would at first glance appear that the number for the combined flank companies is disproportionally high relative to the strength of the two battalions, it should be understood that neither was fielding a full complement of eight centre companies.
4. Replacing Maj. Gen. Mackenzie.
5. Replacing Maj. Gen. Gibbs.

Second Brigade: *Major General Herbert Taylor*
    33rd (1st West Riding) Regiment   (502)
    2nd Battalion, 35th (Sussex) Regiment   (432)
    3rd Battalion, 56th (West Essex) Regiment   (255)
    2nd Battalion, 78th (Highland) Regiment   (262)
Divisional Artillery
    Fyers's Brigade
Cavalry: *Lieutenant Colonel Baron Linsingen*
    2nd King's German Legion Hussars   (451, with 517 horses)
In Garrison
    Centre Companies, 2/21st (Royal N. British) Fusiliers   (107)
    Centre Companies, 2/37th (N. Hampshire) Regiment   (179)
    1st Royal Veteran Battalion   (330, plus 131 detached)
Unassigned Artillery: *Lieutenant Colonel Sir George Wood*
    Truscot's Brigade
    Tyler's Brigade
    Hawker's Brigade

With Merxem captured, the siege train could be brought up and the bombardment opened, but, as the following listing of the ordnance employed on each of the three days makes clear, this operation was severely hampered by the poor quality of the majority of the weapons employed. As a result of failures either of the pieces themselves, or of their carriages, the weight of fire that could be brought to bear was never as substantial as had been hoped.[1]

Ordnance Employed on 3 February 1814

English Ordnance   Four 10-inch mortars
                        Two 8-inch howitzers
                        Six 24-pounders
Dutch Ordnance   Three 12-inch Gomer mortars
                        Four 11-inch mortars
                        Six 7½-inch mortars

    Total, twenty-five pieces

1. As detailed in Graham to Bathurst, 6 February 1814, TNA, WO1/199, pp. 569–78.

Ordnance Employed on 4 February 1814

English Ordnance	Four 10-inch mortars
	Two 8-inch howitzers
	Six 24-pounders
Dutch Ordnance	Three 12-inch Gomer mortars
	Two 7½-inch mortars

Total, seventeen pieces

Ordnance Employed on 5 February 1814

English Ordnance	Two 10-inch mortars
	Two 8-inch howitzers
	Three 24-pounders
Dutch Ordnance	Three 12-inch Gomer mortars
	Six 7½-inch mortars (without beds)

Total, eighteen pieces

Further Reinforcements and Reorganisation

Major General Taylor left the army on 22 February, having been recalled to take up his duties at court as Private Secretary to Queen Charlotte. Lieutenant Colonel Brown of the 3/56th again assumed command of the Second Brigade, until Mackenzie was fit to return to duty in early March. Upon Mackenzie's return Gibbs reverted from divisional command to commanding the Light Brigade, but until this happened the Second Division was left with Gibbs as its only general officer.[1] In early February further reinforcements arrived in the shape of the 2/30th and 2/81st from Jersey, along with the 4/1st and 2/91st which had marched overland from Germany under Brigadier General Arthur Gore. Gore, late commanding officer of the 33rd until his promotion the previous year, had been left in command at Stralsund after the departure of Gibbs. The two battalions from Jersey were assigned to the Second Division, going to the Light and Second Brigades respectively; the two battalions from Stralsund remained as an independent brigade under Gore. This brigade does not seem to have been assigned to either division: although it operated with the First Division, Graham

1. See 'Description of the Troops under the command of his excellency General Sir Thomas Graham KB', TNA, WO1/658, p. 567.

still speaks of it as an independent entity in his dispatch of 10 March 1814.[1] Gore also brought with him nine men detached from those units brought from Stralsund by Gibbs, and '100 foreign recruits for the 33rd Regiment'.[2] The arrival of these reinforcements, and the changes in command already noted, created the following order of battle for mid–late February, during which time Graham had the majority of his troops concentrated to the rear to prepare for the eventuality of a French counter-attack into the Low Countries whilst leaving the Second Division to observe Antwerp.[3]

Commander of Forces: *General Sir Thomas Graham*
First Division: *Major General George Cooke*
   Guards Brigade: *Colonel Lord Proby*
      2nd Battalion, 1st Foot Guards   (692)
      2nd Battalion, Coldstream Guards   (546)
      2nd Battalion, 3rd Foot Guards   (601)
   First Brigade: *Major General John Skerrett*
      2nd Battalion, 44th (East Essex) Regiment   (300)
      55th (Westmoreland) Regiment   (272)
      2nd Battalion, 69th (South Lincolnshire) Regiment (416)
      Flank Companies, 2/21st and 2/37th   (326)[4]
   Divisional Artillery
   Rogers's Brigade

Second Division: *Major General Samuel Gibbs*
   Light Brigade: *Lieutenant Colonel W. G. Harris*
      2nd Battalion, 25th (King's Own Borderers)   (311)
      2nd Battalion, 30th (Cambridgeshire) Regiment   (449)
      2nd Battalion, 52nd (Oxfordshire) Light Infantry   (171)
      54th (West Norfolk) Regiment   (401)
      2nd Battalion, 73rd Regiment   (417)
      Rifle Battalion   (242)

1. Printed in *The Times*, London, 15 March 1814.
2. See return of Gore's Brigade, dated Breda, 28 February 1814, TNA, WO1/200, p. 37.
3. Derived from Table of Cantonments for 10 February 1814, TNA, WO1/199, p. 613; strengths from return of 25 February 1814 TNA, WO17/1773.
4. Calculated as above, with the same caveat applying.

Second Brigade: *Lieutenant Colonel John Brown*
    33rd (1st West Riding) Regiment   (348)
    2nd Battalion, 35th (Sussex) Regiment   (413)
    3rd Battalion, 56th (West Essex) Regiment   (223)
    2nd Battalion, 78th (Highland) Regiment   (257)
    2nd Battalion, 81st Regiment   (351)
Divisional Artillery
    Fyers's Brigade

Independent Brigade: *Brigadier General Arthur Gore*
    4th Battalion, 1st (Royal Scots) Regiment   (729)[1]
    2nd Battalion, 91st   (442)

Cavalry: *Lieutenant Colonel Baron Linsingen*
    2nd KGL Hussars   (393, plus 69 detached, with 517 horses)

In Garrison
    1st Royal Veteran Battalion   (292, plus 131 detached)
    Centre Companies, 2/21st (Royal N. British) Fusiliers   (157)
    Centre Companies, 2/37th (N. Hampshire) Regiment   (119)

Unassigned Artillery: *Lieutenant Colonel Sir George Wood*
    Truscot's Brigade
    Tyler's Brigade
    Hawker's Brigade

Later in February the reinforcements from Wallmoden's corps finally arrived. Despite the arrival of the 3rd KGL Hussars, no cavalry brigade was formed and the regiment operated independently under its commander, Lieutenant Colonel Lewis Meyer. For want of information to the contrary, it is assumed that artillery assignments remained unchanged.

The Attack on Bergen-op-Zoom

On 8 March 1814, Graham launched his attack on the fortress of Bergen-op-Zoom, using forces drawn from the First Division and Gore's independent brigade, plus the 33rd from the Second Division. Other

---

1. This unit had no fewer than 209 men sick at the time of the return, not included here and amounting to 22% of the battalion's strength.

units from the Second Division were also pulled back from the outposts to be on hand if needed, and, indeed, the 2/35th arrived outside Bergen-op-Zoom on the morning of the 9th, just in time to cover the escape of the last British troops to extricate themselves from the fortress after the failure of the storm. Sources that indicate that these battalions were formally transferred from the Second Division to the First are incorrect, but it is conceivable that the 33rd, Gore's old battalion, was slated to join the brigade commanded by that officer, which was otherwise rather weak. If this was the case, these plans were overtaken by events and in the immediate aftermath of the fighting the 33rd resumed its place in the Second Division.

The need to provide a number of storming parties for three genuine attacks and an additional feint or false attack, meant that the established organisation of the brigades involved was largely broken up, creating the organisation given below. Unit strengths are all taken from those given by Graham in his dispatch.[1] Although round numbers, they may not be far off the actual figures since it would seem that in most cases the forces committed to the storm were picked detachments rather than entire units; only the battalions assigned a supporting role seem to have gone in at full strength.

Commander of Forces: *General Sir Thomas Graham*

Commander of Assault: *Major General George Cooke*
    Left Attack: *Colonel Lord Proby*[2]

        Foot Guards Detachments   600 (Storming Party)
        Foot Guards Detachments   400 (Supports)

    Centre Attack: *Lieutenant Colonel Charles Morrice, 2/69th*
        55th   250 (Storming Party)
        2/69th   350 (Storming Party)
        33rd   600 (Supports)

1. Dispatch of 10 March 1814, printed in *The Times*, London, 15 March 1814; see also Anon., *Minor Expeditions*, pp. 84–5.
2. Proby's command consisted of the flank companies of all three Foot Guards battalions, plus detachments from their centre companies.

Right Attack: *Lieutenant Colonel Hon. George Carleton, 2/44th*
   2/44th   300 (Storming Party)
   Flank Coys, 2/21st and 2/37th   200 (Storming Party)
   4/1st   600 (Supports)[1]

False Attack: *Lieutenant Colonel Benjamin Ottley, 2/91st*
   Centre Companies, 2/21st   100
   Centre Companies, 2/37th   150
   2/91st   400[2]

Major General Cooke accompanied the Left Attack; Major General Skerrett and Brigadier General Gore the Right Attack. Each column had a detachment of the Royal Sappers and Miners with Carmichael Smyth, in command, accompanying the Left Attack. Graham's figures give a total attacking force of 3,950 rank and file.

It will be noted that this order of battle differs from that given in all secondary sources published prior to *A Bold and Ambitious Enterprise* in that it assigns command of the False Attack to Ottley rather than Brevet Lieutenant Colonel Robert Henry of the 2/21st. Henry is named by Graham in his dispatch as the officer who held this command, but this stems from his apparent failure to allow for the last-minute changes that added Ottley's 2/91st to the False Attack. It would seem that centre companies of the 4/1st and 2/91st were not originally intended to participate in the operation, with only their flank companies being assigned to the Right Attack. This was then changed on the evening of the storm, with the assignments being changed to those given as above. Since Ottley outranked Henry, he naturally assumed command of the False Attack.[3]

The operation failed with heavy losses, Major General Skerrett, Brigadier General Gore, and Lieutenant Colonel Carleton being amongst the killed. Since Skerrett was responsible for the False and Right Attacks, and Gore was ordinarily the brigade commander of

1. Eyewitness accounts would suggest that the flank companies of this battalion joined those of the 2/21st and 2/37th as part of the Storming Party.
2. Some accounts suggest that the flank companies of this battalion may also have been detached.
3. For more detail, see Bamford, *Bold and Ambitious Enterprise*, pp. 185–6.

the 4/1st and 2/91st, it is easy to see how Graham failed to pick up on the change of command in the False Attack; the more so since both Ottley and Henry were also wounded during the fighting. Cooke was taken prisoner and Morrice wounded; only Proby remained free and unwounded out of those officers who had been assigned command roles. Total casualties amounted to 3,183 all ranks, the bulk of these being prisoners. The distribution of casualties by type and rank was initially reported as follows:[1]

	Killed		Wounded		Missing	
	Officers	*R&F*	*Officers*	*R&F*	*Officers*	*R&F*
Royal Artillery	0	0	1	0	0	0
Royal Engineers	0	0	1	0	0	0
Sappers & Miners	1	7	0	11	0	9
2/1st Foot Guards	2	20	0	16	9	275
2/Coldstream Guards	0	2	1	6	0	33
2/3rd Foot Guards	1	7	1	39	1	35
4/1st	3	38	5	70	17	519
2/21st	0	37	9	76	0	98
33rd	0	36	10	57	0	49
2/37th	1	70	5	44	0	79
2/44th	2	104	11	86	4	135
55th	0	5	6	31	7	62
2/69th	1	8	4	23	2	89
2/91st	0	36	3	20	10	202
Totals	11	370	57	479	50	1,585

The above figures come from 'Return of Killed Wounded and Missing of the Army under the Command of His Excellency General Sir Thomas Graham KB in the attack upon Bergen op Zoom by storm on the Night of the 8th and Morning of the 9th March 1814'. The accompanying 'List of Officers Killed Wounded and Missing' additionally lists one officer killed, five wounded, and two missing from the staff of the army.[2] Missing, in this context, equates to prisoners of war although when the final count was complete the total of prisoners came

1. Data from Anon., *Minor Expeditions*, p. 87.
2. TNA, WO1/200, p. 211217.

out at 1 major general, 4 lieutenant colonels, 2 majors, 20 captains, 62 subalterns, 4 surgeons, 93 sergeants and 1,872 rank and file, for a total of 2,058 all ranks.[1] The men taken prisoner were returned on parole, with the exception of three officers and 119 men exchanged immediately for French prisoners taken by Graham's forces; it is unclear whether or not this last group are included in the figures for prisoners given above.[2]

Reorganisation after Bergen-op-Zoom

The failure to capture Bergen-op-Zoom left Graham with his army badly reduced and its command structure gutted. Having borne the brunt of the losses, the brigades previously under Gore and Skerrett were combined, the former being incorporated into the latter as part of the First Division. Graham then authorised the reorganisation of the effective line infantry of the First Division into two provisional battalions, this organisation becoming effective as of 28 March. The First Provisional Battalion comprised the 4/1st, 2/69th, and 2/91st, and the Second the 2/21st, 2/37th, 2/44th, and 55th. To command the brigade formed from these units, Graham appointed Brevet Lieutenant Colonel Robert Crawford, whose regimental rank was that of captain in the 73rd.[3] Pending the release from parole of Cooke, and the arrival of replacement general officers from home, Gibbs took over the First Division, Lieutenant Colonel Harris again having the Light Brigade. Proby was granted a month's leave to take effect from 25 March, being replaced as brigade commander by Captain and Lieutenant Colonel Francis Hepburn, 1st Foot Guards. By the end of March, the organisation of the army as a whole therefore worked out as follows:[4]

1. 'State of English Prisoners included in the Capitulation', TNA, WO1/200, p. 223.
2. Anon., *Minor Expeditions*, p. 88.
3. Philippart, John, *The Royal Military Calendar or Army Service and Commission Book* (London: A. J. Valpy, 1820), Vol. V, pp. 391–9.
4. See 'Description of the Troops under the command of his excellency General Sir Thomas Graham KB', TNA, WO1/658, p. 567; strengths from return of 25 March, TNA, WO17/1773. The departure of Proby, and identity of his replacement, are also from the latter return, and were erroneously omitted from the information given in *A Bold and Ambitious Enterprise*.

Commander of Forces: *General Sir Thomas Graham*

First Division: *Major General Samuel Gibbs*

    Guards Brigade: *Captain & Lieutenant Colonel Francis Hepburn*

        2nd Battalion, 1st Foot Guards   (503)

        2nd Battalion, Coldstream Guards   (596)

        2nd Battalion, 3rd Foot Guards   (412)

    First Brigade: *Lieutenant Colonel Robert Crawford*

        First Provisional Battalion   (572)[1]

        Second Provisional Battalion   (646)[2]

    Divisional Artillery

        Rogers's Brigade

Second Division: *Major General Kenneth Mackenzie*

    Light Brigade: *Lieutenant Colonel Harris*

        2nd Battalion, 25th (King's Own Borderers)   (295)

        2nd Battalion, 30th (Cambridgeshire) Regiment   (429)

        2nd Battalion, 52nd (Oxfordshire) Light Infantry   (165)

        54th (West Norfolk) Regiment   (419)

        2nd Battalion, 73rd Regiment   (460)

        Rifle Battalion   (227)

    Second Brigade: *Lieutenant Colonel John Brown*

        33rd (1st West Riding) Regiment   (448)

        2nd Battalion, 35th (Sussex) Regiment   (402)

        3rd Battalion, 56th (West Essex) Regiment   (234)

        2nd Battalion, 78th (Highland) Regiment   (257)

        2nd Battalion, 81st   (355)

    Divisional Artillery

        Fyers's Brigade

Cavalry: *No brigade commander*

        2nd King's German Legion Hussars   (423, with 510 horses)

        3rd King's German Legion Hussars   (620, with 683 horses)

In Garrison

        1st Royal Veteran Battalion   (141, plus 295 detached)

---

1. Comprising the 4/1st, 2/69th and 2/91st.
2. Comprising the 2/21st, 2/37th, 2/44th and 55th.

Unassigned Artillery: *Lieutenant Colonel Sir George Wood*
      Truscot's Brigade
      Tyler's Brigade
      Hawker's Brigade
      1st Troop, King's German Legion Horse Artillery
      2nd Troop, King's German Legion Horse Artillery
      2nd Rocket Troop, Royal Horse Artillery

Final Changes and Reorganisations

The priorities for Graham after Bergen-op-Zoom were replacing the manpower and command losses that had been incurred there. For political reasons, various obstacles prevented a speedy exchange of the men taken prisoner at Bergen-op-Zoom, who were not finally released from parole until early April. Even then, the men of the 4/1st were exempted from the exchange; instead the whole battalion was withdrawn from Graham's command and reassigned for duty in Canada. This took advantage of a clause in the parole agreement in which it was promised that, prior to exchange, paroled men would not serve against the French or their allies *in Europe*. Once the exchange of the paroled men had been completed the temporary organisation of the First Brigade into provisional battalions was abandoned, with the exception that the 2/21st and 2/37th were still too weak to function independently – the former, in addition, having lost all its field officers at Bergen-op-Zoom – and so continued as a combined unit for the remainder of the war.[1]

Prior to the decision being taken to go ahead with an exchange, it had been intended to reinforce Graham with the Brigade of Provisional Militia that eventually joined Wellington at Bordeaux, and, in addition, a plan was set in order to form three battalions of detachments from weak units stationed in the British Isles, which were slated to join Graham as a brigade under the command of Major General William Eden. In the event, this formation was still incomplete when the war ended, although Eden was placed on the staff in the Low Countries, and Graham had him earmarked as a new commander for the First Brigade.

1. Graham to Bathurst, 15 April 1814, TNA, WO1/200, pp. 553–7.

In the event, Eden, like his intended command, never left Britain.[1] However, Graham did obtain the services of Lieutenant General Sir Ronald Ferguson to act as his second-in-command, and Brigadier General Colin Halkett was also placed on the staff. Ferguson took command of the First Division, displacing Cooke to the Second and Mackenzie to a newly created Reserve. This last formation replaced the old Light Brigade, which disappeared from the order of battle and was replaced in the Second Division by a new Third Brigade under Halkett. The 1st Foreign Veteran Battalion was sent out to join the army. With these arrivals and changes, Graham's order of battle at the end of the war stood as follows:[2]

Commander of Forces:	*General Sir Thomas Graham*	
First Division:	*Lieutenant General Sir Ronald Ferguson*	
Guards Brigade:	*Captain & Lieutenant Colonel Francis Hepburn*[3]	
2nd Battalion, 1st Foot Guards		(633)
2nd Battalion, Coldstream Guards		(499)
2nd Battalion, 3rd Foot Guards		(527)
First Brigade:	*Lieutenant Colonel Robert Crawford*	
33rd (1st West Riding) Regiment		(486)
54th (West Norfolk) Regiment		(437)
Provisional Battalion[4]		(229)

Divisional Artillery
    Rogers's Brigade

1. On the battalions of detachments, see Bamford, Andrew, 'Battalions of Detachments in 1814 – the Duke of York Responds to Britain's Manpower Shortfall', at http://www.napoleon-series.org/military/battles/1814/c_BritishDetachments1814.html.
2. Organisation as per Graham to Bathurst, 15 April 1814, TNA, WO1/200, pp. 553–7. Unit strengths are effective rank and file, taken from Monthly Return of 25 April.
3. Proby outstayed his leave and did not resume command of his brigade until June, being again recorded as present in the return of the 25th of that month, in TNA, WO17/1773. Hepburn received a brevet promotion to full colonel as of 4 June.
4. 2/21st and 2/37th.

Second Division: *Major General George Cooke*
   Second Brigade: *Major General Samuel Gibbs*
      2nd Battalion, 25th (King's Own Borderers)   (296)
      2nd Battalion, 44th (East Essex) Regiment   (107)
      55th (Westmoreland) Regiment   (233)
      2nd Battalion, 73rd Regiment   (473)

   Third Brigade: *Brigadier General Colin Halkett*
      2nd Battalion, 35th (Sussex) Regiment   (473)
      3rd Battalion, 56th (West Essex) Regiment   (384)
      2nd Battalion, 69th (South Lincolnshire) Regiment   (210)
      2nd Battalion, 91st Regiment   (183)

  Divisional Artillery
  Fyers's Brigade

Reserve: *Major General Kenneth Mackenzie*[1]
      2nd Battalion, 30th (Cambridgeshire) Regiment   (430)
      2nd Battalion, 52nd (Oxfordshire) Light Infantry   (248)
      2nd Battalion, 78th (Highland) Regiment   (268)
      2nd Battalion, 81st Regiment   (351)
      Rifle Battalion   (260)

Cavalry: *No brigade commander*
      2nd King's German Legion Hussars   (417, with 512 horses)
      3rd King's German Legion Hussars   (590, with 632 horses)

In Garrison
      1st Royal Veteran Battalion   (228, plus 209 detached)
      1st Foreign Veteran Battalion   (167, plus 301 detached)

Unassigned Artillery: *Lieutenant Colonel Sir George Wood*
    Truscot's Brigade
    Tyler's Brigade
    Hawker's Brigade
    1st Troop, King's German Legion Horse Artillery
    2nd Troop, King's German Legion Horse Artillery
    2nd Rocket Troop, Royal Horse Artillery

---

1. Mackenzie also had a squadron of hussars and four guns of the KGL Horse Artillery under his command, but it is not specified from which units these came.

This organisation remained in force until after the closing of hostilities, with only a few small changes. Major General Victor von Alten came out in June to assume command of the cavalry.[1] In May the 1st Royal Veteran Battalion and two troops of the Royal Waggon Train were ordered home to be reduced, whilst the 55th also returned to England, 'being ord[ere]d home about a Court Martial by the Commander in Chief'.[2] Graham, or Lord Lynedoch as he had become in May, finally left the army in July, being relieved by Lieutenant General the Prince of Orange.

1. Table of Cantonments dated 30 June 1814 TNA, WO1/201, p. 13.
2. Lynedoch to Castlereagh, 30 May 1814, TNA, WO1/201, pp. 769–70; the circumstances of this court martial are detailed in Bamford, Andrew, '"Dastardly and atrocious": Lieutenant Blake, Captain Clune, and the Recall of the 55th Foot from the Netherlands, 1814', *Journal of the Society for Army Historical Research*, Autumn 2014, pp. 210–22.

Appendix II

Officers and Officership

With four of our six eyewitnesses being recently commissioned officers, all of them – if we allow Thain's service under Graham as a continuation of his time in the Baltic under Gibbs – serving overseas for the first time, it seems appropriate to draw some comparisons between these accounts and to place them in the context of prevailing ideas about officership and attitudes towards the military, its duties and responsibilities. Doing so also allows an exploration of some of the incidents described in the various eyewitness accounts, relating to how officers viewed one and other and the ways in which the commissioned elements of a battalion functioned as a body.

One thing that will have surely struck readers of the accounts of Duncombe, Shaw, Thain, and Moodie, is the extreme youth of all four officers. Duncombe, as we have seen, was gazetted an ensign before he had even left school, and Thain, if we count his time with the Militia, had made his first step towards a commission at an even younger age. None of the four had obtained any formal training as officers prior to being commissioned, although Thain's having briefly served as a volunteer with a Militia regiment – that is to say, a candidate for a commission serving as a gentleman-ranker until a free vacancy might arise – probably came to the regular service with more practical knowledge than the other three. Thereafter, though, Thain had largely to learn on the job, as did Moodie and Duncombe, although it is harder to tell from their accounts just how much practical soldiering either of the latter two had managed to pick up. Shaw, by contrast, went through the rigorous regime practised by the 52nd and several of the other light infantry corps, in which a new officer worked his way through the training necessary to do duty first as a private and then upwards through the NCO ranks until fully conversant not only with his own duties as a subaltern but also of those who would serve under him in action. It is telling that Shaw, thanks to this training, and Thain, by dint, one suspects, of hard work and application, are the two men whose accounts ring with an obvious professionalism that is largely missing from Duncombe's diary or Moodie's memoirs. Shaw, it is true, retained a boyish sense of humour into the bargain whereas Thain seems to have been an altogether more serious individual, but both were evidently competent young officers as is evidenced in particular by their each serving for a spell as acting adjutants – Thain of his battalion, Shaw of the detachment sent by the Light Brigade to help take Fort Batz. Lest we think too harshly of Duncombe's and Moodie's more cavalier attitude to their professional responsibilities, however, their youth should be taken into account as at least partly accounting for what seem like substantial lapses of duty. Duncombe, in later civilian life, evidently matured considerably, and no doubt would have done so just as well had he chosen to continue in a military career. That said, some of their shenanigans – Moodie's absence from his station at Bergen-op-Zoom in particular, but also Duncombe's thoughtless treatment of his men on occasion – suggest a lack of the leadership, discipline and supervision needed from above in order to shape such callow youths into useful officers. Instead, one feels, these young officers were left too much to their own devices, without useful instruction. This might be expected in the 2/21st, understrength and rushed on service at short notice, but is rather more surprising in the case of Duncombe, whose battalion contained a substantial number of Peninsular veterans amongst its officers.

That Thain in particular sought to become master of his profession despite his youth marks him out – and would probably do so even without the additional evidence of his family circumstances – as one of a growing body of professional officers for whom military service was a career and an end in itself rather than a suitable occupation for a gentleman in a time of war, and/or a springboard to higher things. Moodie, too, would no doubt have continued a peacetime career if he could have done, although one cannot help but think that he would have needed to buck up some of his ideas if he wanted to make a success of it. Shaw, equally unable to progress in the British Army, took service overseas instead. Duncombe alone is representative of the older mind-set, for whom military service was a brief interlude before setting out on a political career. Thain, on the other hand, needed to make the Army his life and establish himself in a secure footing from which a successful future military career could develop. Such career officers can be seen back through the eighteenth century and beyond, in some manner the equivalent of the Royal Navy's 'tarpaulin officers', and the sort of reliable men who could be counted upon to do their duty day in and day out, but who lacked the connections to rise beyond field rank. If, as was the case for Thain, this meant accepting peacetime service in the potentially deadly West Indies, or the decidedly unfashionable India, then so be it; there was, in truth, no real alternative. The closest Thain seems ever to have had to a patron or protector was his commanding officer from the 33rd, William Elphinstone, and, alas, it was Elphinstone's incompetence as a general officer that eventually proved fatal for the pair of them.

Another such career officer seems to have been the irascible Major Evatt at Willemstad, who had managed the rare feat of making it from private to field rank – albeit by brevet – and who proved such a bane to Shaw and his comrades. The officers of the 2/52nd were not alone in feeling the rough edge of his tongue, and another eyewitness left his own opinions of the same officer. This was Neville McCready, not strictly an officer at the time, but someone who, as a volunteer attempting to earn a free commission through meritorious service in the ranks, was very much of the same class and mind-set as his commissioned counterparts in these pages. Of his experience at Willemstad he wrote:

> This town, which had been fortified by the enemy, now served as a depot for our stores and a hospital for our sick and wounded. It was well built and fortified. Major Evatt, 55th Regt., was Commandant, and appeared to exercise his authority in a style which caused him to be disliked by all and insulted by a large proportion of the officers of his garrison. He had risen from the ranks and was one of the strongest proofs that good clerks or brutally severe Sergt. Majors seldom become amiable or respectable officers. They labour under an evident inferiority of manners and ideas, and affect to elevate themselves by a domineering severity. They ought to be promoted, but they should form regiments by themselves – honourable bands of veterans whose habits and associations would be such as they had been accustomed to and such as they could enjoy – infinitely more revered and esteemed than in their present state, as the failings which are now too truly adduced against them

would, amongst themselves, pass unnoticed, or more probably
would never have existed.[1]

Quite evidently, a considerable element of social snobbery still prevailed, and would continue to blight officer attitudes to one extent or
another for decades to come. Duncombe's obvious contempt for any
officer outside of the Guards is, in similar fashion, an obvious strand
running through his diary of the campaign.

Such officers, however they might be perceived socially, had at least
obtained their commission and subsequent promotions through merit
and service, much as Thain himself would go on to do in due course. Far
less palatable still than having to serve with a perceived social inferior
was having an officer – any officer – put in over one's head, and it is for
this reason that Thain, no doubt along with the rest of the 33rd's ensigns,
was aghast at the arrival of Lieutenants Oliver and Oddie when the two
men joined the 33rd from the Militia. The concept that brought these
two men into the line in return for persuading sufficient of their men
to volunteer with them, was a sound enough one from the perspective
of a government seeking to maximise the effective use of a dwindling
reserve of manpower, but it served as a block on the promotion of regular
officers of longer service but lower rank. Under ordinary circumstances,
the next two free lieutenancies to become vacant in the 33rd would have
gone to the two senior ensigns; now, with Oliver and Oddie attached
as supernumeraries, they would benefit instead and the promotion of
the regiment's existing ensigns be delayed. The arguments against
this case, here applied with reference to Militia captains blocking the
promotion of deserving lieutenants were put by one styling himself
'Achilles' in a letter to the editor of the *Royal Military Panorama*, dated
4 February 1814, of which the following is an extract:

> I am well persuaded government meant not to *injure* officers of
> the line when they framed that part of the late act of parliament,
> allowing officers of the Militia, with the rank of Captain, to go into
> regiments of the line *with the same rank* as they held in the Militia;
> and I am aware it was a case of urgent necessity, as the men were to
> be got at every risk of temporary inconvenience to the service; yet
> it is, in its very nature, so inimical to the interests, and those the

1. NAM 6807-209: Journal of Edward Nevil McCready, Chapter II.

best interests, of the officers of regulars, that I am sure they never can be subjected to the evils and mortification thus entailed on them, without meeting with that protection and redress from the Royal Commander-in-Chief their case seems so urgently to call for. In many regiments of the line, which have served in the Peninsula for four or five years past, two, three, or four Militia Captains are thrust in as *supernumeraries*; by bringing men for the regiment, when vacancies occur, the eldest Lieutenants, who have probably served with it during all its hard service in the field, and are probably as *one* out of *three* of their companions who landed with them, are *thus* excluded, for a considerable time, from *that* promotion they have looked forward to and *deserved*; this is a peculiarly hard case, and it is universally and acutely felt throughout the army: and as necessity, and nothing else, could at all justify the incorporation of Militia Captains with those of the regulars, certainly government *ought* to correct the mischief by the only means now in their power, viz. to continue the promotion in the army on *death* vacancies, without adverting to supernumeraries *until* peace takes place. Perhaps I may be told there has been already unprecedented promotion in those regiments; if so, I ask to what is this owing? it is in consequence of unprecedented Casualties in the field – of continued fighting, hardships, and severe service; and are the residue of these brave officers, who have now become seniors on the list of Lieutenants, are they to be thus thrown out of their turn of promotion for a length of time, perhaps, and can they think themselves treated as gallant soldiers, who have bled, perhaps, and fought so long for their king and country ought to be? The answer is obvious: and I assert, without fear of contradiction, that for one of these veterans, tried, and experienced Lieuts. who leave the service in disgust (for who that can will not do so), a dozen Militia Captains will not be equivalent to this loss. I mean no disparagement to the Militia, far from it; but they cannot be equal in the field, for some time, to officers of the line, accustomed to action and every kind of service. It is perhaps determined on to continue the promotion as heretofore, without waiting until the present supernumeraries become *fixtures* in the regiments of the line. I trust this is the case: that it will bring some additional expence [*sic*] on the country, I allow; but, heavily burthened as it is, surely the extreme injustice which a contrary line of policy would entail on the Senior Subalterns of the British army, renders it necessary it should be submitted to, rather than the promotion of such meritorious men, or the sinews of the army [be] stopped for any length of time. I hope this matter will be viewed in the same light by the Royal Commander-in-Chief, who is constantly disposed to promote the good of the service and the welfare of the officers, than whom, no class of men are surely more deserving of *all* the advantages fortune throws in their way – they in general earn them dearly.[1]

Lastly, considering the comments made above about a lack of sufficient higher leadership as a contributory factor to the sometimes less-than-professional conduct of Duncombe and Thain, it is also instructive to look in a little more detail at the case mentioned by Thain relating to the eventual court martial of Captain Edward Fitzpatrick of the 33rd. The charges brought against Fitzpatrick related to drunkenness during the operations against Antwerp, with the deliberations and outcome of the resulting court martial being detailed as follows:

Horse Guards, 7 July, 1814. At a General Court Martial, held at Schild,[2] in Holland, on the 25th April, 1814, and continued by adjournments to the 27th of the same month, Captain Edward Fitzpatrick, of the 33d Regiment of Foot, was arraigned upon the undermentioned charges, viz.

1st. For conduct highly unbecoming the character of an Officer and a Gentleman, in appearing in a state of intoxication on the public parade, or place of assembly of the 33d Regiment, on the evening of the 5th of February last, when that regiment was preparing to go into the trenches, under St. Ferdinand's Dyke, and in front of the enemy.

2d. For conduct highly unbecoming the character of an Officer and a Gentleman, and prejudicial to His Majesty's service, in being drunk upon duty, on the evening of the 19th of February last, and for having joined with a reinforcement, when in a state of absolute intoxication, on the out-lying

1. 'Achilles', 'Further Observations on the Bill for rendering the Militia disposable for Foreign Service', *The Royal Military Panorama, or Officer's Companion*, Vol. III (1813–14), pp. 550–2; see also ibid., pp. 362–72.
2. Schilde, now an eastern suburb of Antwerp.

picquet, under the command of Captain Haigh, of the 33d Regiment, on the evening abovementioned.

Upon which charges the Court came to the following decision:

The Court, having maturely and deliberately considered the evidence in prosecution, as well as what the prisoner has adduced in his defence, are of opinion, with respect to the 1st charge, that the prisoner is Guilty.

With respect to the 2d charge, the Court are of opinion that he is Guilty, with the exception of its being an in-lying, instead of an out-lying picquet.

The Court having found the prisoner, Captain Edward Fitzpatrick, Guilty of both charges, do sentence him to be cashiered.

In consideration of the long services of the prisoner, and the very high character he has received as an Officer, the Court beg leave to recommend him, in the strongest manner, to the clemency of His Royal Highness the Prince Regent.

His Royal Highness the Prince Regent has been pleased, in the name and on the behalf of His Majesty, to approve and confirm the finding and Sentence of the Court; and the Commander in Chief directs, that the foregoing charges, preferred against Captain Edward Fitzpatrick, of the 33d Regiment, together with the finding and Sentence of the Court, shall be read at the head of every corps, and entered in the general order book.

By command of H.R.H. the Commander in Chief.

HARRY CALVERT, Adj. Gen.[1]

On the face of it, a just sentence for a serious transgression of duty. The point, of course, was that whilst it was bad enough for an officer to be drunk on duty, and be incapable of serving effectively, the discipline of the whole battalion was undermined as a result. How, after all, could the men be expected to stay sober with such an example, and how, too, could any officer of the 33rd discipline a man for drunkenness when a fellow officer went unpunished? In passing, it must be remembered here that the 33rd had long served in India prior to its recall to Britain in 1812, and a culture of heavy drinking was decidedly pronounced on the subcontinent at this time, to the detriment of good order and discipline alike.

1. Quoted in James, C., *A Collection of the Charges, Opinions, and Sentences of General Courts Martial* (London: T. Egerton, 1820), p. 634.

Yet, the fact that this case only came to a court of inquiry and then to court martial because of the trouble-making of Lieutenant Beauclerk suggests that more was going on here than meets the eye. Evidently, the senior officers of the 33rd had elected to deal with the matter internally rather than bring the whole battalion into disrepute by having one of its officers publicly tried. Regimental pride and identity meant that there was a need for a balance between maintaining internal order and maintaining the wider reputation of the unit. That Fitzpatrick's transgression had, until Beauclerk's intervention, been dealt with within the regiment does not need to be taken as evidence that his conduct was condoned, but rather, perhaps, that his fellow officers – like the court in their appeal for clemency – recognised a passing error by an otherwise competent officer. It is easy to conceive that matters were originally allowed to rest in return for a promise of future good behaviour and, indeed, we have evidence of similar solutions being applied to transgressions by otherwise-respected officers in other regiments. Considering that Fitzpatrick had been drunk on duty on two occasions, one hopes that it was at least made clear to him that his third chance was his last, but in the event it did not matter as Beauclerk ensured that the case came to trial anyway. A cover-up, perhaps, and one in which the importance of regimental prestige surely played a part, but one that tells us much about the tensions between different conceptions of conduct, duty, and loyalty co-existing within the officer corps of this era.

Britons and Russians

Graham's campaign was one of the very small number of occasions during the Revolutionary and Napoleonic Wars when British and Russian troops fought side by side. Discounting the small British detachments – mostly from the KGL – that had fought in Germany in 1813, the last major campaign to see the combined service of appreciable forces from the armies of both nations had been the ill-fated 1799 expedition to North Holland. Much since then had changed, Russia having been for some time an enemy of sorts, then an ally, then an enemy again, and finally an ally again under circumstances that did much to redress previous poor perceptions. This shift in perception came most obviously through the awareness in Britain of the epic campaign fought by the Russian Army in the defence of its homeland in 1812, and the nation's subsequent major role in the 1813 German campaign. These actions were well reported in Britain, and John Philippart's book, referenced by Ensign Thain as being part of his pre-campaign reading, was only one offering that brought its readers up to date with the Russian forces and their activities.

From a reading of *Northern Campaigns*, therefore, Thain would have become well acquainted with the structure of the Russian Army, its corps and regimental organisation, its principal commanders, and its operations in the field. Philippart's study was for the most part factual, designed to familiarise his readers with 'the great and important Political and Military events on the Continent'; with that in mind it eschewed 'all party feelings, principles, or exertions', but it generally painted a picture of stoical Russian defence against French aggression and emphasised the key role that Russia's actions had had in turning the course of the war against France. 'High destinies', Philippart wrote in one of his more flowery passages, 'were prepared for [Russia] in the womb of fate; and she omitted no opportunity of calling into action every energy that she possessed to confront the danger with which she had so long been threatened; to commence a struggle, not for honour and happiness alone, but for her liberty, her religion, and her existence.'[1] Certainly, these recent events were sufficiently embedded into the British consciousness to become an obvious term of reference, with Shaw readily drawing the parallel with Napoleon's retreat from Moscow when attempting to contextualise the sufferings encountered by Graham's troops upon their first withdrawal from before Antwerp.

That said, the reality of meeting the Russians in the flesh was rather different, and the accounts contained within this work share a distaste for Russian disciplinary practices, in particular the arbitrary nature of punishments and the poor officer–men relations. The Cossacks, of course, were widely accepted as being something apart, but, even here, meeting them in the flesh evidently served to dispel any lingering romanticised perceptions of these tough but undisciplined warriors. Strict discipline was accepted by the British Army, but it was – by and large – fair discipline; for blows to be casually dispensed by Russian officers and NCOs struck against British ideas of liberty. Similarly, whilst it would be foolish to claim otherwise than that the British Army was on occasion responsible for theft and looting, the widespread and sanctioned theft by the Cossacks in particular was alien to the British military culture of the time. There was a world of difference between, for example, Corporal Meuller ensuring that he and his companion got a good feed from their temporary landlady at no charge because Meuller recognised 'the difference between Continental and British quartering', and the Russian practice of simply taking what was wanted with no intention of paying. All such incidents, therefore, as well as allowing Graham's troops to see for themselves the men who had defeated Napoleon, also allowed them to compare themselves, and for the most part favourably at that, with a foreign 'other' and thus, in their own minds, enhance their own self-image. Only when the Russian regular infantry was briefly encountered, men who were veterans of the 1812 campaign, did the opportunity for self-congratulation disappear

1. Philippart, John, *Northern Campaigns, from the Commencement of the War in 1812, to the Armistice Signed and Ratified June 4, 1813* (London: P. Martin & Co., 1813), Vol. I, pp. v–viii, 10.

and it was the British who instead found themselves the worse off by the comparison.

It is, therefore, also worth clarifying here the identity of the various Russian forces operating in the Low Countries and encountered by the various British eyewitnesses, for there were actually three distinct bodies, all of them different in their origin, command and organisation, and the way in which they were perceived differed somewhat as a result. The first of these two groups – the large number of Cossacks, and the smaller contingent of regular troops, the bulk of them forming the command of Major General Benckendorff – need little additional introduction. The regulars, in particular, had little contact with the British, as the small infantry contingent – two battalions of the Tula Infantry Regiment and one of the 2nd Jagers – was used to take Breda, and remained there in garrison thereafter: it was these troops that Carmichael Smyth and Thain saw when they visited the town, and it is interesting that Thain, who alone has anything positive to say about the Russians, did so based on these men rather than the rather different sets of troops encountered by the other eyewitnesses. A little more was seen of the single regular cavalry regiment under Benckendorff, the Pavlograd Hussars, and rather more of the Cossacks. Graham was obliged to rely on these troops for his outposts until his own cavalry were ashore, and a sorry task they made of it, albeit much hindered by the lack of a common language. All the Russian regulars, and the majority of the Cossacks, left the area soon afterwards when Benckendorff was recalled to the main allied armies in late December

The last body of troops – encountered by Moodie and Shaw, and of whom the former gives a most detailed account – were not, strictly speaking, soldiers at all but, rather, sailors, as Shaw indeed realised. That Moodie thought them soldiers is hardly surprising, however, for their officers wore a green uniform in the same style as their military counterparts, whilst the men were in a green double-breasted jacket and trousers, and a round hat.[1] Russia possessed marines as well as sailors, but these had been formed into regiments for service ashore during the 1812 campaign, hence the need to drill seamen to act as soldiers in

1. Haythornthwaite, Philip J., *The Napoleonic Source Book* (London: Arms & Armour, 1990), p. 281.

their stead. It is extremely unlikely, however, that Moodie was correct in granting them a light company; no doubt the party to which he refers by this name were merely an advance guard of some description.

It might well be wondered what these men were doing in the Low Countries at all: the answer is that they were made available at short notice to replace the detachment of Royal Marines who had taken part in the initial landings and who had been employed in coastal operations ever since. They came not, as Shaw supposed, from the Russian ships taken in the Tagus back in 1808, but rather from elements of the Russian Baltic Fleet that had taken shelter in British ports in 1812. The force initially numbered 300 men who were landed on South Beveland from the troopship HMS *Nemesis* on 3 February 1814.[1] Upon acquainting Graham of their impending arrival, Lord Bathurst informed Graham that a further 2,000 Russians were at readiness for the same service 'as soon as I shall be informed of your opinion as to the assistance which you may consider this Description of Force able to afford to you in your future operations'.[2] Graham's reply was initially favourable, although he worried about the strain that would be placed on his commissariat as a result, but Admiral Young, commanding the North Sea Fleet, considered the Russians completely undisciplined and wished to see them gone. Graham, desperate for manpower, remained uncertain, telling Bathurst that:

> If any sudden necessity of recalling the Russian Seamen had occurred the order I should suppose would have been more imperative as in the case of the Brit. Marines who were to be immediately sent back on the arrival of these Russians – had that been the case, there would be nothing to be said, except to repeat that this diminution of numbers, obliging me to detach meanwhile to replace them, would probably cripple entirely any further operations of this Corps. But I am rather inclined to suppose that the Russians are to be taken away on the ground of their being useless. I am not prepared to say whether they are deficient in discipline as Ad'l Young seem'd to think when he wrote on the 2d, before he had received any detailed report – but allowing this to

1. See Muster Book in TNA, ADM37/2464.
2. Bathurst to Graham, 28 January 1814, TNA, WO6/16, pp. 59–60.

be the case I should still think they might be disposed of so as to be very useful. We are obliged to occupy Tholen, Steenbergen & Willemstadt with considerable numbers of troops – these are of a description the least fit for bearing discipline in the field but I should consider them quite equal to the duty in South Beveland, where there might certainly be some hundred Russians left who, mix'd w'th the Marines & the troops from Garrisons of these places, would do Extremely well & I would garrison the three places above mentioned almost entirely with Russians – say 500 in each place, & 500 left in S Beveland. There is a force of 2000 usefully disposed of at once & who must be replaced by the best troops, if recall'd. I should on the contrary very much wish to have the number of Russians increased to 3000 as Your L'dship proposed because they will daily make progress in Discipline & would be at hand to assist in work in the event of undertaking a siege.[1]

Graham went on to remark that he had to rely on Young's assessment because he himself had, 'had nothing to do with the Russians – except directing a detachment sent to Tholen to be provisioned by our Commissariat like British troops'; these may well have been the men encountered by Moodie. It is unclear if the initial detachment was reinforced, but it certainly was not withdrawn either, as Shaw encountered them during the preliminary operations against Fort Batz on the very last day of the war.

1. Graham to Bathurst, 21 February 1814, TNA, WO1/199, pp. 659–62.

The Duke of Clarence and the Battles of Merxem

One of the best-known sets of stories relating to Graham's campaign in the Low Countries are those surrounding the adventures of HRH the Duke of Clarence – the future William IV – on the battlefield at Merxem. As is famously known, the Duke was found wandering amongst the allied skirmishers during the First Battle of Merxem, came so close to being wounded that he had several musket balls through his coat, and was eventually rescued from further danger by Lieutenant Thomas Austin of the 2/35th's Light Company. Further embellishments of the story – and we have already heard one of them from the account of Charles Shaw – relate that the plainly dressed Duke was mistaken for a commissary officer and that his identity was only later revealed, to the embarrassment of those concerned. There is, however, one serious problem with all this, and that problem is that HRH the Duke of Clarence was nowhere near the battlefield of First Merxem. Indeed, he was not even in the Netherlands at the time, although he would arrive there shortly afterwards, was indisputably present at the Second Battle of Merxem, and remained with the army for the subsequent operations against Antwerp. All this therefore begs the question of how these stories came about, how and why the myth evolved, and what, if any, grounding in reality the tale of royal heroics – or, if one prefers, royal foolhardiness – actually possesses. Such an investigation provides the historian with a fascinating exercise in the difficulties of working with primary-source accounts – particularly eyewitness memoirs composed after the fact – and provides a salutary lesson in unquestioning reliance on any one version of events.

The best way to trace the evolution of the myth is to analyse the various accounts in the order in which they appeared, but it is first worth clarifying just what a royal duke, whose pretensions to arms were decidedly naval rather than military, was doing accompanying a British army on campaign in the first place. Born on 21 August 1765, Prince William Henry was the third son of George III and as a young man served as an officer of the Royal Navy, commanding several small warships before obtaining the rank of rear admiral in 1789. In that year he was also created Duke of Clarence, and a year later his active naval service came to an end; this was much to his regret, and he continued to seek employment at sea, something that became increasingly unlikely due to his seniority within the naval service. His presence in the Low Countries in 1814 therefore owed at least a little to a desire to see active service, even if only as a spectator, but was also due to the parlous state of his personal finances, caused in part by the need to make a financial settlement with his former mistress, the actress Mrs Jordan, with whom he had had ten children but from whom he had separated in 1811. As well as some relief from his creditors, it seems that the Duke was spreading his net further afield in his search for a suitable – for which read wealthy – bride, a search that eventually ended with his 1818 marriage to Princess Adelaide of Saxe-Meiningen.

All the sources suggest that the Duke landed in the Netherlands on 19 January 1814. Certainly he was at Tholen on that date, as Graham was obliged to miss a meeting with Bülow in order to attend upon him, sending Major General Taylor to liaise with the Prussians in his stead.[1] Since Tholen would be an obvious point of landing, and with etiquette demanding that the commanding general greet his guest on arrival, it may safely be inferred that the Duke had then just arrived. This is confirmed by one of the anonymous *Letters from Germany and Holland*, dated Tholen, 20 January 1814, recording that 'yesterday the Duke of Clarence reached this place on his way to the Hague', and would leave that afternoon to join Graham's headquarters.[2] Graham himself informed Bathurst on 24 January that the Duke had arrived at headquarters in Oudenbosch 'three days ago', which is to say the 21st, and this date is confirmed by several of our eyewitnesses. Looking through the accounts contained in this volume, Carmichael Smyth makes no mention of the Duke at all, and neither does Moodie.

1. Taylor to Graham, 19 January 1814, in TNA, WO1/199, pp. 485–95.
2. Anon., *Letters from Germany and Holland*, pp. 107–8.

Duncombe agrees with Graham in placing his arrival with the troops in the field as 21 January, and Thain confirms his presence at a review on that date; Meuller gives no date of arrival, and Shaw's dating is suspect for reasons that will be returned to. First Merxem, it will be recalled, had been fought on 13 January; the second battle took place on 2 February.

From the outset, every opportunity was taken to praise the Duke. Thus, in the anonymous letter already cited above, it is related that the royal personage immediately made a good impression on all who saw him:

> The British officers had the honour of being introduced [to the Duke] this morning, and the authorities of the town also waited upon the Prince to congratulate his Royal Highness on his arrival in Holland. The senior Protestant Minster of the town was appointed to deliver the address, which he did very much in the style of a sermon. Among other things, he complimented the Duke on having had the *courage* to sleep within three short miles of an Enemy's garrison. Here His Royal Highness stopt the Divine, and with a benevolent smile informed the good Pastor, that *a British Prince always slept in security where he had a British soldier to guard his pillow.*

This letter forms part of a selection that was edited for publication in 1820, forming as such one of the earliest full histories of the campaign. The anonymous writer served with Gibbs in the Baltic and then under Graham in an unspecified staff role, possibly as an attached volunteer rather than in any official capacity. On several other points, the letters show indications that, even if tidied up for publication, they were not influenced in this process by other printed sources: they are, for example, one of the few accounts correctly to list Lieutenant Colonel Ottley rather than Lieutenant Colonel Henry as commanding the False Attack at Bergen-op-Zoom, thus ignoring an error perpetuated in print from Graham's own dispatch onwards. We can therefore be reasonably confident that they reflect things as the writer viewed them in 1814, and – it goes without saying – be absolutely certain that they reflect his opinion in the year of their publication. They therefore represent one of the earliest printed accounts to include elements of the Duke of Clarence story. Contained within a letter dated at Roosendaal on 10 February, and outlining the details of the second advance on Antwerp and subsequent bombardment, the writer gave a fairly extensive account of the Duke's involvement in events:

> No man amongst us shewed more anxiety [over the progress of the bombardment] or more determined bravery than His Royal Highness the Duke of Clarence, who, the moment he heard of our advance, left the Hague and joined us on the evening of the 1st at Breschat. He accompanied the advanced guard of the 1st division on the morning of the 2d, and had several very narrow escapes during the attack upon Merxem.
>
> Being on foot at the head of the column a musket ball passed through his cloak and great coat, carried off the hilt of his sword, and afterwards hit an artillery officer in the throat, but being too much weakened in force it was unable to penetrate the doublings of his silk handkerchief, though it bruised him considerably. The Prince entered Merxem with the first of the troops, and, notwithstanding the severity of the weather, did not leave it till very late in the evening. He remained from day-light till dark in the tower of the church, during the whole period of our bombardment. A bundle of straw in a farm house, at a short distance in the rear, served him for a bed during the night; and so much was his Royal Highness interested in the operations going on, that he seemed quite regardless of hunger, fatigue, or cold, all of which he suffered to as great a degree as the poorest soldier in the ranks. He is become quite the idol of our little army.[1]

Although this account lays the printed foundation for much of what came after, it does itself contain a number of problems which, taken together, suggest that the writer was relaying army gossip rather than a personal view of events. For a start, it would be mutually incompatible for the Duke to have been simultaneously at the head of the First Division and present with the lead troops going into Merxem. Merxem was taken by the Second Division: of the two brigades of Cooke's First Division, the Guards were in reserve and the First Brigade delayed in its intended southerly flanking movement by extensive inundations. Certainly, as is discussed below, the Duke did ascend Merxem's church tower once the

---

1. Anon., *Letters from Germany and Holland*, pp. 139–41.

village was captured, and in doing so certainly placed himself within range of the enemy's guns. Direct evidence for any additional heroism is, however, lacking, but that, in a sense, is not really the point. Whilst the Duke was clearly under no obligation to expose himself in action – or even, indeed, to be with the troops in the field at all – the fact that Graham's men believed him to have done so says more about their own morale and self-image than about anything else: here was this small force, operating in adverse conditions and out of the limelight of great events, yet it was graced with the presence of the King's own son. As is evident here, the Duke's presence was quickly seized upon, and his role and activities exaggerated, as part of the identity of Graham's little army. What these letters do tell us, therefore, is that exaggerated stories relating to the Duke of Clarence were current at the time, and would – it must be assumed – have been widely known across the army. Thus, later written accounts need to be viewed with the caveat in mind that their writers were very likely aware of, and their narratives influenced by, this contemporary exaggerated belief in the nature of the Duke's role in the campaign.

After this early offering, the real influx of printed material relating to the Duke's 1814 adventures came in the year that he acceded to the throne as King William IV. Thus the 1830 edition of the *United Service Journal* contained, after a précis of the new monarch's naval career, a short account entitled 'The Duke of Clarence at Merkhem in 1814 (Communicated by an Officer Present)'.[1] The author is identified only as 'P. W.', a set of initials which, if they indicate a Christian name and surname respectively, do not match those of any officer serving with Graham. Since it contains some other useful details that are of wider interest to this work, this account is reproduced in full below:

> I would not have intruded on the pages of the United Service Journal, had it not been to discharge a debt of personal gratitude to our Sovereign King William; to the King's contempt of danger I am indebted for the preservation of my life.
>
> I feel that it is a work of supererogation to speak to the members of the United Services of the courage of any individual of the

---

1. P. W., 'The Duke of Clarence at Merkhem in 1814 (Communicated by an Officer Present)', *The United Service Journal and Naval and Military Magazine* (1830, Part II), pp. 523–5.

Royal Family; now that we know more of fighting than we used to do, it is admitted that few love fighting for fighting-sake; but amidst those few might be placed the members of the House of Guelph. My object is to record a fact, for the information of the very honest and worthy John Bulls, who will not love their King the less for knowing that, as soon as parental authority and state necessity admitted of it, he was most anxious to be at their natural-born enemy, the French.

When the British troops, in 1814, advanced on Antwerp for the purpose of destroying the French fleet, we quitted the village of Bircham about an hour before daylight,[1] on one of the most intensely cold mornings of that rigorous winter; it was, however, a positive comfort to be again in motion, as the march of the preceding day had been tedious, and our roads covered with wet snow. When darkness brought us to our halting-place, the rest we had anticipated proved to be visionary; after providing for the shelter of the men, the only place left for the officers was a small room without either doors or windows; I say doors, for in addition to the door from the passage, a doorway led by a few steps to the garden, so that Boreas had free scope for his gambols, which he performed in such perfection, that the recollection of them always brings on an attack of rheumatism.[2] For our bed we had a little damp straw, on which we were obliged to lie as close as possible, to prevent suffocation from the dense smoke with which the room was filled from the few green sticks it cost us much labour to collect; it was not at all 'Kilkenny fashion', for we had smoke without fire. Sleep was out of the question, and it was only the good-humour and brotherly affection which existed (and to which all who have served must look back with gratification) that made such miseries endurable. It was, therefore, (notwithstanding the pleasantry of our Assistant-Surgeon, who passed the night in apostrophizing a pair of shoes which he kept greasing whenever the smoke admitted of his sitting up,) a positive happiness to be called on to turn-out. The frost had become intense, so we were glad to push on; snow

1. The village is in fact Berchem, now a suburb of Antwerp.
2. Boreas was the Greek god of the North Wind.

was falling heavily when we passed a column of Prussians drawn up on the road, having their arms most carefully covered by their cloaks; it was destined to act on the other side of Antwerp. Shortly after daybreak, and just as we reached a wood occupied by French pickets, the sun broke out in great splendour, disclosing a magnificent scene: but who has not admired the splendid appearance exhibited by trees covered with hoarfrost under the sparkling effect of sunshine?

As the cheering rays of the sun reached us, our ears were saluted by the dropping fire of the skirmishers, which the frozen earth and wood made to reverberate with a thousand echoes. As our pace increased, so did the fire, and some heavy volleys, close upon our right, told of our near approach to the enemy. On clearing the wood, we discovered the village of Merkhem, and advanced on it in double-quick, passing the dead bodies of several of the enemy behind low walls and hedges that guided us to the entrance of the village by the church. On entering the main street, expecting to be saluted by the fire of the enemy, the leading companies commenced cheering, but were checked by the lion-hearted Sir Thomas Graham's calling 'silence.' An advance of a few paces brought us up with the skirmishers, and exhibited the French broken and escaping over a sheet of ice. Numbers of them were overtaken by the gallant 95th, and brought back, to my utter amazement, in the highest spirits. They were certainly to all appearance in much better humour than their captors, whose havresacks they commenced rummaging for bread, and on finding it, with an 'Obligé, Monsieur,' seated themselves on some trees which had been felled, and commenced eating most greedily.

Being halted and standing at ease, all quiet except a few straggling shot to the right, I went to the head of the column to see how matters were going on, and had just got to the extremity of the village, and obtained a glance of a road that turned off at a right angle, when a gentleman in a blue frock coat advanced from a house on the opposite side of the road, and laying his hand on my arm, said, 'You had better retire, or you will be fired on.' At the moment he said so, several balls struck the earth close to us and went ricocheting past; I was so confounded that I had not the power of thanking him, nor could I at the moment avail myself of the hint; when I did, I did it well, for I did it quickly. As the gentleman moved off, smiling at my perturbation, (it was the first time I had seen duck-and-drake played after that fashion,) I observed he had got a shot through the skirt of his great coat. I was not long in getting to the rear, where I found the men piling their arms, and was attracted to a door by seeing a crowd round it; I learned that the smell of new bread had brought them together; they were rapping in vain, when a hopeful son of St. Patrick, placing the muzzle of his firelock to the keyhole, said, it was quite a convenient implement for picking a lock with; he was, however, prevailed on to stop, and Mynheer, being told we were friends and that he should be paid, we were admitted. As I saw the soldiers were paying cheerfully, I obtained as much as I could well carry off, to the great solace of my brother officers, as we had subsisted the previous day on a small quantity of bread and gin. When I mentioned my blue-coated friend, (the army at that time wore grey great coats) it was suggested, that although he must have had a bellyfull of fighting by that time, yet some new bread might be very acceptable: just then an officer came up and informed us, that he of whom we were in search was no less a personage than the Duke of Clarence; for, that his Royal Highness had spent a part of the previous night with him in a most miserable Picket-house; shortly after his Royal Highness had left him, and while he was lamenting having met so pleasant a person when his canteen was empty, he was roused from a fit of blue devils by an aide-de-camp of Sir Thomas Graham inquiring for the person who had just left him, and who, he stated, was the Duke of Clarence.

It is correctly stated in the third number of the United Service Journal, that his Royal Highness occupied the house at the extremity of the village next Antwerp, and which was knocked about his ears; to the right and left of it were erected the batteries, in front were the furnace for heating shot, and the windmill and dike from which we had been fired on; from the window was obtained a view of Antwerp, the fleet, and all that was going on, but it was too hot a berth to attract many visitors. It was nearly in front of this house, and on the morning after we took possession of the village, that a singular circumstance occurred. Three officers of the 37th regiment, walking arm-in-arm, two of them, by the same cannon-shot, lost each a leg, the one in the centre escaping unhurt. I shall not trespass on your pages with an account of the occurrences of the week we remained at Merkhem in the attempt to destroy the French fleet. I am, however, certain, that the most vivid imagination among the 'Gentlemen of England who live at home at ease,' cannot picture to itself what his present Majesty must have suffered from exposure to the intense cold; it was such as to make me frequently wish myself in the other world. It is true, at home they were holding fairs and roasting oxen on the Thames; but then, John had his fireside and roast beef to return to, and he and his lady went snugly to sleep, without thinking of fools campaigning on the Continent, unless, perhaps, to long for another list of killed and wounded.

There is quite clearly a not inconsiderable amount of flattery in here, and even if the narrative is completely truthful, it is taking things rather to an extreme to suggests that the Duke's actions, even if exactly as reported, were directly responsible for saving the writer's life. A point of note here is that nowhere does the writer specify which of the two Merxem actions his narrative relates to, nor does he supply a date. It is nevertheless fully apparent that this set of reminiscences comes from the second action, fought immediately prior to the bombardment of Antwerp, since the details of that operation are related directly after the two anecdotes concerning the Duke and the fresh bread. Indeed, that bread and the Duke are so closely linked could, although rather an oblique reference, be read as implying that the blue-coated figure was assumed to be a commissary, thus providing a grounding for the more developed story of mistaken identity related by Shaw.

This was one of the earliest accounts of these events to make it into print, and neither it, nor Meuller's brief and passing mention of the Duke in his own account of the action, specify which of the two Merxem battles were graced by a royal presence. Indeed, because Meuller omits to mention the first action at all, the Guards not being engaged therein, a superficial reading of his account might even leave the reader believing that his account is of the first battle. Certainly, after the very definite dating of the anonymous 1820 account, things quickly become vague, or, at least, unspecified, as to just which battle the Duke was at. In the same way that the influence of earlier writings can often be seen in memoirs of the Peninsular campaigns composed in later years – particularly those that post-date Napier's history – it is not inconceivable to suggest that later memoirs of Graham's campaign may owe something to those accounts that preceded them. Shaw's account is a case in point: he places his anecdote at First Merxem, even though every circumstance indicates that he is describing the second battle. One response might therefore be to discount Shaw's story completely as a fiction, but so many details ring true – albeit for the later action – that it is tempting to think instead that he had either genuinely misremembered, or else sought the aid of earlier printed accounts to confirm his own memories, and confused himself thereby as to the date. In particular, Shaw's account of his conversations places Graham in the steeple of Merxem's church, and in so doing matches the contemporary account of Major General Taylor, who records in a letter that he, Graham, and the Duke together ascended the tower, at three in the afternoon of 2 February, in order to view the preparations for the bombardment.[1] It may therefore safely be said that the basics of Shaw's account are verifiable, if wrongly dated, even if the more humorous elements relating to his having mistaken the Duke for a commissary may or may not be a poetic embroidering. It is hard for us to judge whether both Shaw and P. W. were aware of a genuine case of mistaken identity relating to the Duke, or whether the former borrowed from the latter in building on this anecdote. On balance, it is probably safest to say that, at the least, the commissary story was current rumour and likely had some grounding in the truth, particularly if the Duke was wearing blue on the day.

Thus, by the time Shaw's account was published in 1837, all the basics of the Duke of Clarence myth were complete and had been stated in print: that the Duke was at the first battle (Shaw); that he was closely enough engaged to have a ball through his coat (Anon. and P. W.); that

1. Taylor to York, 3 February 1814, Taylor, Ernest (ed.), *The Taylor Papers: Being a Record of Certain Reminiscences, Letters, and Journals in the Life of Lieut.-Gen. Sir Herbert Taylor GCB, GCH* (London: Longmans Green, 1913), pp. 138–9; this is also confirmed in Sperling, *Letters*, p. 28, and by the anonymous letter already quoted above.

he was mistaken for a commissary officer (Shaw, and by implication P. W.); and that he exhibited personal courage under fire (all accounts). There was thus a considerable amount of material already in print to be drawn on and engaged with when Thomas Austin penned his account of the campaign.

Austin was born on 18 December 1794, and obtained his first commission, as an ensign in the Middlesex Militia, some months before his fifteenth birthday. Less than a year later, on 17 May 1810, he entered the regular service, exchanging a newly gazetted Militia lieutenancy for an ensign's commission in the 35th Foot. His lieutenancy in that same regiment was confirmed on 6 December 1813, by which time the 2/35th, in which he was serving, was already under orders for the Low Countries. His account of his service was not published in his own lifetime, but, rather, was prepared for publication by his great-nephew, Brigadier General H. H. Austin, and eventually brought out in book form in 1926. The work is titled *Old Stick-Leg*, this apparently being the name by which the editor and his brothers referred to their aged relation, for the very good reason that he had spent the years from 1814 until his death in 1881 stumping around on a wooden replacement for the limb he lost at Second Merxem. Its subtitle, however, which gives a better idea as to its source, is *Extracts from the Diaries of Major Thomas Austin*, with the added note that these have been 'arranged' by the original writer's great-nephew. The work itself consists of a mixture of original text interspersed by linking and summarising passages by the book's editor, but if the text presented as Thomas Austin's own is indeed his diary, then it is surely a diary that has been reworked and rewritten after the fact, for the passages of description and conversation are far too lengthy for it to be otherwise, and extensive mention is made in the final pages of the writer's circumstances long after the war's end. Austin junior even makes reference at one point to a footnoted passage in his ancestor's account, which more than anything suggests a finished piece of writing rather than a series of contemporary jottings. In tone, too, Austin has far more in common with the after the fact recollections of Shaw and Moodie than with the unadulterated diaries of Duncombe and Thain. These caveats need to be kept in mind when considering Austin's contribution to the Duke of Clarence legend.

Austin's account begins uncontroversially enough with his company skirmishing ahead of the Second Division's advance across the snow-covered heath north of Merxem. He recounts how a French outpost was evicted from a château, and then how the skirmishers advanced towards Merxem, driving back their French opposite numbers. It is possible that the precipitate nature of the French withdrawal owed more to the fact that their comrades were hard-pressed by the Prussians, and required support, than to the British advance alone, but this sort of misapprehension is common to many memoirs and can be readily appreciated and forgiven. However, we then get onto more dubious ground, for he goes on state that:

> The Duke of Clarence (afterwards King William the Fourth) now joined the advanced troops, and when the enemy opened fire on us and some casualties had occurred, my commanding officer, Major MacAlester, addressing the Royal Duke, said 'may I entreat your Royal Highness not to remain here, but to retire a little distance until the general rejoins the brigade'. The general had been sent for by Sir Thomas Graham.
>
> 'Retire! Certainly not,' the Duke replied, and continued to go on with the troops.[1]

Austin then explains how the troops attacked a French battery – a circumstance that does not entirely fit with other accounts of the action – and how he was superficially wounded when 'a cannon ball grazed my left side'. He then returns to his adventures with the Duke:

> Whilst engaged in clearing the enemy from the enclosures round the village of Merxem, the Duke of Clarence accompanied the Light troops during a part of the time, and HRH frequently aided the men in getting through the intricate fences which occasionally obstructed their progress. Being the senior subaltern of the Light company, my post was on the extreme left of the skirmishers which covered the advance of the right column of attack.[2]

This passage, it should be noted, as well as setting the scene for what follows, does usefully demonstrate that the 2/78th in its charge was

---

1. Austin, *Stick-Leg*, p. 85.
2. Austin, *Stick-Leg*, p. 86.

supported by the skirmishers of the Light Brigade on its right (the 'right column' in Austin's account) and a detached company of riflemen on its left. This evidence of flank protection, and of reinforcements being on hand, helps explain why a single small battalion was so effective against a larger force. Having provided a useful detail, however, Austin now descends into apparent fantasy:

> When forcing the enemy from hedge-row to hedge-row, behind each of which they made a stand and fired heavily, the Duke of Clarence scrambled through a fence some distance from my left. Turning my head in that direction, I observed a party of the enemy issuing from a house and garden with the evident intention of capturing His Royal Highness. Seeing that delay might prove dangerous, I desired such of the men of different units as had got through the fence to follow me. This was promptly done, and then, with about a dozen of my own men, one or two of the 78th Highlanders, and a few of the 95th Rifles, we moved against the party. It had by this time approached to within twelve or fourteen yards of the Royal Duke, and had already intercepted his retreat, and were about to surround him. Had he attempted to run he would certainly have been shot. My object was to get at the fellows with the bayonet without firing; but when the enemy fired on my party and killed a soldier of the 78th and a rifleman, the fire was returned and a rush made at them.[1]

Austin then continues by giving details of the ensuing combat, in which he recorded that eight of the enemy were killed and eleven taken prisoner. After a digression relating to the good treatment of the French wounded, he then emphasises the gallantry of his future monarch, who 'evinced great coolness and courage throughout the affair, [and] was well pleased at the promptitude in going to his rescue'. One man of the 78th, Austin then tells us, received a commission as a result of his bravery, but, for himself, 'promotion did not come from the north, south, east or west'. This bitterness is a point to return to, but for the moment it is worth asking the question, setting aside for a moment the fact that Austin is talking about the wrong battle, that even if the Duke had indeed been present as Austin states, how

1. Austin, *Stick-Leg*, p. 86.

would the French have recognised him for who he was, in order to make such a risky attempt? Austin makes no mention of the Duke's supposed attire, but he is unlikely to have been in uniform and, even if the commissary-esque blue coat cannot be confirmed, a plain topcoat seems likely wear.

The adventure related above is not quite the end of Austin's account, for he also comments adversely on some of the earlier printed accounts of the incident – confirming thereby that he had read them, and that his diaries were tidied up into a narrative long before his editor prepared them for publication – remarking scathingly on the 'absurd paragraphs' relating the Duke's 'miraculous escape' from death.

> One writer represented that His Royal Highness's coat was perforated by five bullet holes; another, more moderate, made the number only three. For my part, though quite ready to testify to the gallantry and pluck of the Prince, who was as much exposed to the enemy's fire as anyone, I must say that, although I was close to him, I did not see the bullet holes. Bullets are not such respecters of persons as to perforate coats of royal personages without touching bone or muscle.[1]

A rather rich comment, one cannot help but think, from someone who claims to have been grazed by a cannon ball and yet to have escaped with hardly a scratch, a circumstance surely even more improbable than that he ridicules others for attributing to the Duke.

Finally, Austin mentions a little later on that 'Sir Thomas Graham entered the village [of Merxem] along with the Duke of Clarence', adding a detail that serves to confirm that this part of the story is assuredly cribbed by going on to relate that, 'they ascended the church steeple to the belfry, but a shot or two from the enemy striking the steeple, the Duke and Sir Thomas descended to a place of better security'.[2] As has been demonstrated, Graham and the Duke did indeed climb to the belfry, but this was on the afternoon following the Second Battle of Merxem and by that time Austin was in no position to represent himself as an eyewitness, as he was then in the process of being carried to the rear with a shattered leg.

1. Austin, *Stick-Leg*, p. 88.
2. Austin, *Stick-Leg*, p. 90.

That wound, however, and the above-mentioned bitterness over lack of promotion, may perhaps help explain his penning of what is – even if we are being charitable – at the very least a much embroidered version of events. His military career was ended not by his wound but by the peacetime reductions of the Army, and although he obtained a wound pension and a post as Fort-Major at Duncannon Fort in Ireland, he was thwarted in his attempts to obtain further compensation or employment. Although this was not strictly the case, Austin had developed the opinion, by the time he wrote up his diaries, that he was 'wounded and cast aside'. In this light, it is easy enough to see that a gradual embroidering of a basic story may have taken place in an attempt to justify claims for employment or sinecure, leading to the creation of a narrative that contains much useful detail but also much that is harder to reconcile with the known facts. Austin did not, he says, approach William IV due to an unwillingness to be seen as 'presuming on the performance of an accidental service', although he did in 1833 obtain a letter of recommendation from Graham, now Lord Lynedoch. This endorsed his conduct at Merxem and, interestingly and confusingly, mentioned his involvement in saving the Duke in the action of '13th January 1814'. This, it may seem, throws into question the assertions made here that the Duke was not, in fact present at the first battle, but to set against Graham's 1833 letter we have nothing at all with a contemporary date to place the Duke in the Low Countries at so early a stage. A combination of advancing years and the elderly general's well-known desire to do all he could to aid former soldiers suggests that a claim of Austin's was endorsed without any further consideration or checking of details.[1]

What we must ask, though, is whether any of Austin's account of his adventures can be considered reliable. Were we dealing with any other eyewitness giving a 13 January date for an anecdote concerning the Duke, we might, as with Shaw, assume that the events related to the second battle and not the first, and that the writer's memory had become confused or misled by other accounts stating that the Duke

1. Austin, *Stick-Leg*, pp. 198–201. It might be questioned whether the note cited is truly 'in the handwriting of General Lord Lynedoch', as even in 1814 failing eyesight made Graham's own hand extremely hard to decipher and it is unlikely that a further two decades had done it any favours.

was at the first battle. Austin, however, lost a leg in the second battle, an event so significant – and painful – that one would assume it would have remained clear in his mind which day was which. However, the identities of the troops involved, and the circumstances of the fighting described, all suggest that, other than his anecdote of the Duke, Austin is describing genuine events from the 13 January action. Has he, then, simply drawn on stories about the Duke gleaned from other accounts, and added an extra adventure to an otherwise factual narrative? This, it must be said, seems the most likely case, and it has already been demonstrated that this has been done with reference to the Duke ascending the belfry of Merxem's church. The other alternative is that the events took place as described, but it was not the Duke but another who was rescued through Austin's actions, and that Austin came to the conclusion, then or later, that he really had rescued the Duke. Might it even be, in the most supreme of ironies, that an adventurous commissary was mistaken for the Duke rather than the reverse? Perhaps, but even if we ignore the belfry anecdote as a borrowing from Shaw, Austin adds a third instance in which he claims to have seem the Duke of Clarence, this time dining with Graham in a grand house during the first retreat from Antwerp. There are few, if any, personages, who could both have been wandering amongst the skirmishers at First Merxem and present at a grand dinner with Graham and his staff, and Austin should have known them all by sight or, at the least, by uniform. Tempting as this last hypothesis is, therefore, it must be discounted.

What, then, can be drawn from all this? Sadly for those who love a good story, it is safe to say that the actual active involvement of the Duke of Clarence in Graham's military operations was limited. He was initially on his way to The Hague rather than Graham's headquarters, and from the Duke's own brief mention of the campaign it rather sounds as if Graham had dragged him along with the army – in his own words, 'I was so suddenly called away by Sir Thomas Graham' – rather than his attendance being from a desperate desire to see combat.[1] The closest that he got to the action seems to have been the oft-mentioned ascent to the belfry, and for that we only have Austin – who was not there – to say that he came under fire at this juncture, although P. W.

---

1. Clarence to Lord Liverpool, 6 February 1814, Taylor, *Taylor Papers*, p. 141.

and our anonymous letter-writer both assert that the Duke was still in the village when it later came under fire from the French counter-bombardment. Austin's account, which brings together the majority of the earlier legends with the exception of Shaw's commissary anecdote, comes at the end of a process of account-by-account elaborations on some initial basic facts and a lot more contemporary rumour, with an unfortunate confusion over dating thrown in for good measure. It can only be assumed that Shaw, checking his account against others already in print, was misled by ambiguous wording and thus placed his own encounter with the Duke at the wrong battle. Once that affirmed date was in print, it became accepted – certainly by Austin, who seems to have drawn heavily on Shaw for details of the Duke's activities as is evidenced by his inclusion – and elaboration – of the belfry story. The difficulty, which can also be seen in the confusion over who commanded the False Attack at Bergen-op-Zoom, is that once one authoritative source has stated something in print, it is very hard to contradict it. It is therefore repeated, and becomes accepted fact. Add to this the inevitable temptation for a veteran writing years after the fact to check his memory against the printed record, and it is easy to see how confusion can enter the narrative. Finally, when this is additionally combined with memorialists keen, for whatever reason, to enhance their own role in events by claiming to have done and seen things that logically they could not have, the historian is left with quite the tangle to unravel.

Further Thoughts on the Bergen-op-Zoom Disaster

The failed attempt to take Bergen-op-Zoom was one of the most embarrassing defeats suffered by British arms during the Napoleonic Wars. Not since the catastrophe at Buenos Aires in 1807 – an operation with more than a few parallels to the events of seven years later – had so many British soldiers been forced to surrender. As can be seen from the accounts contained in this volume, the shame of failure was deeply felt – particularly amongst those, including Moodie and Mueller, who were taken prisoner – and led in turn to a need to rationalise and explain the reasons for the defeat.

Naturally, the primary narrative was shaped by those who had planned and directed the attack, or, rather, such of them as had survived. In particular can be seen the influence of Graham, who had ordered the attack, Carmichael Smyth, who had produced the basic plan of attack, and Major General Cooke, who had led the attack. The basic premise of this narrative, encapsulated in Graham's own despatch but also very apparent in Carmichael Smyth's reports to Lieutenant General Mann, was that the plan was a good one – as evidenced by the fact that the troops had all got in – but that things had gone wrong thereafter. For Cooke, and, to a lesser extent for Carmichael Smyth, there was a problem with this basic narrative, in that they had been amongst those who were inside the fortress – Cooke, indeed, being the senior officer and in overall command of the attacking troops – and that this explanation, whilst largely exculpating Graham, cast questions over their own role. Thus, a refined narrative developed that blamed failure variously on the actions of Major General Skerrett, Brigadier General Gore, and Lieutenant Colonels Carleton of the 2/44th, and Muller of the 4/1st. The first three officers named were all conveniently dead, whilst the last-named was in disgrace on account of his battalion having lost its colours when it surrendered. The conduct of Colonel Lord Proby's Left Attack, composed of detachments from the three Foot Guards battalions, and accompanied by Cooke and Carmichael Smyth, was passed over. The fact that these were the last troops to engage the enemy was for the most part explained away by the assertion that the other troops had made their attacks too early.

Much of this tendency can be seen in Cooke's report to Graham, made while its author was still a prisoner in French hands, which is reproduced in full here:

Sir,

I have now the Honor [sic] of reporting to your Excellency that the Column which made the attack on the Antwerp side got into the place about eleven o'clock on the night of the 8th by the clock of this town, but at about half past eleven by the time we were regulated by, a delay having occurred at [illegible] occasioned by my finding it necessary to change the point of attack, on account of the state of the Ice at the first intended spot. Every exertion was made by Lt. Col. Smith [sic] & Captn. Sir George Hoste of the Royal Engineers in getting on the ladders & planks requisite for effecting the Enterprise, and indicating placing them for the decent [sic] into the ditch, the passing the [illegible – cut ?] in the Ice, and ascending the Ramparts of the Body of the Place during which operation several men were lost by a fire from the Ramparts. After we were established on the Ramparts, and had occupied some houses from whence we might have been much annoyed, and had sent a strong Patrol towards the Point at which M. Genl. Skerrett and Lt. Col. Carleton had entered, I detached Lt. Col Clifton with part of the 1st Guards to secure the Antwerp Gate and see if he could get any Information of the Column under Lt. Col. Morrice. Lt Col. Clifton reached the gate, but found that it could not be opened by his men, the enemy throwing a very heavy fire up a street leading to it. It was found also that they held an outwork commanding the bridge which would effectively render that outwork useless. I heard nothing more of this detachment, but considered it as lost, the communication having been interrupted by the enemy. Lt. Col. Rooke[1] with part of the 3rd Guards was afterwards sent in that direction, drove the enemy from the intermediate

---

1. Capt. and Lt Col Henry Rooke, Coldstream Guards.

rampart, and reached the gate where he found it useless to attempt any thing and ascertained that the outwork was still occupied.

We were joined during the course of the night by the 33rd, 55th, and 2nd Battn. of 69th Regiments, but the state of Uncertainty as to what had passed at other Points determined me not to weaken the force now collected, by attempting to carry Points which we could not maintain or penetrate through the streets with the certain loss of a great number of men, the more particularly as I knew that the troops at the Water Port Gate under Lt. Col Muller were very seriously opposed I sent the 33rd to reinforce them.

The Enemy continued a galling fire upon us, and at one time held the adjoining Bastion, from the angle of which they completely commanded our communication with the exterior, and brought their guns at that angle to bear against us. They were charged and driven away by Majors Muttlebury and Hog [sic] with the 69th and 55th in a very gallant style.

Finding that matters were becoming more serious and being still without any information from other Points excepting that of the failure of Lt. Col. Morrice's Column near the Wouw Gate, I determined at the suggestion of Col. Lord Proby to let part of the troops withdraw, which was done at the ladders where they entered.

About daylight the Enemy having again possessed themselves of the aforementioned Bastion, they were again driven from it by Majors Muttlebury and Hog, with their weak battalions in the same gallant manner. I soon afterwards began sending off some more men when Lt. Col. Jones who had been taken Prisoner in the night came to me (accompanied by a French officer who summoned me to surrender) and informed me that Lt. Col. Muller and the Corps at the water port gate had been obliged to surrender and were marched Prisoners into the town, when I also learnt the fate of Lt. Col. Clifton's detachment, and of M. Genl Skerrett, M. Genl. [sic] Gore, and Lt. Col. Carleton, and that the troops which had followed them had suffered very much and had been repulsed from the advanced points along the Ramparts where they had Penetrated to. I was convinced that a longer continuance of the Contest would be a useless loss of lives, and without a Prospect of Relief as we were situated – I therefore consented to adopt the mortifying alternative of laying down our arms.

I have now to perform the just and satisfactory duty of conveying to your excellency my sense of the Merits and good conduct of the soldiers in this bold and ambitious enterprise. I have only a knowledge of what passed under my own observation, and I lament that the loss of M. Genl. Skerrett from his dangerous wound, and of the other superior officers employed at the other Points of attack, prevents me from giving such detailed praise of the merits of the officers and soldiers, as I have no doubt they deserve.

I beg to repeat my praise of the distinguished conduct of Colonel Ld. Proby. Lt. Colonels Rooke and Mercer,[1] commanding the 3rd Guards and Light Infantry distinguished themselves by their activity and bravery, and Majors Muttlebury and Hog of the 69th and 55th Regiments deserve my warm praise for the conduct displayed by their Corps in the charges I have before mentioned. I have every reason to know that Lt. Col. Clifton conducted his detachment in the most gallant and officerlike manner, and I have to lament that his death deprives me of receiving his report of the conduct of Lt. Cols. MacDonald and Jones, and the officers and soldiers of the 1st Guards under his command.

I am not yet enabled to have made an exact Return of the Prisoners taken at different times by the enemy, nor of the numbers taken from them.[2]

Cooke's primary purpose, it may well be said, was to explain away the fact that he had ordered his troops to lay down their arms, but his choice – deliberate or otherwise – to praise the conduct of the Guards and the troops with them, whilst for the most part ignoring the deeds of the other regiments, set the tone for the official account contained in Graham's own report. The main report was delivered orally by Graham's aide, Major James Stanhope, but in his covering letter to Lord Bathurst, Graham made it clear that he had accepted Cooke's report, writing that 'had the Royals maintained the Water-port gate, General Cooke would have held his ground, and the place must have fallen'.[3] In private, Graham was even more scathing, writing that 'The right column went on like a pack of fox-hounds into cover, and in all directions, and were annihilated before the Guards got in.'[4]

In *A Bold and Ambitious Enterprise*, I put forward a narrative which challenged this interpretation, demonstrating – insofar as is possible

1. Capt. and Lt Col Robert Mercer, 3rd Foot Guards, who was killed in the fighting.
2. Cooke to Graham, 10 March 1814, TNA, WO1/200, pp. 129–33.
3. Graham to Bathurst, 11 March 1814, TNA, WO1/200, pp. 141–3.
4. Graham to Cathcart, 4 April 1814, in Delavoye, *Thomas Graham*, pp. 732–3.

with conflicting eyewitness accounts from an age before accurate time-pieces – that the Right, False, and Centre Attacks went in on schedule, or possibly even slightly behind it, and that the contribution of the Left Attack – Cooke, Proby, and the Guards – was extremely late. Cooke, indeed, does admit to delay in his own narrative, a point that seems to have subsequently been ignored, but by omitting to note the time at which he should have attacked fails to emphasise just how late he was. In fact, taking Cooke at his word, the Guards were in the region of between an hour and an hour-and-a-half late, and it is, therefore, hardly to be wondered that the leaders of the other columns took action without waiting for them. Indeed, as Thain makes clear, Lieutenant Colonel Morrice delayed the assault by the Centre Attack because he was awaiting the sound of firing from his left – that is, from the Guards – before going in. We can only speculate what would have happened if the Centre Attack had gone in on schedule, and whether Morrice's three battalions might have benefitted from the diversion caused by the False Attack in the same way that Carleton, Skerrett, and Gore were able to make an unopposed assault on the harbour sector. Such speculation aside though, Thain's narrative does allow us to state conclusively that the order of the attacks going in was as follows: False, Right (almost immediately afterwards), Centre (after a delay of a few minutes), and Left (much delayed).

The exact details of what happened during the False Attack remain unclear, as its commander was wounded, along with his replacement, and no reports or eyewitness accounts appear to have survived. We might, on these grounds, wish that Dunbar Moodie had remained in his assigned place with this attack, rather than going off adventuring instead. Again allowing for the confusion over the difference between local time and the time being observed by the British – something made worse by the fact that the majority of eyewitnesses do not indicate which of the two is being employed – the idea that the False Attack went in early and gave the game away can safely be discounted. James Stanhope's assertion that this attack went in as early as 21.30 must be discounted as improbable, but even if the False Attack was early, it does not excuse the Left Attack being late.[1]

1. See Bamford, *Bold and Ambitious Enterprise*, pp.185–8; Glover, *Stanhope*, p. 147.

Exact timings aside, as Moodie makes clear, it is unlikely that the troops making up the Right Attack would have managed to get in, without the diversion caused by the False Attack, and the French concentration against it. The conduct of the Right Attack, which Moodie joined, is well documented, with the excellent and recently republished account of Lieutenant Sperling to add to Moodie's own lively version of events. The activities of these troops can therefore be traced with some certainty, although the actions of Major General Skerrett, and of Lieutenant Colonel Muller and the 4/1st, remain sources of some controversy and will be returned to. Insofar as the Centre and Left Attacks are concerned, the sources that I had at hand when preparing *A Bold and Ambitious Enterprise* enabled the production of a basic narrative that I am still confident in the accuracy of. However, the addition of Thain's and Meuller's accounts – and, in one small respect, that of Duncombe – allows the inclusion of further details which not only tell us more about what happened – or did not happen – but also about why.

Cooke admits that there was a delay on the march by which the guardsmen who would form the Left Attack made their way towards their objective, but gives little more information. This, though, would seem to relate to the difficulties encountered when the attacking troops were close to the fortress and picking out their point of entry, rather than to Meuller's recorded halt at a 'village near the angle of the great road' some miles short of the objective. If Meuller's exhausted state after his spell on outpost duty was anything to go by, it was as well to halt the troops on the march, and it was likewise sensible to await darkness before pushing too close to Bergen-op-Zoom lest the game be given away: equally, neither concern would seem to justify waiting so long as to delay the column appreciably, which is what happened. However, what needs to be questioned here is not why there were delays, but why the troops were not given sufficient time to get into position before the commencement of the attack.

The problem was that the hour of attack was linked to the tides, it being necessary for the Right Attack to go in at low water, and this therefore set the timetable for the whole assault. This, in turn, set a limit on the number of troops that could be brought into the operation. Since the plan was only finalised on the evening of 7 March, not all of Graham's command was close enough to have any chance of taking part. The bulk of the Second Division was observing Antwerp, and thus could not be spared in its entirety in any case: from this formation, only the 33rd and 2/35th could be called upon, and the latter only as a reinforcement to help secure the town – as was hoped – on the morning after the attack. The brigades of Skerrett and Gore were both close enough to be brought in at full strength and by easy marches, but the Guards were billeted further away, in support of the Second Division, and this begins to explain why only a portion of the brigade could be brought in, and also helps contextualise the problems that delayed their attack. Meuller's account makes it clear that proper orders only reached the Guards at Putte on the morning of 8 March, and that the men detailed for the attack had to deposit their surplus kit and then to make a march of ten miles to their objective. This does not, on the face of it, seem an unreasonable object to achieve within what may be calculated as roughly twelve hours, but evidently it was still necessary to rush the preparations, leading, amongst other things, to Ensign Duncombe and his picket being left so long unrelieved. That there were timing problems and that not all the troops made the attack on schedule must therefore be attributed to the haste with which the operation was mounted, and the responsibility for that must ultimately lie with Sir Thomas Graham. Graham, it is true, had good reasons of his own for choosing to risk an attack, but when he gambled on making it that gamble was rendered the more daring by the small time-window within which the operation was mounted.[1] Depending on how one chooses to interpret certain comments made by Cooke, Meuller and Duncombe, some of this already limited time may well have been squandered by poor management within the Guards Brigade, but this was a matter of making a bad situation worse rather than being in itself the cause of all the delay.

Of course, just as it behove those who had served with the Guards in the Left Attack to produce accounts of their experiences that presented the actions of their part of the assault in the best light, so too for those who served elsewhere. Thus, the accounts of Thain and Moodie, and

---

1. For a discussion of the strategic imperatives influencing Graham's decision to attack – which, it must be emphasised, did *not* hinge on the oft-argued desire to do something before his troops were withdrawn – see Bamford, *Bold and Ambitious Enterprise*, pp. 171–6.

particularly the defence presented by the latter for the conduct of Major General Skerrett and Lieutenant Colonel Muller, need to be viewed with this caveat in mind. That said, Moodie makes some good points even allowing for a potential bias, whilst Thain and the 33rd managed to be just about everywhere during the course of the night, first forming part of the abortive Centre Attack, then reinforcing the Left Attack once the Guards had made a lodgement, and ending up in the harbour area supporting elements of the Right Attack; insofar as the reader needs to be aware of the potential for any underlying loyalties affecting the perspective of Thain's account, they can only be to his regiment and not to any one of the attacking columns.

The primary case that can be made against Skerrett is that he split his forces by leading a small detachment to the left – that is, towards the False Attack – rather than moving his whole force to his right, across the harbour, to try and link up with the Guards. Because other forces, led by Brigadier General Gore and Lieutenant Colonel Carleton, did make such a circuit to the right, leaving the remaining troops of the Right Attack to secure the harbour area, this move by Skerrett undoubtedly had the effect of diluting the potential for any effective action by the Right Attack, which was not only the second-strongest of the four attacks but also the only one, as chance would have it, to get inside the fortress undetected and on schedule. Because Skerrett did not survive the attack, he was a convenient scapegoat at the time. Adding to this his less than stellar Peninsular career, it is easy to write him off completely as an incompetent. A better characterisation of Skerrett, however, would be of a man who was personally brave but unimaginative and, based on his Peninsular service, lacking in the moral courage needed to take difficult decisions. As overall commander of the northern sector of the assault, Skerrett had direction of both the Right and False Attacks. Almost as soon as fighting broke out, it became apparent that the False Attack had worked almost too well, inasmuch as that it had drawn upon itself the attention of almost the entire French garrison. No doubt, the correct thing to do would have been for Skerrett to capitalise on this by securing the harbour area and as much of the town as possible whilst the garrison was distracted, but Skerrett nevertheless elected to delegate the movement to the right to Carleton and Gore and to take a small party in the opposite direction. The question that is inevitably asked, and which can never be conclusively answered because if anyone was privy to Skerrett's intentions other than the man himself, they never recorded them, is why?

Moodie speculates that the general had despaired of being able to link up with the Guards – as well he might, since there had been as yet no sign of action from that sector – and that he meant to force the Steenbergen Gate and thereby admit the men of the False Attack to allow them to enter the town as reinforcements. This is a possibility, certainly, but it seems an unlikely one for Skerrett must have been aware how weak a force the False Attack was; the total force that could have been admitted by such a move, allowing for casualties and men separated from their units, could barely have exceeded, if at all, the number of troops that were detached from the Right Attack in order to facilitate its entry. Furthermore, any troops thus admitted would only gain access to the most heavily defended portion of the whole fortress, thanks to the concentration of the French garrison in that sector to meet the False Attack. An alternative piece of speculation – and it is no more than that – is that Skerrett was aware, from the volume of firing coming from the Steenbergen Gate, of the danger facing the False Attack, and was determined to make some effort to join or relieve them. It must be remembered that Skerrett had left the Peninsula under a cloud after a small detachment under his command – Captain Cadoux's company of the 95th – had been left unsupported and thereby suffered heavily at the hands of a greatly superior force. Did Skerrett see the same thing happening here, and seek to avert it, even at peril to his life, rather than have another stain on his reputation? Certainly, such a move fits with a personality type high in personal bravery and sense of honour but lacking in moral courage, for the correct, if cold blooded, response was surely to leave the False Attack to its fate and capitalise upon the diversion thereby offered. Then again, though, Skerrett was hardly abandoning the Right Attack, for its own leader, Lieutenant Colonel Carleton, remained with it and so did the supernumerary Brigadier General Gore; Skerrett may therefore have considered that his wider command responsibility for both attacks entitled him to leave these two capable subordinates to oversee the Right Attack.

Ultimately, we do not know why Skerrett acted as he did. As for the consequences of his actions, they were perhaps less severe than might be assumed. Certainly, the Right Attack was diminished by some 150 men. Then again, however, these men continued the fight in the northern portion of the fortress, between the harbour and the Steenbergen Gate, for longer than would have otherwise been the case, potentially delaying the French counterattack by some hours. Even allowing for the fact that, irrespective of what the other British columns did, the French needed some time to reorganise themselves after the repulse of the False Attack, the point that they thereafter needed to employ a proportion of their forces evicting the survivors of Skerrett's detachment from the bastions in which they had taken refuge further delayed their ability to move in overwhelming force against the troops in the harbour area and ultimately against Cooke's main force in the 'Oranje' bastion. Had this hard-bought time enabled the remaining forces to secure the rest of the town and thus achieve success, Skerrett's actions might well be remembered as the sacrifice of a hero, rather than the errors of a scapegoat. Indeed, some thought him heroic even so; Moodie, certainly, as we have seen, considered Skerrett 'a most gallant, zealous, and active officer', and regretted his death as a significant cause of the eventual disaster.

When Skerrett turned to the left, Carleton and Gore took a second party in the opposite direction, intending to link up with the Left Attack. Finding no sign of the Guards, they pushed on around the ramparts and eventually met their end at the hands of a large body of French troops who seem to have been part of the force that had earlier thwarted the attempted entry by the Centre Attack. Carleton and Gore were killed, and their surviving troops dispersed, eventually linking up with Cooke and the Guards in the 'Oranje' bastion when the Left Attack made its belated appearance. There, too, assembled the surviving troops of the Centre Attack – the 33rd, 2/69th and a wing of the 55th – who made an external circuit of the walls eventually to gain access to the fortress by the ladders belatedly erected by the Guards. Thain's account adds useful detail to the early experiences of the Centre Attack, and helps counter the unfounded suggestion of widespread panic that comes from the pen of James Stanhope,[1] but does not serve to alter the basic

1. For which see Glover, *Stanhope*, p. 149, and refutation in Bamford, *Bold and Ambitious Enterprise*, pp. 198–9.

narrative of this portion of the operations that was presented in *A Bold and Ambitious Enterprise*; however, with respect to the closing stages of the fighting in the harbour sector, where the 33rd were lately shifted as a reinforcement, Thain does provide additional insights into the actions of the other major scapegoat of the night, Lieutenant Colonel Frederick Muller of the 4/1st.

The version of events given in *A Bold and Ambitious Enterprise* contained a defence of Muller's conduct, drawing primarily on Moodie's narrative of events during the course of the night, when the 4/1st and its commander were essentially left to their own devices, to paint a picture of a far more active and enterprising officer than the standard narratives of events – right back to Graham's own despatch – allow. Only at the end did Muller fail, first in his inability to extricate his surviving men in an effective manner, and secondly – and most grievously in the eyes of his contemporaries – in his battalion losing its colours. To assert, as Graham did, that all would have been well if only Muller had held the Waterport Gate is a distortion that attempts – and, in the light of all the evidence, fails – to shift the blame for the surrender from Cooke, the man who authorised it, and from Lord Proby whose defeatist attitude did much to colour Cooke's thinking and actions. By the time the French regained control of the harbour after evicting the last of Muller's troops there, the bulk of Cooke's potential offensive capability had already been frittered away, and the troops under his command were in essentially the same position as when they were later forced to lay down their arms. Thus, Muller's contribution to the defeat may be deemed negligible. Against this version of events, however, Thain raises additional criticisms of Muller that need to be addressed if a more rounded understanding of this officer's role and conduct is to be obtained.

Specifically, Thain reports that the 4/1st fell back without Muller making any effort to notify the men of the 33rd who were deployed to his right, facing the upper harbour, and that that battalion was left in peril as a result. If the 33rd had indeed been placed under Muller's direct command, as Thain suggests, then this indeed was a serious dereliction. It is unclear, however, whether this was actually the case. Cooke, in his report, simply notes that the 33rd were sent to reinforce Muller's battalion, although since Muller outranked the 33rd's Major

Parkinson it may have been simply taken as given that Muller had the command in the harbour area. Whether or not he had been given formal command responsibility, however, the fact remains that to fall back without notifying the other battalion was a poor showing on Muller's part, and needs to be set against his record during the events of 8–9 March. Otherwise, however, that record seems to be a good one. For the bulk of the night, as can be seen from Moodie's account of events prior to the arrival of the 33rd, Muller did as good a job as could be expected of someone who had been left largely to his own devices by the departure and subsequent deaths of Skerrett, Carleton and Gore. Only in the morning did his performance begin to fall short, perhaps an indication of physical and emotional exhaustion, and whilst he cannot be faulted for beginning to withdraw his men under heavy French attack it is undeniably the case that the withdrawal of the 4/1st, and the eventual surrender of the greater part of the battalion, stands in unfortunate contrast to the far more deftly managed withdrawal of the 33rd under the direction of Major Parkinson. The very fact that the 33rd got off in such good order must indeed stand as at least partial rebuttal of the idea that Muller left Parkinson's men completely in the lurch, although at the same time it cannot be denied that had the two units been able to cooperate effectively it could well be that they could have both got to safety with far fewer casualties and without the loss of the 4/1st's colours. What we have, therefore, are several legitimate criticisms of Muller's action in the closing stages of the action, which led to the loss of many of the men in his battalion, and to the loss of its colours, and which also placed the 33rd in some peril. For these errors at the end of a long and trying night, Muller may justly be faulted. His actions, however, only served to make the disaster worse; they were not, as Graham and Cooke suggest, the cause of the disaster in itself.

We might well therefore ask, what were the causes of the disaster? In general terms, the answer remains that which was given in *A Bold and Ambitious Enterprise*: a complex and risky plan, executed at too short notice with an insufficient force. Two key factors can be identified within this. Firstly, the late arrival of the Foot Guards detachments under Lord Proby, who made up the Left Attack. Had these troops, and Cooke with them, managed to enter the fortress on time, or even slightly late, other errors would have mattered far less: in particular,

Carleton and Gore would have been able to link up with Cooke and Proby and complete a secure link across the harbour area between the Right and Left Attacks, rather than continuing on around the ramparts to their doom. The reasons behind this delay to the Left Attack have already been discussed above. The second factor relates to poor control of troops within the fortress, with substantial – and ill-fated – detachments being made not only from the Right Attack but also from the troops assembled under Cooke at the 'Oranje' bastion. It is strange indeed that Skerrett is so often vilified for taking off a detachment from the Right Attack, yet Cooke gets little blame for frittering away the Guards in penny packets leading to their loss in the desperate street fighting described by Corporal Meuller. Many of the details of the failure can well be laid at the door of Cooke, Skerrett, Proby, Muller and the other senior officers with the attacking troops, and in that sense it is tempting to accept the Graham and Carmichael Smyth thesis that the plan failed because of what happened after the troops got in. This, however, remains a shifting of the final responsibility, which must lie with the man who took the gamble and ordered the attack, the same man, it might be added, to whom the credit would have accrued had things gone well: Sir Thomas Graham.

Appendix VI

Monuments and Commemoration

Unsurprisingly for a campaign that culminated in an action as disastrous as that at Bergen-op-Zoom, there is little in Britain by way of commemoration for the men who fought under Graham, and such memorials as there are pay tribute to particular fallen individuals. Generals Skerrett and Gore get a single shared plaque in St Paul's Cathedral, watched over by two classical female figures, but the wording carefully glosses over the fact that the action in which they fell was a disaster, noting only that both men 'fell gloriously while leading the troops to the assault'. Captain John Purvis of the 4/1st, meanwhile, is commemorated by a plaque in Canterbury Cathedral, erected by his brother-in-law and standing tribute to nearly three decades of military service that culminated in a mortal wound at Bergen-op-Zoom from which he expired eight days later. None of these officers, however, are buried in British soil; they lie, along with the others who fell, in churches and churchyards in the Netherlands, and, until recently, lacked any marker of where they lay. It was only when this book was in the final stages of preparation that I was contacted by members of a Dutch group who were in the process of replacing the monuments that had once stood to these men, and it is to them that I am indebted for the information which follows.

The majority of the British officers who fell at Bergen-op-Zoom were interred at Wouw, which was safely within the British lines in the aftermath of the failed assault. Nevertheless, commemoration was later made in Bergen-op-Zoom itself, with two engraved tablets being placed in the town's medieval Gertrudiskerk. This was the same church in which many of the British prisoners were held after Cooke's surrender. The first of these tablets, almost two metres tall, commemorated by name the officers buried at Wouw, whilst a second, smaller, tablet commemorated the fallen officers of the Foot Guards. Although the latter was considered to be of finer quality, neither tablet was heavily decorated. Some years afterwards, the descendants of Lieutenant Colonel Carleton came to Bergen-op-Zoom in search of his grave. Upon eventually establishing that Carleton had been buried at Wouw, the family erected a new gravestone and monument, which remain there to this day, its restoration in 1988 having been funded by the local authorities. Unfortunately, all trace of the monuments at Bergen-op-Zoom had been lost until recently.

Sadly, the interior of the Gertrudiskerk was gutted by fire in 1972. The memorial tablets could not withstand the heat of the fire and were destroyed that day. Restoration has continued ever since, although the basic work was completed, and the church rededicated, in 1987. Even this work cost over a million euros, but it did not permit the restoration of all the monuments. Over the centuries, hundreds of people were buried in this church and many of them are commemorated by the beautiful memorials and tombstones which dominate the interior. The tombstones in the floor have frequently been moved, so that an individual stone may not be near the spot where that person was buried. Furthermore, the fires – there had been another in 1747, when the French stormed the place during the War of the Austrian Succession – also destroyed the lists of memorials, which made the process of reconstructing the church interior all the more difficult. Progress has been made in restoring and replacing many of the older monuments, but until recently nothing was done about replacing the two plaques commemorating the British officers who fell in 1814. Much of the impetus behind the restoration work came from Mr Kees Booij who was appointed project leader and supervisor on behalf of the local authorities of Bergen-op-Zoom. Sadly, Mr Booij died in 2002, and subsequently the project faltered until it was picked up again by the Church Study and Workgroup, who began the process of commissioning replacement tablets to the highest possible standard. The replacement tablets are to be a gift from the citizens to the town of Bergen-op-Zoom, and are to be formally unveiled in March 2016.

Bibliography

Archival Sources

The National Archives, Series PRO30/35: Sir James Carmichael Smyth
Papers
  PRO30/35/1: Miscellaneous. Letters, observations, memoranda and
  reports. Entry book.
  PRO30/35/6: Letters to Lieutenant General Mann December 1813–
  December 1818

Secretary of State for War, and Commander-in-Chief, In-letters and
Miscellaneous Papers
  WO1/199–201: Dutch Expedition (1813–1814): Commander's Dispatches

The National Archives, Series WO6, War Department and successors:
Secretary of State for War and Secretary of State for War and the Colonies,
Out-letters
  WO6/16: Holland, Flanders, and France. 1813–1818

The National Archives, Series WO17, Office of the Commander in Chief:
Monthly Returns to the Adjutant General
  WO17/274–282: Regiments of Foot, 1814
  WO17/1773: Germany, 1813–1814 [includes Holland]

The National Army Museum
  NAM 6807-209: Journal of Edward Nevil McCready

Printed Primary Sources

Anon., *Letters from Germany and Holland, During the Years 1813–14; With a
Detailed Account of the Operations of the British Army in those Countries, and
of the Attacks Upon Antwerp and Bergen-op-Zoom, by the Troops under the
Command of Gen. Sir T. Graham* (London: Thomas & George Underwood,
1820)
'Achilles', 'Further Observations on the Bill for rendering the Militia
disposable for Foreign Service', *The Royal Military Panorama, or Officer's
Companion*, Vol. III (1813–14), pp. 550–2
Austin, Brigadier General H. H. (ed.), *Old Stick Leg: Extracts from the Diaries
of Major Thomas Austin* (London: Geoffrey Bles, 1926)

Cooke, Captain, et al., *Memoirs of the Late War* (London: Henry Colburn & Richard Bentley, 1833)

Delavoye, Alex. M., *Life of Thomas Graham, Lord Lynedoch* (London: Richardson, 1880)

Duncombe, Thomas H., *The Life and Correspondence of Thomas Slingsby Duncombe, Late MP for Finsbury* (London: Hurst & Blackett, 1868)

Glover, Gareth (ed.), *Eyewitness to the Peninsular War and the Battle of Waterloo: The Letters and Journals of Lieutenant Colonel the Honourable James Stanhope 1803 to 1825* (Barnsley, Pen & Sword, 2010)

James, C., *A Collection of the Charges, Opinions, and Sentences of General Courts Martial* (London: T. Egerton, 1820)

Meuller, A. F., *Letters from Spain* (Dundee: J. Chalmers, 1823)

Morris, Thomas, *Recollections of Military Service, in 1813, 1814, & 1815, through Germany, Holland, and France, including some Details of the Battles of Quatre Bras and Waterloo* (London: James Madden, 1845)

P. W., 'The Duke of Clarence at Merkhem in 1814 (Communicated by an Officer Present)', *The United Service Journal and Naval and Military Magazine* (1830, Part II), pp. 523–5

Shaw, Charles, *Personal Memoirs and Correspondence of Colonel Charles Shaw* (London: Henry Colburn, 1837)

Sperling, John, *Letters of an Officer of the Corps of Royal Engineers from the British Army in Holland, Flanders, and France to his Father, from the Latter end of 1813 to 1816* (London: James Nisbet & Co., 1872)

Taylor, Ernest (ed.), *The Taylor Papers: Being a Record of Certain Reminiscences, Letters, and Journals in the Life of Lieut.-Gen. Sir Herbert Taylor GCB, GCH* (London: Longmans Green, 1913)

Van Gorkum, Jan Egburtus (ed. L. J. F. Janssen), *De Bestorming der Vesting Bergen op Zoom, op den 8sten Maart 1814* (Leiden: Hooiberg & Zoon, 1862)

Secondary Sources

Anon., *British Minor Expeditions 1746 to 1814* (London: HMSO, 1884)

Ballstadt, Carl P., 'Moodie, John Wedderburn Dunbar', in *Dictionary of Canadian Biography* (Toronto: University of Toronto/Université Laval, 2003), Vol. 9; available online at http://www.biographi.ca/en/bio/moodie_john_wedderburn_dunbar_9E.html

Bamford, Andrew, *Sickness, Suffering, and the Sword: The British Regiment on Campaign 1808–1815* (Norman: University of Oklahoma Press, 2013)

———, *A Bold and Ambitious Enterprise: The British Army in the Low Countries 1813–1814* (Barnsley: Frontline, 2013)

————, '"Dastardly and atrocious": Lieutenant Blake, Captain Clune, and the Recall of the 55th Foot from the Netherlands, 1814', *Journal of the Society for Army Historical Research*, Autumn 2014, pp. 210–22

————, 'Battalions of Detachments in 1814 – the Duke of York Responds to Britain's Manpower Shortfall', *Napoleon Series* website, at http://www. napoleon-series.org/military/battles/1814/c_BritishDetachments1814. html

Brown, Steve, 'British Artillery Battalions and the Men Who Led Them 1793–1815: Royal Engineers/Royal Sappers and Miners', *Napoleon Series* website, at http://www.napoleon-series.org/military/organization/ Britain/Engineers/RoyalEngineers.pdf

Burnham, Robert (ed.), 'Lionel S. Challis' "Peninsula Roll Call"', *Napoleon Series* website, at http://www.napoleon-series.org/research/biographies/ GreatBritain/Challis/c_ChallisIntro.html

Cochran, John, *A Catalogue of Manuscripts, in Different Languages on Theology, English and Foreign History, of Various Dates, from the Twelfth to the Eighteenth Century* (London: Ibotson & Palmer, 1829)

Connolly, T. W. J., *The History of the Corps of Royal Sappers and Miners* (London: Longman, Brown, Green & Longman, 1855)

Cope, Sir W. H., *The History of the Rifle Brigade (The Prince Consort's Own) Formerly the 95th* (London: Chatto & Windus, 1877)

Courthope, William (ed.), *Debrett's Complete Peerage of the United Kingdom of Great Britain and Ireland* (London: J. G. & F. Rivington, 1838)

Dalton, Charles, *The Waterloo Roll Call* (London: Eyre & Spottiswoode, 1904)

Davidson, Major H. (ed.), *History and Services of the 78th Highlanders (Ross-shire Buffs) 1793–1881* (Edinburgh & London: W. & A. K. Johnston, 1901)

De Santis, Lieutenant Colonel Edward, 'Quartermaster Sergeant James McKay, Royal Sappers and Miners', at http://www.reubique.com/ mckay.htm

Duncan, Francis, *History of the Royal Regiment of Artillery* (London: John Murray, 1873)

Fisher, David R., 'Duncombe, Thomas Slingsby (1796–1861), of 20 Queen Street, Mayfair, Mdx.', *History of Parliament Online*, at http://www. historyofparliamentonline.org/volume/1820-1832/member/duncombe-thomas-1796-1861

Goff, Gerald Lionel Joseph, *Historical records of the 91st Argyllshire Highlanders, now the 1st Battalion Princess Louise's Argyll and Sutherland Highlanders, containing an account of the Regiment in 1794, and of its subsequent services to 1881* (London: R. Bentley, 1891)

Hamilton, Lieutenant General Sir F. W., *The Origin and Service of the First or Grenadier Guards* (London: John Murray, 1874)

Haythornthwaite, Philip J., *The Napoleonic Source Book* (London: Arms & Armour, 1990)

Jones, Major General Sir John T., *Journal of Sieges Carried on by the Army under the Duke of Wellington* (London: John Weale, 1846)

Lewis, Stephen, 'Officers Killed – Afghanistan 1838–42', at http://glosters. tripod.com/FAfghan.htm

MacKinnon, Colonel, *Origins and Services of the Coldstream Guards* (London: Richard Bentley, 1833)

O'Byrne, William Richard, *A Dictionary of Naval Biography* (London: J. Murray, 1849)

Philippart, John, *Northern Campaigns, from the Commencement of the War in 1812, to the Armistice Signed and Ratified June 4, 1813* (London: P. Martin & Co., 1813)

——, *The Royal Military Calendar or Army Service and Commission Book* (London: A. J. Valpy, 1820)

Uglow, Jenny, *The Pinecone* (London: Faber & Faber, 2012)

Index